TALES FROM A SOUTH AMERICAN STORM DRAIN

2nd Edition

The Jaw-Dropping Adventure Of A Lifetime

By
MIKE PLUMMER
with Tim Foster

Copyright © Mike Plummer 2023
This book is sold subject to the condition that it shall not, by way of trade or otherwise, be lent, resold, hired out, or otherwise circulated without the publisher's prior consent in any form of binding or cover other than that in which it is published and without a similar condition including this condition being imposed on the subsequent publisher.
The moral right of Mike Plummer has been asserted.
ISBN: 9781097460625

While all the stories in this book are true, some names and identifying details have been changed to protect the privacy of the people involved.

CONTENTS

Day

1 and 2	January 26-27, 1981	8
3	January 28, 1981	22
4	January 29, 1981	28
5	January 30, 1981	32
6	January 31, 1981	36
7	February 1, 1981	39
8	February 2, 1981	42
9	February 3, 1981	47
10	February 4, 1981	51
11	February 5, 1981	55
12	February 6, 1981	59
13	February 7, 1981	66
14	February 8, 1981	69
15	February 9, 1981	72
16	February 10, 1981	76
17	February 11, 1981	80
18	February 12, 1981	85
19	February 13, 1981	89
20	February 14, 1981	92
21	February 15, 1981	95
22	February 16, 1981	101
23	February 17, 1981	106
24	February 18, 1981	109
25	February 19, 1981	112
26	February 20, 1981	117
27	February 21, 1981	124
28	February 22, 1981	131
29	February 23, 1981	137
30	February 24, 1981	140

31	February 25, 1981	143
32	February 26, 1981	145
33	February 27, 1981	149
34	February 28, 1981	154
35	March 1, 1981	159
36	March 2, 1981	162
37	March 3, 1981	165
38	March 4, 1981	169
39	March 5, 1981	173
40	March 6, 1981	177
41	March 7, 1981	183
42	March 8, 1981	187
43	March 9, 1981	189
44	March 10, 1981	192
45	March 11, 1981	197
46	March 12, 1981	202
47	March 13, 1981	207
48	March 14, 1981	211
49	March 15, 1981	219
50	March 16, 1981	225
51	March 17, 1981	231
52	March 18, 1981	236
53	March 19, 1981	240
54	March 20, 1981	249
55	March 21, 1981	252
	ABOUT THE AUTHOR	264

ACKNOWLEDGMENTS

I would like to thank Roman Kurowski for being a true friend and helping me out when the shit started flying in the Amazon!

I literally owe you my right hand and wrist because without your help they'd have probably been amputated due to gangrene.

Cheers mate.

Day 1 and 2

January 26-27, 1981

Shitting myself.

That is how I felt as I checked in my ridiculously oversized and overpacked Karrimor rucksack at the monster of all British airports, London Heathrow. Here I was, a former junior sales assistant at John Lewis, with career prospects and opportunities that most young people in the early eighties could have only dreamt of, about to embark on an adventure of epic proportions. My plan was to travel around the world, starting off in South America. I felt that if I could survive South America, I could survive anywhere!

Let me put this into context: imagine a tall, skinny, pale, fresh-faced male, twenty-five years old, blond hair, blue eyes, who had never set foot out of Europe. I was travelling alone, having put my burgeoning professional career as a college lecturer completely on hold, to discover what lay on the other side of the 'big bad' world.

I had just spent the last eight years toiling away building up a career: having left school virtually unqualified with one 'O' level, I had by now successfully completed my first post-graduate degree and was working as a BTEC National

Coordinator at Matthew Boulton Technical College in Birmingham, with over three years' lecturing experience under my belt, and was standing at a crossroads in my life.

One route led to a guaranteed career, promotion, safety and security – especially as I was the hero of the hour, having single-handedly stopped a riot in the college canteen between a large number of drunken engineering students and police cadets a few days before the Christmas holidays. Furthermore, I had rescued my vice-principal, a nervous little man who meekly stood or rather cowered in the middle of this rabble, surrounded by some fifty to sixty inebriated students who towered over him, boisterously threatening to rearrange his face! The other route, however, led to risk, danger and the unknown, and its mesmerising allure was so overpowering, like the song of the mythical sirens, that I resigned my post, bought a pair of hiking boots and a map of the world.

It was a real 'life is too short, so grab it by the throat and squeeze the blood out of it' moment. But now here I was shitting myself, metaphorically speaking, and I hadn't even arrived at my departure gate.

This wasn't the first time I had done something completely manic without thinking things through properly: aged seventeen, I decided that it would be a most wondrous idea to play 'Chicken' with my friend's car, once a week, at the end of our day-release course at a local tech college (I spent the rest of the week working at Knight and Lees department store, in Southsea). For those of you who do not know what the game 'Chicken' is, let me paint a vivid picture for you. 'Chicken', in ordinary terms, consists of one person dodging an object or objects coming at them, generally at high speed. These objects could be anything that can be thrown, kicked or could even be runners in a race or a cyclist on the road, although unfortunately my version involved a car.

'Car dodging' had become a weekly tradition at Highbury Technical College and, to my own credit and being an adrenaline junkie, I was pretty good at it: standing in the middle of the road waving my arms and laughing as one of my classmates would drive out of the car park and head straight for me. Then at the critical moment, I would successfully leap out of the way and, with a manic smile on my face, I'd bathe in the surge of adrenaline that would rush through my body, leaving me elated, breathless and wanting more. However, on one occasion – just one week before my first year exams, I might add – I toyed with fate one too many times and in one misjudged feint, was completely taken out by the car. I rolled, by some stroke of luck, over the bonnet and roof, only to land unconscious in the gutter by the side of the road, rather than under the wheels.

My friend driving the car, believing we were about to collide, lost his nerve at the very last moment just as I was about to jump out of the way and, unfortunately, swerved in the same direction as I had leapt. Realising his mistake he immediately slammed his foot on the pedal, missing the brake and by pure chance hitting the accelerator instead. This actually proved to be a saving grace, for as the car was speeding up when it actually hit me it propelled my body over the top of the car. If it had been braking and slowing down when it had hit me I would probably have gone under the wheels and been run over, probably fatally.

As a result, I was admitted to the intensive care unit at the local hospital in a coma, where I lay unconscious for the first week, then half awake, thankfully, for a further ten days, strapped up to an array of assorted medical machinery before being released. I spent another five weeks recovering at home, on the Isle of Wight, before starting work and 'normal life' again. My family and friends who visited me and helped me through this difficult time probably thought that this would, at long last, curb my antics and make me appreciate the value of my life a little more. However, unfortunately for them, surviving a collision like that only made me realise just how short life really was and how much more there was to see and experience before the final curtain falls. As clichéd as it may sound, the memory of the crash and my daredevil approach to life got me onto the tarmac, up those steps and onto that plane on that cold winter's day in January 1981.

My palms were sweaty and my fingers trembled nervously as I fumbled with the seatbelt by my side, which, for some unapparent reason, was refusing to lock together. I let out a disgruntled sigh and proceeded to carefully study the offending apparatus, convinced that the seat had been wrongly equipped with two identical halves. Finding this not to be the case, I sheepishly began looking around me trying to see if anyone else was experiencing similar difficulties. However, it appeared not, so I once more turned to the matter in hand with renewed vigour and agitated frustration.

'Can I be of some assistance?' chirped a tall, slender air stewardess who had suddenly appeared beside me, hovering in the gangway. She must have caught the distressed look forming upon my face as, without further ado, she seductively lent over me to fasten the belt before smiling sweetly and saying, 'Don't worry, many people get nervous about flying.'

Yes, I thought, as she left my side, *but it's not the flying that worries me, it's what happens when we land!*

She continued up the aisle in search of other passengers in need of her assistance, her shapely hips tastefully wrapped in a figure-hugging uniform, rhythmically swaying from side to side. This receding vision of beauty momentarily bewitched me, before I reluctantly came to and sank back into my chair.

Can this really be happening to me, I thought to myself, *or am I just dreaming and, if so, what sort of dream will it turn out to be?*

I sat there, silently pondering over the answer, oblivious to all the commotion around me until, as if in answer to that very question, the plane's engines promptly roared into life and filled the cabin with their deafening cries. Yes, I decided, *this is reality,* and before I knew it, the *'Fasten Your Seatbelt'* and *'No Smoking'* signs were flashing above my head and the plane began slowly rolling across the tarmac, edging towards the awaiting runway and its destination of Miami, Florida. There was a moment's hesitation while the pilot readied for the 'clear for take-off' signal from the control tower. Then, the signal received, the plane set off down the runway, picking up great speed as it went along, until its nose gently tilted skywards and it majestically ascended into the heavens.

I took a long, deep breath and closed my eyes. I couldn't decide whether to laugh or cry. I was extremely excited but at the same time very, very scared. *What will happen to me? How, when and from where will I return? WILL I RETURN!!!!?* Questions like these kept flashing into my mind, thrown out by an overactive brain that was fast becoming intoxicated on an endlessly rising tide of adrenaline.

Suddenly, all of those months of planning were over. Here I was on the verge of the single greatest adventure of my life, but I was afraid. Afraid to take that first step, that initial jolt that would lead me into the unknown, the harsh and often frightening reality of another world. I was finally leaving the confines of a protective environment, an industrialised nation with all of its social benefits and handouts, which are all too often taken for granted. Out there lay the third world, full of underdeveloped countries where sufficient food, clothing and shelter were the exclusive rights of the rich and an all-too-often hopeless ambition of the poor.

From Miami, I caught a connecting flight on to Santa Cruz in Bolivia, via Caracas in Venezuela and Manaus, the capital of the Amazon.

Santa Cruz Airport, which was probably the Mecca for all Bolivian airplane enthusiasts, unfortunately left much to be desired as far as European standards went. I remember looking out of the plane's window as it approached the runway, alarmed to see several concrete runways, each carefully placed in-between the remnants of what at first sight looked like a number of crashed planes. However, upon closer inspection, as we came into land, I realised that they were, in fact, the remains of abandoned aircraft in various stages of decomposition. It became apparent later on that the scrap metal was being used for spare parts. In third-world countries, nothing went to waste.

The airport also included a few whitewashed concrete

buildings, the occasional much-valued, scraggy-looking chicken foraging around for food and the inevitable soldiers. Armed to the teeth, they stood ominously dotted around outside the buildings like acorns on an oak tree, but looking fearsome and unfriendly. Evidently, Bolivia was recovering from its latest revolution. In fact, the country seemed quite partial to revolutions and actually held the world record, having had approximately one hundred and fifty in the last one hundred years.

The plane taxied slowly to the end of the runway, veering off towards the airport's unimpressive collection of buildings. Whereupon, reaching its destination, the aircraft lurched to a halt, prompting me to unclip my safety belt, before following the other passengers apprehensively off the plane. I climbed carefully down the mobile gangway and stepped onto Bolivian concrete. The glare from the sun made me instinctively reach for my Polaroids, while my lungs began trying to adjust to the unfamiliar warm, damp, stale-smelling air. It was like stepping into a sauna fully clothed, under the watchful gaze of an immensely powerful searchlight.

Inside the main building, I was met by a babbling mass of people milling around in what, to my eyes, seemed disorganised chaos. Momentarily, I stood perfectly still, almost stunned, allowing the array of strange sights, sounds and smells to bombard my senses all at once. I was confused, disorientated and perspiring profusely. The place reminded me of a scene from the Hollywood blockbuster 'Casablanca', but I could not see Bogart anywhere, and where was the pianist?

I eventually came to and, after staring all around with a 'young little boy lost' look written across my face, I realised that no one was going to come and help me. I was out here on my own.

For a short moment, I closed my eyes, took a deep breath and clenched my fists before tentatively approaching an official-looking man who was suitably attired in his airport uniform and standing diligently behind a counter. I proceeded to ask him how, when and where I had to check in for my connecting flight to Buenos Aires. However, there was an unfortunate communication problem, as the official could not speak a word of English and my limited command of the Spanish language consisted of – 'Si, si, señory and señorita!'

Consequently, either the official misunderstood my question or I his answer, or, as the case may well have been, we both misunderstood each other. The eventual outcome of which was that I went straight to passport control, from where I was ushered by an armed soldier up a creeping wooden staircase and into the 'International Lounge'.

Lounge, I thought as I emerged through the doorway. Why, I had seen better furniture in a Glaswegian unemployment office (but that's another story).

The elaborately decorated room, upon which the Bolivian authorities had obviously spared no expense, measured roughly twelve metres by nine. It contained eleven wooden benches covered with bodies in varying degrees of consciousness, a small wooden bar and the top of a flight of stairs that led out onto the runway. In one corner was situated a mixed toilet, the stench of which could be smelled from most parts of the room and was guaranteed to put the faint-hearted off any thought of eating. The concrete floor had never heard of, let alone seen a carpet and the windows, which adorned the two outer walls of the room overlooking the runway, stood proudly, naked to the eye, without a pair of curtains or set of blinds in sight to cover the gently distorted curves of their frames and the peeling paintwork.

The only form of entertainment, apart from watching the locals scratch themselves, was a small black and white television, positioned some two metres off the ground and surrounded by a wall of awestruck locals; each one seemingly mesmerised by 20th-century technology. The monochrome talking picture box was showing dubbed over reruns of the 1960s British serial 'Robin Hood', starring Richard Greene. He was, surprisingly, an accomplished bilingual and managed to perform the amazing feat of miming in English while speaking in Spanish with apparent ease.

Several hours later, an ancient-looking 1940s Douglas DC3 twin-propeller plane crawled along the runway and the flight to Buenos Aires was announced. A queue quickly formed in the lounge, from the now fully conscious bodies, who began slowly moving down the stairs in an orderly fashion. It felt surreal being the only foreigner in the queue. I towered like a colossus over the rest of the travellers, many of whom were Gauchos from the Pampas. They wore colourful ponchos, thick cotton trousers, cowboy hats and weather-beaten, leathery, tanned faces.

At the bottom of the stairs stood a ticket collector who was carefully checking each boarding pass, while at the other end of a short passageway stood an armed soldier guarding the exit to the runway and the awaiting aeroplane. He was brandishing a sub-machine gun held firmly in his hands and it was fairly obvious that he took his job very seriously. Slowly, one by one, the passengers walked past the soldier and out into the sunlight to board this dinosaur from a bygone age. At least, that's what everyone else was doing. I, however, handed my ticket over and started walking along the short corridor leading to the outside, when the ticket collector suddenly called after me. I was abruptly brought to a halt by the armed guard who swung the sub-machine gun he was holding and thumped the barrel into my stomach.

I immediately broke out into a cold sweat and realised that I had an allergy to guns, especially loaded ones! My heart started pumping like a hungry woodpecker attacking a tree and I was beginning to wish that I had worn an incontinence pad in case of nervous leaks! Luckily though, it was not needed as the ticket collector called me back and proceeded to explain, in broken English, that I could not board the airplane, as I had not yet checked my rucksack in from the previous flight. This was something that I had stupidly assumed would automatically have been done for me when the luggage was taken off the plane, as I was on a connecting flight.

Furthermore, and in typical South American style, the plane to Buenos Aires had been overbooked so I could regrettably do little more than helplessly watch it take off and disappear in to the clouds without me. As a result, I ended up spending several hours longer than I had anticipated in Bolivia, hanging around the airport manager's office, anxiously awaiting news of an available plane. In the meantime, I was on my best behaviour, trying to be as nice as possible to everyone, especially the armed guards, by wearing a permanent Nancy Reagan grin (the wife of the then American President, Ronald Reagan, had a strong penchant for facelifts which left her face with a permanent grin) and waving frantically to anyone whenever I stepped outside the office to stretch my legs.

By the time I had reached Buenos Aires, all I was dreaming of was a cool shower and a bed but it seemed, for the time being at least, that even these simple pleasures were to elude me.

At the airport, I rearranged my flight to Montevideo as, due to my unexpected stopover in Bolivia, I had missed my connection. It was here that I discovered my ticket was actually valid for six months and that I could have stopped over in Caracas, Manaus and Santa Cruz if I had wished too. *Oh well*, I thought, *it's a little late to find out now*. Still, I quickly decided that my introduction to South America would be done in style, so I accordingly changed US$30 worth of travellers' cheques into 60,960 Argentinian pesos and went to buy a bus ticket to the city centre. I was convinced that this would be more than enough to cover the bus fare, a room for the night and still enable me to do some sightseeing the following day. After all, I was travelling through South America.

Unfortunately, Buenos Aires turned out to be very expensive to visit (it was the most expensive city in the world for commercial office rents). In fact the bus fare alone, which only took approximately twenty-five minutes, cost an incredible 27,000 pesos (that was approximately US$13.30 or £35.69 in today's money)!

Upon reaching its destination in the city centre, I alighted from the bus and set about scouring the backstreets and alleyways, in search of some form of cheap accommodation. While sitting at home, half-heartedly reading through a selection of South American travel books that had listed pages of accommodation, it had all seemed so easy. All I had to do was simply turn up and walk down any side-street that I chose and cheap hotels would be fighting for my custom. However, now that the daydreaming was over and reality had taken its place, I saw everything in a somewhat different light.

There I stood, alone in the middle of a crowded bus station somewhere in Buenos Aires, the capital of Argentina, 10,500km away from home. It was half past ten at night (01:30am GMT), I could not speak the local language and was tired, hungry and thirsty. Still, I was British and proud of it. *One of the Bulldog breed*, I kept on telling myself. So, with rucksack firmly strapped to my back and bulging kitbag in hand, I reluctantly marched out into the night, with my only comfort being the thought that at least things couldn't get worse. Alas, I was wrong.

After several minutes, the threatening sound of thunder rang in my ears and before long I was gaining first-hand experience of a South American rainstorm as the great sink-plug in the sky was removed and water poured down in ever-increasing quantities. Droplets the size of marbles plummeted down at a considerable speed, stinging everything in their path including me; and immediately drenching me to the skin. I began to wonder if visiting South America was really such a good idea after all.

I tried several seedy-looking hotels but had little success, as they were either fully booked or didn't seem to like letting out rooms to drowned rats with rucksacks. Unknowingly, I had arrived at the peak of the Argentinian holiday season. *So much for foresight and meticulous planning!* I thought to myself. By now, I was starting to become paranoid over the predicament I found myself in and the more I walked, the more concerned I became; half expecting to come face to face with a knife-wielding mugger who would leave me crumpled in a heap up a dark side-alley with my throat slit. It was like a bad dream except for two things: I wasn't tucked up in a warm bed and I most definitely couldn't wake up from this one.

Eventually, with the help of an English-speaking student that by chance I happened to ask directions from, I located a hotel called "The Pit", or at least after spending one night there, that's what I christened it.

For the princely sum of 20,500 pesos (approximately US $10), I managed to procure a room. However, it looked more like a toilet cubicle, consisting of a cast-iron bed, paper-thin mattress and a wooden chair with an assortment of different-sized legs.

The hotel itself looked like a Victorian slum: old, smelly and practically falling down; a ramshackle remnant of a bygone age. It was also infested with the Argentine equivalent to meals-on-wheels – i.e. *"Meals on legs"*. The place was a miniature game reserve for cockroaches, which seemed to be crawling all over it.

They were literally everywhere except, that is, in my room, which reinforced my belief that insects weren't stupid. After all, even cockroaches had limits beneath which they would not stoop. I had my first close encounter with one of them as I was climbing up a dimly lit, rickety old staircase which led to my bedroom. It seemed that one of them was scurrying down the banisters for a quick bite to eat when I accidentally put my hand on it. I shuddered at the feel of its hard shell-like body writhing under my palm and instinctively withdrew my hand before racing up the stairs like a scared child, to the comparative safety of my room.

At 3am local time (6am GMT) while sitting on my bed, listening to my neighbour's television, which remained on all night, I wrote the day's closing comments in my diary:

'I'm off to bed now, or at least, I think that's what it is: something long and thin that sinks in the middle and doesn't move very much when you sit on it.'

'At last we're alone,' I softly whispered to the bed bugs. *Oh happy days are here again!*

***

In 1987 when an army sergeant at Murtala International Airport in Lagos, Nigeria, was faced with a problem of overbooking, he came up with an original and amusing solution. The plane had been overbooked to the point that every seat was occupied and the gangways between the seats were choked with sweating obese bodies. Meanwhile outside the mobile stairway leading up to the plane was also full and there were a large number of people trying to get onto the stairway. Consequently, the sergeant brandishing his sub-machine gun ordered everyone off the plane and made them all run around it three times, promising that the first people back would be guaranteed a seat. It evidently resembled a huge dodgems car race, as in West Africa the staple diet is Fou Fou, a starchy breadfruit, which invariably causes the development of obesity. Fortunately though, in West Africa, fatness is a sign of good health, prosperity and beauty and so it is highly respected and admired.

*

In July 1987 grave robbers broke into former Argentine president Juan Peron's tomb and cut off his hands (he had died in 1974). They then demanded US$8,000,000 for their safe return, threatening to burn them unless the ransom was paid.

*

In October 1988 a poodle fell to its death from the thirteenth floor balcony of a tower block in Buenos Aires, killing three people in the process. It landed on a woman, killing her instantly, causing a shocked bystander to step back in horror off the pavement and straight into the path of an oncoming bus, whilst an elderly man witnessing the whole regrettable incident from across the road, dropped dead from a massive heart attack.

*

In November 1991, Argentinian anger boiled over into violent demonstrations when it was revealed that France had donated 32,000 tons of dried human excrement as a goodwill gesture to Argentina, to be used as fertiliser. The arrival of the 'detritus humanus' on a converted container ship only came to light when a somewhat perplexed Argentinian customs chief asked officials for a ruling over whether imported human faeces was subject to import tax.

However, medieval physicians in England regularly used animal dung in their treatments:

- Greek white, the white coating on dried dog dung, was prescribed for sore throats, tonsillitis and lung ailments.
- Mice excrement was useful for intestinal worms.
- Oxen dung for rheumatism or fever.
- Sheep manure was used to help treat jaundice.
- Freshly dropped cow dung was often applied to aching joints.

As gross as this may seem today dried dung from healthy animals does actually contain antimicrobial and even antibiotic properties.

*

In South America they tended to do things their own way. Argentinian bandits had recently held up a coach, and having robbed everyone of their valued possessions, proceeded to lock them all up in the boot, until some hours later they were released by an elderly peasant walking past with his donkey!

*

The Patagonian cavy or Mara is a large rodent living in the arid regions of Argentina. Unusually for a rodent it is monogamous and will mate with the same partner for life. The young are well develop at birth and can start to graze within twenty-four hours of being born. They are kept in a large communal den where up to fifteen pairs of cavy deposit their young and then take turns to look after them during the day. Each mother returns several times during the day to feed and nurse their young and look after the crèche.

*

The Pampas are the fertile South American lowlands that cover over 750,000 square kilometres of the continent. They stretch across large parts of Argentina, Uruguay and Brazil.

*

An Argentinian farmer, Pedro Martin Uretas, created a stunning tribute to his late wife on their farmland at Laboulaye in the central Argentinian province of Pampa, by planting 7,000 trees in the shape of a guitar which stretches for almost a mile, and is so large that it can only be properly appreciated from the sky. However, Pedro has never been able to fully appreciate his own handiwork, as he is afraid of flying!

*

All apartments in Chile are fitted with suction vents in each room, so you sweep the mess in to one corner and the suction vents take it away.

*

According to legend, a Pishtaco is a mythical beast that dwells in the Andes region that lures its victims into the jungle where it sucks out their body fat with an elongated vampire like tooth.

Andean natives have long prized fat, as they believe excess body fat is a sign of good health, strength and beauty, and even used to worship a deity called Viracocha (meaning sea of fat).

It was also rumoured that Spanish conquistadors used to kill native Indians and boil their bodies in order to produce fat to grease their metal muskets and cannons which used to rust in the humid climate.

It was recently reported that many Andean people have rejected food aid, believing it was a cunning plan to plump them up in order to steal their body fat at a later date.

*

Bolivia is home to the world's largest butterfly sanctuary, near Santa Cruz.

*

Duelling was only outlawed in Uruguay in 1992.

*

Uruguay has over twelve million cattle which outnumber the population by three to one

*

Uruguay has over 12 million cattle which outnumber the population by 3 to 1.

Day 3

January 28, 1981

Although the room was somewhat squalid and depressing to look at, I still slept well and arose the next morning feeling refreshed and ready to face the rigours and torments of a new day. I sat on the bed, slowly munching my way through a breakfast of cheese rolls and home-made quiche Lorraine. *'Thanks, Mum.'* This was washed down by a canteen full of chlorinated swimming pool water, or at least that's what it tasted like once I had added the correct dosage of purification tablets. Then, having satisfied my hunger and thirst, I quickly packed up my rucksack and left my previous night's refuge. The thought of its sinking bed, sandbag pillow and view of a local poverty trap from the doorway, spurred me on towards the backstreets of Buenos Aires.

The room was situated on the fourth floor off an open veranda that clung to the side of the building like a limpet mine and overlooked a local slum area tucked away in-between several impressive-looking skyscrapers.

Once outside, I began trying to locate the city's other airport by asking for directions to the nearest bus station, from where I hoped I would be able to catch a bus. It appeared that the city had two airports and that I had flown into one on the previous night and was due to fly out of the other sometime later that afternoon. The local people were friendly and extremely helpful, especially when they found out that I was British. After all, it had been a contingent of British mercenaries that had helped liberate Argentina from the perilous clutches of its colonial masters, the Spanish. I had also arrived a year before the Falklands crisis erupted onto the scene.

Unfortunately however, the police were suspicious of everyone, especially people who looked out of the ordinary. So, it wasn't long before I had been stopped in the street by two gun-toting policemen, frisked spread-eagled against the side of their police car, questioned in broken English and made to produce my passport. I was later informed by a fellow traveller, that if I had not been carrying my passport at the time, I would have automatically been thrown into jail for a couple of days and in the process have probably lost any valuables that I had had in my possession! Moreover, I was assured that this would be the least of my worries, as if there was a revolution during my stay in prison – which seemed to occur throughout South America with alarming regularity – the reasons for and the length of my imprisonment might easily be lost in the chaos and confusion that would inevitably follow. Consequently, I could end up becoming a long-term guest of the new military junta.

Somewhat shaken by my first encounter with the Argentinian authorities, I carried on with increasing apprehension, but, as the old saying goes, it was a case of 'out of the frying pan and into the fire.'

Before long I had, quite by accident, stumbled across the headquarters of the Argentinian commandos, the grounds of which were next to a park littered with tanks and anti-aircraft guns, each neatly placed in-between rows of brightly coloured flowerbeds. I got the impression, however, that the weaponry on display was not there for decoration purposes. As I walked by, head bowed low under the weight of my rucksack, my attention was drawn towards the front of the building as an aggressive shout rang out above the droning hum of passing traffic.

I looked up to find two armed guards standing at the top of an elegantly sweeping concrete staircase looking down at me through the sights of their Kalashnikov rifles. In between them stood a young army officer, pistol in hand, loudly gesticulating with his arm while shouting out a command, which I guessed was ordering me to immediately cross over the road and walk past the building on the other side. Remembering my allergy to guns, I quickly obeyed. I carefully negotiated my way across the busy dual carriageway, realising that I was but a hair-trigger away from having my head blown off, as the commandos carefully followed my progress with their rifles.

Having wasted most of the morning wandering through the backstreets of the city lost, I eventually stumbled upon a bus station, where fortune smiled on me as a couple of extremely helpful Argentinian sailors, one of whom was studying English, advised me on which bus to catch. Within the hour I was boarding a plane for Montevideo, the capital of Uruguay, and by late afternoon I had settled into a cheap hotel close to the city centre.

I was glad to have left Argentina, for although the people had been very friendly, the police and military authorities were well-renowned for their ruthless and barbaric methods of dealing with people. They ruled with a rod of iron and a simple promise: if you caused trouble, you would be permanently removed from society.

During what became known as the "Dirty War" (1976-1983), the military used to regularly abduct people from their homes, usually in the middle of the night, and they would disappear, never to be seen again by their family or friends. Initially they would be taken to one of 364 secret interrogation centres, where they would be tortured.

Once the authorities believed that they had obtained all useful information from the victim, they would be driven to a nearby airfield, bundled onto a helicopter and then flown out several miles into the Atlantic Ocean. Once there, they would have their hands tied behind their back, their stomachs sliced open with a machete and the bleeding body would be dumped into the dark waters below. Needless to say, few bodies were ever washed up onto the coastline.

In 1977 a number of mothers whose children or partners had disappeared started protesting peacefully at the Plaza de Mayo in Buenos Aires, in front of the Casa Rosada Presidential Palace, in open defiance of the government's attempts to ban all forms of protest. Each week they would meet together and silently dance with the ghosts of their missing husbands, partners or children. In 1987 Sting released the song 'They Dance Alone', in veneration of their plight. Unfortunately, several founding members of this movement were abducted and ended up on one of those 'death flights'. The military later admitted that over 9,000 people had disappeared under these circumstances but the Mothers of the Playa de Mayo believe that the figure is closer to 30,000.

Like all other South American countries, Argentina consisted of two classes, two extremes: you were either rich and powerful or poor and powerless. This fact was later highlighted by a friend who explained to me the different funeral arrangements available in Buenos Aires.

At the poor man's cemetery, the procedure was simple – the authorities dug a huge pit, filled it up with bodies and then covered it up with earth. Four years later, they dug it up again, burnt the remains and buried another collection of unknown people in their place. Whereas, the rich person's cemetery, called 'The Cemetery of Ricoleta' – which roughly translated means the 'little city of the dead', followed a somewhat different practice.

The cemetery was like a museum of architecture, with a Greek colonnade at its entrance and a huge bronze statue of the resurrected saviour at the far end. These were linked by a main avenue that had a number of paths, each paved in stone and lined with cypress trees, branching off it. Along these paths, huddled close together like houses in a street, stood the family vaults of the region's influential and affluent nobility. The list of permanent residents reads like an Argentinian hall of fame and includes: Eva Perón, a granddaughter of Napoleon; past presidents of Argentina; the founder of the Argentine Navy, and Nobel Prize winners to name but a few.

Each tomb was shaped like a building, which ranged from the simple to the extravagant, with practically every conceivable style of architecture represented. There were Georgian houses, miniature banks, war memorials and even a small pyramid. Inside, the coffins were laid out on shelves and the families even employed servants to go in every day to dust the coffins, clean the floor and windows and polish the front door! Outside each family vault was mounted a large strategically positioned plaque that contained a list of the people permanently in residence, along with their date of arrival.

That night, I ventured out and sank a few bottles of local beer. This was more like it: sat in a bar, a crisp 'cerveza' in hand, happy and relaxed for the first time since leaving England.

***

Uruguay is the same size as England and Wales, although its population is less than that of Wales alone. Well over a third of the country's total population lives in the capital Montevideo and there are three times as many cattle as there are people in Uruguay.

*

In October 1992, a treasure hunter, Ruben Callado, successfully located the wreck of the 'El Preciado', a Spanish galleon sunk by English pirates 200 years earlier off the coast of Montevideo. The ship's manifest which had been found after a detailed search of shipping archives stated it was transporting 47 tons of gold, 147 tons of silver and a six-foot-high, gold-plated statue of the Virgin Mary.

Shortly afterwards the find was discussed at a specially convened cabinet meeting as it was thought the treasure from the ship could be equivalent to Uruguay's total foreign debt. Regrettably though this proved not to be the case, although it was still worth over $400 million!

*

One of the most popular beverages throughout Uruguay is 'Mate': a tea-like drink made of dried 'yerba mate' leaves. It is said to offer the 'strength of coffee, the health benefits of tea, and the euphoria of chocolate' all in one beverage. Legend has it that 'mate' was presented as a gift from the gods to humanity after a man stopped two goddesses from being eaten by a jaguar.

*

Uruguay has the longest national anthem in the world: it has eleven verses and can take approximately six minutes to sing through, but it's worth waiting for with lines such as 'No one insults the image of the sun!'

*

Nahuelito is a monster that is reputed to live in Nahuel Huapi, Lake Patagonia, Argentina. Like Nessie, the Loch Ness Monster, the Argentine plesiosaur is named after the lake it resides in and has been described as a giant serpent with a huge hump.

*

The Palacio de Sal is a hotel with a difference, as it is entirely built of salt blocks. It used approximately one million 35-cm (14-inch) salt bricks, to build the floor, walls, ceiling and furniture, including beds, tables, chairs and sculptures. The hotel has a dry sauna and a steam room, a saltwater pool and whirlpool baths.

It took two years to construct the building from blocks of salt which were extracted from Salar de Uyuni, the world's largest salt flat. The hotel is located 350 km (220 mi) south of the Bolivian capital of La Paz, on the edge of Salar de Uyuni. Some parts of the 4,500 square feet complex have to be rebuilt every year due to water damage after the rainy season.

The hotel has one rule "DO NOT lick the walls or furniture !".

*

Uruguay's President Jose Mujica (2010 – 2015) refused to reside in the official presidential palace during his tenure and instead lived in a one-

bedroomed house. He also donated around 90% of his salary to charity and once adopted a dog that he accidently ran over in his tractor

Day 4

January 29, 1981

At first light, I caught a bus along the coast to Maldonado, a popular seaside resort that I had read – *'Should not be missed at all costs, due to its beautiful sandy beaches.'* However, having dragged my rucksack around the hotels for nearly two hours, I finally came to the conclusion that there must have been a printing error in my South American handbook. It should have read – *Maldonado should be missed at all costs* – and at an average cost of US$45 per night on my meagre finances, could you blame me? Consequently, I got the next bus back to Montevideo and decided to push on that night to the country that I had come to South America to visit: Brazil. The fourth largest country in the world (it covers over 8.5 million square kms, approximately 48% of South America), Brazil is full of spectacular scenery, exotic food, idyllic weather and, so I had been reliably informed, beautiful women.

The return journey from Maldonado to Montevideo was

particularly cosy, as the driver appeared to be attempting to gain a place in the Guinness Book of Records for squeezing the largest number of passengers onto a bus. In fact at one time there were more people standing than sitting. Following this 'take my breath away' experience, I promised myself to never again complain about London's Underground at rush hour. Within a comparatively short space of time everyone was joining in with the occasion by 'getting to know their neighbours', which became a very intimate experience whenever someone from the back of the bus attempted to get off.

The bus eventually reached its final destination after having crawled along the road at an excruciatingly slow pace and opened its doors to release countless hordes of passengers onto the streets of Montevideo.

Upon regaining the circulation in my legs, I proceeded to make my way to the ticket office in the bus station, where, after fighting my way through the crowds to get served, I booked a ticket to Porto Alegre. I then spent a lazy afternoon wandering around the city before returning to the station to board the awaiting overnight coach.

This coach was excellent and the scenery breathtaking, but what made the journey so memorable was the way in which the driver and co-driver doubled up as waiters. Every two or three hours they would pull off the road, stop the coach and come around serving refreshments. The first time it was with boiled sweets, the second time coffee and biscuits and finally chilled drinking water.

In the early hours of the morning the coach neared the Brazilian border and I began to feel a little nervous, as this was one moment that I had not been looking forward to. I had noted when carrying out some background research on South America that the Brazilian border police often gave people travelling with rucksacks a bad time; carefully searching through their packs for anything looking vaguely suspicious and asking numerous personal questions.

The coach came to a halt outside the border post and I joined the exodus as everyone filed off to collect their luggage and carry it into the building for inspection. Once inside though, I was somewhat relieved when they only made a token gesture of checking my belongings, by casually opening up my kitbag and half-heartedly looking inside. In fact they didn't even bother to make me open up my rucksack and instead simply drew an 'X' on the side of it with a piece of chalk, before walking along to the next person's luggage. Obviously, the early hours of the morning were the best time to cross the Brazilian border with a rucksack. It seemed the guards were only too willing to pass everyone through as quickly as possible and then stamp their passports so they could get back to sleep.

During one of the refreshment stops, I got talking to an elderly widow sitting close by who enquired if I was English and upon her return, immediately introduced me to her daughter, Silfide, who had taken the opportunity to get off the coach and stretch her legs. They both spoke perfect English and Silfide was quick to grab the opportunity to find out what had been happening back in England since she had returned home.

It turned out that her father had been the Uruguayan Consulate General to England and since her return to Montevideo upon his death, she had been homesick for London and English-speaking people, who were sadly lacking in Uruguay. She had so many questions to ask that we ended up talking throughout most of the night. By the early hours, I had gained first-hand knowledge of how the inner circle of the diplomatic corps lived, played and worked in London. It appeared that her social calendar had been one long continuous cycle of banquets, balls and socialite parties; during which she rubbed shoulders with the men and women (or at least their sons and daughters), who personally advised many of the world's leaders.

***

You should never burp, fart, spit or pick your teeth in public in Uruguay as it is frowned upon and regarded as extremely disrespectful to the people around you.

*

In La Paz, Bolivian people dressed up as zebras help pedestrians safely cross the road while educating the locals and children about the importance of road safety.

*

Bolivia is one of only two landlocked countries in South America, and every year on March 23rd the country commemorates the Battle of Calama which led to the loss of the "Litoral". This was a mainly desert region of approximately 120,000 square kilometres which gave Bolivia access to the Pacific ocean but was conceded to Chile at the end of the War of the Pacific in 1879.

At the Battle of Calama Commander Eduardo Abaroa was defending a small bridge over the River Topáter with a small company of less than a hundred men against a battalion of 500 well-armed Chilean soldiers. The Chilean commander seeing the hopeless position that the enemy was in, ordered Abaroa to surrender. However he refused, uttering the immortal words, "Me, surrender? Tell your grandmother to surrender!," upon which he was shot dead and the rest of the Bolivian soldiers were massacred.

Despite being landlocked for 140 years Bolivia still has a navy of over 5,000 sailors who are largely employed on Lake Titicaca (one of South America's largest lakes and the world's highest navigable body of water, where they work in the tourist industry offering day trips on the lake to help pay for the upkeep of their boats.

At midday on March 23rd the crowds observe five minutes of silence while they listen to recordings of seagulls squawking and ships' horns tooting being played over loudspeakers

According to Bolivia's former president Eduardo Veltze, the country's annual GDP growth could be 20 percent higher if it still had direct access to international waters.

Day 5

January 30, 1981

Upon arrival at Porto Alegre, capital of the state of Rio Grande do Sul, I tentatively joined Silfide and her mother outside the bus as they waited for their respective luggage to be unloaded. I had decided to stick to them like a leech and was secretly hoping to be invited home to stay. I felt like a blood-sucker. The prospects seemed most promising and my mind began to mull over the possibilities. A soft bed instead of a hard sack, wallpaper instead of crawling cockroaches and yes, real food, although I meant no disrespect to my mother's sandwich-making abilities that had sustained me for the first three days of my travels.

Unfortunately for me however, they both lived in a large house in Montevideo and were just up visiting Porto Alegre to look at some property. It seems that for the duration of their stay they had rented a small apartment, large enough for two, but not spacious enough for three.

I felt disappointed, but tried to hide it as I best I could and soon perked up when Silfide cordially invited me around that evening for a meal and even offered to help me find a reasonably priced hotel.

Upon reaching a suitable place of habitation near the city centre, Silfide suggested that I should wait outside while she enquired within. It appeared that the managers of these establishments often kept two price lists: one entitled 'Locals' and the other 'Foreigners'. Having successfully negotiated a reasonable price, she then reappeared outside the building and led me in, much to the amusement of the official behind the front desk.

Registration documents completed, she left me to settle into my room, leaving her address and suggesting that I should come around for a drink and bite to eat once I had unpacked.

The room was small and primitive looking, but clean and comparatively insect-free as far as South American standards went. There was only one slight problem, while the manager was demonstrating how to operate the shower unit along the corridor, he indicated that I should always open the window whenever I took a shower. The trouble was, the hotel backed onto a block of high-rise apartments and, as the window had no blinds or curtains, I wondered whether the manager was running a private peep show for the bored housewives across the way, for a small remuneration of course. I only hoped they wouldn't demand a refund!

The hotel was situated in the centre of town at the top of a very steep hill. As I was soon to learn, Porto Alegre was actually built on a series of hills which ensured that all sightseeing would not only improve your mind, with regards to Brazilian architecture, but also your body. I also noticed that the fashionable dress for most of the nubile young women of the area consisted of a figure-hugging leotard, short pleated skirt and sandals. No bra of course, as it would have been out of the question to wear one in the uncomfortable humidity of the tropics.

I readily approved of such common sense and felt that the sight of such liberated freedom, especially on some of the more well-endowed passers-by, was at times breathtakingly spectacular and well worth a closer inspection if at all possible.

In the afternoon Silfide, who regrettably did not partake in the local fashion, gave me a personalised sightseeing tour of the city. I was particularly surprised, while walking through a busy indoor market, to come across a voodoo shop neatly slotted in-between a designer clothes shop and a local butchers.

The place was filled with numerous herbs, charms and a large assortment of carvings in various sizes. There were glass jars full of animal eyes: evidently snakes' eyes were supposed to be particularly good for solving love or money problems. I could imagine the instructions – *'one to be taken three times a day after meals'*. There was also a collection of assorted lizard skins piled high in a corner. These it seemed, would be sold and then at a later date cut into strips, ground into powder using a mortar and pestle and sprinkled over food. This evidently had the power to calm the high-spirited. Yet other containers were filled to the brim with lizard tails, which Silfide assured me made very good back scratchers! They even sold powdered dog's tongue which, when added to a man's food, was supposed to make him a loyal lover, while a naked ceramic couple once bought and displayed in the bedroom was guaranteed to significantly improve your love life, rectify impotency and increase fertility!

By the doorway stood a six-foot-tall carving of a black woman, brightly painted and lacquered so that it stood out amongst its dull surroundings. Its deeply set eyes gazed out from a solid face of mahogany with a stare that sent a cold shiver down my spine. I refused to enter the shop for a closer examination and, much to my relief, we left the area shortly afterwards, heading for a nearby park.

It seemed that witchcraft was a recognised and often accepted form of medicine in Brazil and voodoo shops were commonplace in many towns and villages throughout the country.

In the evening I was treated to a most enjoyable meal, washed down by a liberal supply of chilled wine. Silfide and I talked on until late about London and the life of a diplomatic family, before I left to slowly retrace my steps back to the hotel, where I collapsed into bed and drifted off into a deep and restful sleep.

***

Twenty-four kilometres along the coast from Porto Alegre is the seaside resort of Cassino that uses, among other things, a novel method of public transportation: railway flat cars powered by sail.

*

In a swampy area of the Parana Delta near North-eastern Argentina, lies an island with a difference. Named "The Eye", the island is a near-perfect round circle of land surrounded by an equally round thin circle of water. The water is very clear and very cold in comparison to the other bodies of water in the area. The diameter of the island is said to be 130 yards (119 meters) across the outer circle. On top of all this strangeness, the island also seems to rotate (or float) slowly around its own axis. Comparing first images taken of it in 2003 and using the slider tool on Google Earth, clearly shows that the circle of land has moved around within the hole it is located in.

Most people share the opinion that the island is too perfectly shaped to be a natural formation, but if it was indeed man-made, what is the purpose of it?

Conspiracy theories are rife, with the most popular of the lot being that the island is concealing an alien base below its surface !

*

Uruguay has had problems with obesity and blood pressure. To combat this, the government banned the use of salt shakes in public places!

Day 6

January 31, 1981

I awoke to the sunlight shining through the curtainless window. Then, abruptly stirring from my bed, I grabbed a towel and with knobbly white knees jutting out before me, I made a quick dash down the corridor towards the bathroom. By the time I had finished, I felt sure that the neighbours would probably be demanding financial compensation from the hotelier and the initiation of a government rehousing scheme, declaring the immediate vicinity unsafe for window-watchers!

I spent the morning with Silfide and her mother, where once again the larder doors were opened as food and wine were placed before me in ever-increasing quantities. In the afternoon, Silfide took me hill-climbing around the city, revealing some of its lesser-known tourist attractions. Regrettably, however, these did not include herself.

On the way back to their apartment, I mentioned how surprised I had been that morning, to turn on my radio and, quite by accident, tune into a local station playing British and American music. Silfide explained that if the local radio stations had their own way they would probably play western music and little else. However, the Brazilian authorities, realising this to be the case, passed a law stating that all radio stations must play a higher proportion of Brazilian samba music than western music, as in this way they hoped to preserve their musical heritage for future generations.

At 18:30, Silfide walked me to the bus station where I caught the overnight coach to Curitiba. The coach was spacious and comfortable but sadly lacked one important feature: air-conditioning. Consequently, I had a restless night in the still unfamiliar humidity of the tropics. Furthermore, I noted that the toilet was worth avoiding if at all possible. In fact, I found the sanitation in most parts of Brazil to be of an extremely poor standard. You could tell the British Empire had never stretched this far! Here, as with many other developing countries, the toilet paper was not supposed to be flushed, but instead placed into an open waste paper basket close by. This was periodically emptied when it became full to overflowing, although in the tropical humidity it could have practically walked off and emptied itself!

***

In 1500, Pedro Cabral sailed from Lisbon with thirteen ships and 1,200 men following Vasco da Gama's navigation charts to India. Unfortunately for the natives of Brazil, his ships were of a bulkier design than da Gama's and were consequently much slower. This resulted in them being carried further west than intended by the strong equatorial currents of the region.

When Cabral first sighted the coastline of Brazil he believed it to be an island and, upon landing, sent out a small search party to walk around it. There is no recorded evidence that they ever returned! Cabral set sail for Portugal nine days later, the holds of his ships filled with the timbers of the Brazil tree, leaving behind two convicts to learn the Indians' language and customs.

At first, little interest was shown in the country until a small number of merchants who had successfully extracted a red dye from the Brazil tree's timbers approached the king and were granted the rights to the Brazil wood trade.

The country was originally named 'The land of Santa Cruz' (Holy Cross) until, in the years that followed, vast numbers of merchant ships plied the Atlantic Ocean back and forth transporting huge quantities of hardwood from the Brazil tree. Over a period of time people started referring to it as 'The Land of Brazil' which in turn was abbreviated to 'Brazil'.

*

The Uros people of Lake Titicaca live on 62 artificial islands made entirely out of layered reeds up to 4 metres thick that float and move around freely on the lake, they rely primarily on fishing and a barter system to fulfil all their basic needs.

Each island lasts for approximately 25 years before they start sinking, hence after 23 years the inhabitants start building a new island to move on to.

*

Pope Francis once worked as a bouncer at a night club in Buenos Aires, a cleaner sweeping floors and a chemical tester in a laboratory, before he became a Jesuit priest.

*

Uruguay was the first country in the world to provide free laptops and Wi-Fi to its school children.

*

Bolivia's infamous 'Death Road' claims the lives of 200-300 people each year.

*

Argentina was the first country to use fingerprinting in criminal investigations.

Day 7

February 1, 1981

The bus pulled into Curitiba (capital of the Brazilian state of Parana, built on the 900-metre-high plateau of Serra do Mar), at approximately 08:00, whereupon I alighted with the other passengers. Having carefully rummaged through my belongings and repacked my kitbag, I checked my rucksack into the left luggage office for three days and bought a ticket on the overnight coach to Foz de Iguaçu. I then spent the rest of the day wandering around Curitiba biding my time and taking things easy.

Within a comparatively short period of time I was yet again following in the footsteps of those less famous and often unknown explorers.[1]

Yes, I was lost, somewhere in the backstreets, but for want of

---

[1] *Thomas Nuttall (1786-1859) was a British botanist who in 1812 conducted a study of plants in the remote parts of North West America. Unfortunately, however, he later became better known for his ability of getting lost whenever he went out collecting samples rather than for his classification of flora. In fact, on one such occasion, upon his failing to return to camp, a search party was sent out to look for him. However, as they approached the botanist, he mistook them for bloodthirsty Indians and proceeded to run away. The rescuers doggedly followed him for three whole days through the bush and across rivers until he accidentally stumbled back into his own camp.*

something better to do I decided to carry on regardless and eventually came across the Passeio Público: the city's central park.

The cool shade of the trees attracted my sweat-stained body and I quickly vanished into their shadows. I was greeted by an array of lush green vegetation and colourful flowers which scented the air with sweet-smelling aromas. Venturing further into this Aladdin's cave of tropical flora, I came across a lake which had two small artificial islands situated at its centre. These were inhabited by a number of monkeys who spent their time either basking in the sun, carefully grooming each other's coats, or noisily chattering away amongst themselves. The islands were linked together by a long rope suspended between two poles which, periodically, one or more of the monkeys would cross, casually swinging back and forth, hand over hand as they precariously dangled above the water.

By the water's edge sat numerous ducks of varying sizes while, close by, several popcorn sellers paraded up and down the pathway, noisily attacking passers-by with a barrage of sales talk as they attempted to sell their merchandise. I sat down to fully appreciate my surroundings while trying to ignore the continual drone of noise that kept battering my eardrums. Then, much to my surprise, I noticed several people stopping to buy popcorn: to feed, not themselves or the ducks as one would have automatically assumed, but the fish in the lake. The ducks would noisily hover around these human food dispensers but their frantic quacking came to no avail as the people simply ignored them and carried on feeding a seething mass of hungry and seemingly ferocious fish. Wherever popcorn landed, the smooth surface of the water erupted into a boiling inferno of activity. No wonder few ducks actually ventured into the water. Better to be hungry than fish food! In England ducks ate fish, but somehow over here the roles of predator and prey seemed to have been mixed up in translation, as they looked like they were reversed.

The park also contained a small zoo with a varied collection of animals, including thirteen lions – seven male and six female.

No wonder Africa was running short of them, they were all over here!

I continued on through the park to find my exit guarded by two naked stone statues, each one over six metres in length. On one side lay a woman reclining on her elbow, head thrown back in gay abandon. While on the other, stood a man staring into the distance, a look of pensive concentration carved onto his face and, by the size of his enormous erection, I had little difficulty imagining what he was thinking of.

At 19:00 I caught a coach to Foz de Iguaçu but, unfortunately, it turned out to be both crowded and uncomfortable, so I spent another uneasy night drifting in and out of sleep. While sleeping, I had a weird dream of being repeatedly beaten on the head by a monkey wielding a large fish, only to half-awake to find I was actually hitting my head against the side of the window.

***

The Yacumama, which translates to 'Mother of the water', is a mythical, monstrous serpent that lives in the Peruvian part of the Amazon basin and is said to be over 130 feet long and six feet wide. The villagers say that it can suck up water and spit it out like a water cannon to knock monkeys out of trees which are its staple diet. Rather like the Amazon archerfish that can spit droplets of water to knock insects onto the water.

*

'Ya-Te Veo' or the South American Man-Eating Tree is supposed to inhabit the Chako forest region of Argentina and Bolivia. It is said to have an abundance of beautiful flowers that hang down from its canopy which exude a powerful sleeping agent. Its prey are initially attracted by its powerful scent, but are then overwhelmed by its toxicity and become paralysed and die by this poisonous perfume. Over a period of time, the victim is drained of blood via suckers contained within the flowers themselves. The plant is said to feed on all manner of large animals and supposedly even human beings.

Day 8

February 2, 1981

Foz de Iguaçu was a drab, dirty-looking town with streets full of litter, pavements full of beggars and shadows full of prostitutes. I made a half-hearted attempt at trying to locate a hotel but wasn't particularly disappointed when my efforts were left unrewarded. The place seemed to have a general dislike towards tourists and there was a noticeable lack of sleeping accommodation in the area. Of the few that I did come across though, they were either full, grossly overpriced or unfit for human habitation. In fact, the only serious offers I received were from the local prostitutes, stood lurking in the doorways.

From here, the town that is and not the local prostitutes, I joined an excursion to the Argentinian side of the Iguaçu Falls and suddenly, everything seemed worthwhile.

Set on the borders of Argentina, Brazil and Paraguay and surrounded by a lush tropical rainforest – where wild orchids and numerous other flowering plants blossomed and bloomed in abundance – were situated the Iguaçu Falls. They were the holy burial place for the Tupi-guarani and Paraguas Indians for thousands of years, prior to the arrival of the Portuguese, and, in my opinion, were probably the most impressive falls in South America, if not the world. Fed by over thirty rivers and streams, it was here that the River Iguaçu fanned out to a width of well over 4km before crashing down some sixty metres into the turbulent waters below with a thunderous roar. It has been estimated that approximately 1,755 cubic metres of water per second poured over the falls, and that during the flood months of May to July, this could rise up to 12,750 cubic metres per second.[2]

The falls were approached by following a small, partly overgrown mud track that threaded its way through the trees and lush undergrowth. On either side, a myriad of creatures continued a life-and-death struggle, oblivious to the passing human traffic. Among the trees, spiders, some the size of my fist, hung motionlessly in wait surrounded by their gossamer fishing nets, several as large as two metres across, while other more industrious neighbours busily climbed around their webs repairing broken threads or surveying their latest catch of fat, juicy insects.

The path led to a narrow walkway approximately 110 metres in length which consisted of a large number of wooden planks. Each plank was placed on steel supports that had been driven into the rock-bed below the water and was fitted with its own accompanying handrail to offer support to those visitors of a nervous disposition. This led out over the fast-flowing river, which rushed past below, to a small viewing point approximately seven metres in length, perched precariously on the very edge of the falls at a point known as the 'Devil's

---

[2] *Niagara falls is actually made up of two falls: the American falls and the Canadian falls, which are separated by a small island called Luna Island. The combined width of the falls is one kilometre and it is fifty-six metres high. The highest falls in the world are the Angel Falls in Venezuela, which are a phenomenal 979 metres high.*

Throat'.

From here you could watch the waters plummeting down directly beneath you, only to send great clouds of mist rising 150 metres up into the air, through which the sun continually painted vivid and colourful rainbows for all to see.

High above, birds of prey majestically soared through the airways gracefully tracing wide circles across the sky, until one of them would hit a warm air pocket and suddenly rise several hundred metres into the air. Below them, the rich brown waters of the Rio Iguaçu flowed downstream to become a tributary to the Rio Paraná.

I looked upstream to watch with fascination as the carcass of some unfortunate animal slowly drifted towards the precipice of the falls. Perched on its bloated body stood a vulture hungrily pecking at its hide until, as the lifeless body dropped over the edge, it spread its wings and gracefully flew away.

In the distance, flocks of parrots noisily chattered amongst themselves, occasionally spilling out from the thick, choking blanket of trees to fly to pastures new, with a brilliant blaze of colour, before once more disappearing, swallowed up by the never-ending rainforest which stretched for as far as the eye could see. Meanwhile, magnificent butterflies in all their beauty and splendour fluttered among the colourful blooms of the tropical flowers, in search of their rich stores of nectar.

For a long, timeless moment I stood, my mouth wide open, in awe at the sight in front of me. My eyes and ears hungrily absorbed their surroundings, yet my brain seemed confused and unable to handle everything at once. I kept on blinking, unable to believe everything around me was reality and not merely a fantastic illusion, created within the dark recesses of my own vivid imagination. I reluctantly left the falls and returned to Foz de Iguaçu, silent and speechless, the corridors of my mind still revelling in the breathtaking visions of beauty and perfection that had appeared before me.

That night I travelled back to Curitiba. The coach was once more crowded and uncomfortable but, unlike before, it didn't seem to bother me. I was at peace within myself and nothing could wrench this tranquillity away from me.

***

Downstream from Iguaçu Falls is the Itaipu Dam, the world's largest hydroelectric power station, which has the capacity to produce up to 12.6 million kilowatts of power. That's enough electricity to supply the energy needs of the whole of Paraguay and Southern Brazil. The joint venture between the Brazilian and Paraguayan governments cost US$18 billion and contained enough concrete to build a two-lane highway from Moscow to Lisbon. Unfortunately, however, in completing this colossal monument to man-made technology, the world's largest waterfall, the Sete Quedas Falls (Seven Falls) – which had thirty times the water capacity of Iguaçu Falls – was destroyed while at the same time creating a lake of 1,400 square kilometres.

*

If you're on your own with time to spare near the river's edge, you don't get easily embarrassed and are interested in butterflies, then try urinating on a flat rock and return approximately half an hour later: butterflies will tend to congregate around pools of urine, feeding off the mineral salts left behind after evaporation!

*

Urine can be a very useful commodity: in Bermuda if you are stung by a jellyfish, the locals advise as a temporary measure, to urinate upon the sting to help neutralise it until you can receive proper medical attention. It's best to try and get out of the water before you attempt this though.

*

An old English remedy for chilblains was to soak your feet in maiden's water.

*

In fact over the last 4,000 years, urine has had many uses:

- Roman authors such as Catullus wrote about people using both human and animal urine as a mouth wash and teeth whitener.

- *Cloth dyed with madder root pigment and mixed with urine created an excellent red dye and had been used to dye clothing found in the tomb of the Pharaoh Tutankhamun, as well as in the ruins of Pompeii. In fact, the emperor Vespasian levied a tax on urine around 70 AD, and when his son Titus expressed disgust at the tax, Vespasian retorted, 'Pecunia non olet,' (money doesn't stink). His tax was so famous, that his name is still used today for public urinals e.g. vespasiennes in French and vespasiani in Italian.*

- *In Tudor times, Norwich, then the second largest town in England due to the wool trade, had several hundred ale houses and outside each one stood a giant bucket used to collect its patrons' urine, which was later emptied each night. At the height of its trade, it is estimated that over 200,000 litres of urine was required each year for the dyeing of wool. In the 1880s, there were over 450 pubs within Norwich's city walls.*

- *When left out for a period of time, urine decomposes into ammonia, which can be used as a cleaning product for removing stains, as well as a sanitiser and disinfectant.*

- *Medieval doctors recommended fresh urine to treat sores, burns and insect bites.*

- *Stale urine, when mixed with ash, was often used to treat a rash on a baby's bottom.*

- *Medieval ladies used their own urine on their skin as a beauty treatment.*

- *On the battlefield soldiers would often urinate on each other's wounds in order to clean them; this made sense as the urine was probably a lot cleaner than any nearby water.*

- *During WWI, British-made Vicker's machine guns needed a 'waterjacket' to keep the weapon cool as it fired off hundreds of rounds. The trouble was, this water would evaporate, so if they ran out of water to replenish it, they would use urine instead.*

Day 9

February 3, 1981

Upon arriving back in Curitiba, I carefully extricated my weary body from my seat and gingerly alighted from the bus. The entire length of my legs, from my toes to my backside, tingled with pins and needles, and for several minutes I could do little more than stand around stamping my feet and flexing my aching muscles until the uncomfortable sensation slowly ebbed away. Whereupon, I proceeded to drag my exhausted body out of the bus station and steer it into the adjoining railway station in plenty of time to catch the 7am train to the port of Paranaguá. The journey, said to be the most spectacular in Brazil, easily lived up to its reputation, as the train gently meandered along the 110 kilometre track for several hours. It threaded its way through lush tropical rainforests, past mountains, deep gorges and breathtaking waterfalls. The most spectacular of these was a waterfall that spurted out of the middle of a sheer rock face some forty metres up, sending water cascading down onto the rocks far below. It appeared and swiftly disappeared while I was changing the film in my camera! Timing: *you've either got it or you haven't*, and today I had left it back in Curitiba.

On the way, the train stopped at several sleepy little hamlets that the 20th century seemed to have left behind. Here, time stood still or at least appeared to have passed by at a slower pace. The small villages could have fallen out of the pages of a Brazilian history book, with their dust, dirt and flaky plaster.

Upon reaching Paranaguá, I immediately began trying to locate a cheap hotel for the night and, up one of the side streets close to the station, I homed in upon a particularly shabby-looking building. It looked perfect for my needs and, after making initial enquiries inside, I found that the price lived up to my hopeful expectations. The inside of the building was shaped like a Roman villa, with a central open courtyard and a circular concrete fountain, which had long since dried up, as its centrepiece. On the first floor, there was a large, open, wooden balcony that ran right the way around the inside of the building with a number of tiny rooms located off it.

I quickly found my room on the first floor, dumped my belongings on the bed, stripped off down to my shorts and, with a towel nonchalantly draped around my waist, headed for the shower. I was so ready to cleanse my body of three days of sweat, dirt and dust. Unfortunately though, the shower, rather like the building, had its weaknesses, i.e. the water was ice-cold and stopped working whenever someone flushed the toilet next door. I guess things could have been worse though it only worked when someone flushed the loo!

Once back inside my room, I managed to locate the hot water. It was coming out of the taps in the sink; in fact it was coming out of both taps. I briefly contemplated the idea of reversing the roles, by bathing in the sink and cleaning my teeth under the shower. However, I couldn't find a shower mat of the correct dimensions, i.e. small enough to fit in the basin.

I got dressed and began my well-rehearsed routine of checking for bed bugs and other unfriendly creatures lurking in the murky corners of my room. Having successfully completed my manoeuvres, I lay back on the bed well satisfied. My roommates seemed harmless enough and as the old saying goes, variety is the spice of life. The floor was literally crawling with a fine piled carpet of tiny ants. There were the inevitable cockroaches scurrying around and the ceiling was an intricate mosaic of spider webs: each one with its respective creator lying in wait for any unsuspecting visitors to their domain. They were not particularly large but I hoped would entertain any uninvited 'guests' that might happen to drop in for a quick night-cap; namely mosquitoes.

When I had first arrived in South America, I quickly realised that there was nothing more irritating than trying to sleep with a squadron of Kamikaze mosquito pilots flying around the room. No sooner would the light go out, than in the distance I would hear the faint sound of these tiny, portable blood-banks warming up their engines with a quick "BBBZZZZZPP, BZZPP," after which they would take off, one after another, switch on their radar and home in on their potential target: any warm-blooded creature in the immediate vicinity. The mosquitos' code of combat was simple: if it breathes, suck the blood out of it!

With bated breath, I would often lie there waiting, straining my ears listening to their approach, as they drew ever nearer, until their very sound seemed to fill the room with its deafening roar. A bead of cold sweat would invariably break out upon my brow and trickle down my forehead, and then, quite suddenly and without prior warning, a deathly silence would descend upon the proceedings. They've arrived! I would lie there motionless, scarcely daring to draw breath, thinking about where they were and when they would attack. My questions would soon be answered as I would feel a pin prick of pain, as one of the blood sucking parasites would begin drilling in the hope of striking a thick, juicy vein.

Unfortunately for me though, the little blighters in Brazil must have been avid followers of Dallas, the 1970s US soap about an oil and cattle ranching dynasty, or at least the insect world's equivalent, as they were usually successful. During the night, I would often wake up and break into a bout of masochistic practices: repeatedly slapping myself, to no avail, as the mosquitoes invariably got away unscathed, their bloated bodies filled with my blood, ready to suck another day.

I spent the afternoon wondering around Paranaguá, and that evening found an excellent little café, where I tucked into a large steak and all the trimmings, washed down with a couple of beers for a modest 240 cruzeiros (that's approximately £1.50).

***

Due to a lack of bees in Kenya, most flowers there are pollinated by flies, hence the vast majority of flowers smell like putrefied meat in order to attract their pollinators.

*

Paranaguá is a free port for the landlocked country of Paraguay.

*

When building a new house in certain parts of Bolivia, it is normal practice to bury a llama foetus in its foundations as a sacrificial offering to Pachamama, the Mother Earth, goddess of the ancient Aymaran religion. It is believed that the foetus will keep the construction workers safe and will give the resident wealth, health, happiness and good luck.

*

In Biritiba Mirim, forty-five miles east of Sao Paulo, the Mayor has outlawed death. Unfortunately, the current cemetery is filled to the gunnels and the regional authorities have banned opening up a new cemetery or crematorium. As a result, he proposed the immortality legislation to the town council. You don't die, just probably fall into a deep sleep!

*

In 2017, the case of Ashutosh Maharaj, the founder and spiritual leader of the 'Divine light awakening mission' in the Punjab, came to light when his family petitioned the courts to allow them to remove his body from a freezer where he had been stored since he died in 2014 so that he could be thawed and cremated. However, his followers, who placed him in the freezer, believe him to be merely in a state of deep meditation from which he will eventually return to life! Much to the joy of his followers, the petition was thrown out by the judges.

Day 10

February 4, 1981

The following morning I returned to Curitiba by bus, where I collected my rucksack and caught the afternoon coach to my next port of call: São Paulo. It was the largest city in South America (the fastest growing city in the world), and renowned for its industrial might and polluted atmosphere. The River Tietê that flows through São Paulo is so toxic that the gases given off from it are corroding the office equipment of nearby businesses. A recent story that hit the headlines in all the São Paulo newspapers was that an alligator had been found living in the river. What amazed everyone was how it could survive in such polluted waters and what it could be living on.

São Paulo city covered more than 1,500 sq. kms (three times the size of Paris), and had a total population of well over twelve million, which was growing at the rate of 4.2% a year. By July 2018 the state of São Paulo had a total population of over 45.6 million and rising.

No sooner had the coach reached the outskirts of the sea of shanty towns (known as favelas) that surrounded the city, than my nostrils were greeted by a multitude of obnoxious odours:

ranging from rotten oranges and sickly spaghetti Bolognese sauce, through to industrial toxic fumes.

Upon venturing out onto the streets of São Paulo, I was once more attracted to yet another reject of habitation, this time situated close to the coach station itself. My room was at the back of the hotel towards the end of a dark, unlit alleyway which was enclosed by a three-metre-high wall topped with broken glass. The alleyway had a cluster of tiny rooms positioned off it on either side, rather like two rows of shabby-looking beach huts, although I'd seen a lot nicer beach huts before.

By now I was becoming so proficient at checking a room for insects that I was seriously considering throwing away my lecturing career and becoming a security guard. With a casual glance I noted that the cockroaches were steadily getting larger the further north I went. In São Paulo they were averaging out at approximately 6cm in length, although I had trouble verifying this as they wouldn't stand still long enough for me to measure them! I also happened to notice that a gang of lizards had muscled in on the action and had practically taken over the premises: running around as if they owned the place, they would greedily plunder the tasty fruits of victory, such as an occasional fat, crunchy cockroach. It was like listening to someone munching their way through a packet of crisps. *Cockroach flavour?* I thought. No, I doubt if it would catch on in England. Pity though, there'd be an endless supply of raw materials...

It seemed to me that Brazilian showers were just like fingerprints – each one had its own unique, distinguishable characteristics. The shower in this particular establishment resembled the famous Wasserspiele on the outskirts of Salzburg in Austria, as jets of hot and cold water shot out from everywhere and in all directions, especially where you least expected it to!

The Wasserspiele was the playground and innovative masterpiece of a mad fountain designer, Markus Sittikus von Hohenems. He booby-trapped the gardens of his chateau with hundreds of hidden water jets which invariably drenched unwitting visitors as they wandered through the gardens.

***

Some fascinating facts about cockroaches include:

—Recent studies have shown that the species has been around longer than the dinosaur, with some specimens living over 359 million years ago.

—There are over 4,600 species of cockroach and they can be found in every continent except Antarctica.

—A cockroach can live for up to a week without its head, as they can breathe through little holes in each of their body segments.

—A cockroach can hold its breath for forty minutes and can even survive being submerged under water for half an hour.

—They can run up to three miles an hour.

—Because they are cold-blooded insects, cockroaches can live without food for one month and survive without water for approximately one week.

*

In 1888 the regional government bought an old farmhouse on the outskirts of São Paulo and set up the first-ever snake farm. The scientist in charge of it believed that snake serum could be used to help save the life of someone bitten by a venomous snake. He started off with sixty-four snakes and his first patients were horses from the Paulista Cavalry, who were the military police of São Paulo state. Today it is the largest snake farm in South America and a major tourist attraction with over 70,000 snakes along with thousands of poisonous spiders and scorpions. The antidotes made from the venom have reduced the number of deaths from snake bites in Brazil by 80%.

*

In 1959, as a protest against local government corruption, a five-year-old female rhinoceros named Cacareco was voted onto the city council of Sao Paulo, winning over 100,000 votes. Unfortunately, however, she was unable to take office as Cacareco couldn't get up the stairs and into the council chambers to be sworn in. Today, the term

"Voto Cacareco" is commonly used to describe protest votes in Brazil.

Other animals that have been elected to public office include;

1981: Bosco a Labrador-Rottweiler mix, served 13 years as the mayor of Sunol, California;

1986: Henry Clay III a beer-swilling billy goat, was elected Mayor of Lajitas, Texas. He often consumed up of 40 bottles of beer a day;

1997: Stubbs the cat was elected the mayor of Talkeetna, Alaska for 15 years;

1998: Goofy the German Shepherd was elected mayor of Rabbit Hash, Kentucky. He was replaced by Junior, a black labrador who was eventually succeeded by a border collie called Lucy Lou, who is the town's current mayor;

2014: Duke a Great Pyrenees dog became the mayor of Cormorant, Minnesota;

2018: Sweet Tart a cat was elected the mayor of Omena, Michigan. There were 13 dogs, a peacock, another cat, and a goat also on the ballot but Sweet Tart was the runaway winner. They also elected a Special assistant for fowl issues which was a chicken called Penny;

2019: A 3-year-old Nubian goat named Lincoln was elected mayor of Fair Haven, Vermont, defeating a Samoyed dog named Sammie by two votes.

*

Dustin the Turkey, was a well-known puppet with a strong Dublin accent character that appeared on RTÉ television's The Den between 1989 and 2010 and has been described as "the most subversive comedy force on Irish television".

Being multi-talented he also had a successful music career with chart-topping singles. He won the public vote to represent Ireland at the Eurovision Song Contest 2008 with the song "Irelande Douze Pointe", although he unfortunately did not progress past the first semi-final stage.

Day 11

February 5, 1981

The day was spent wandering around the city visiting several local tourist attractions. This included tentatively peeping out of a window at the top of the forty-one storey Edifício Itália (the tallest building in South America) to see if I suffered from vertigo. The view from here revealed the awesome size of São Paulo, where approximately fifty percent of the country's industrial output was produced. Evidently, the main reason behind the city's industrial growth and its ever increasing population was the availability of unlimited electrical power. São Paulo was built on a plateau with several rivers running through it, two of which had been dammed to form two huge artificial lakes – Lake Guarapiranga and the Rio Grande Reservoir which were used to power the turbines of a nearby hydroelectric plant.

The city centre seemed to be inundated with three things: beggars, shoe-shine boys and the Brazilian equivalent of sandwich-board men. These duly walked around carrying long, thin poles, looking like a bedraggled collection of Roman standard bearers whose uniforms were in the wash. On the end of each pole was attached a rectangular-shaped board advertising local photographers and displaying samples of their handiwork. Personally speaking, however, I was not impressed, as it looked more like a collection of mug shots, a kind of tatty rogues' gallery, rather than a mobile exhibition of a photographer's workmanship. What's more, they also exhibited a number of miniature X-ray photographs revealing people's innermost secrets, or at least their internal organs, for it seemed that in São Paulo most photographers doubled up as radiographers.

I also noted that members of the city's emergency services looked extremely helpful and friendly! Why, even the firemen wore pistols, and the mounted police carried a particularly nasty-looking, three-foot sabre attached to their belts, in addition to their standard-issue handguns. I quickly decided not to ask them for directions, and instead wandered around the streets until I came across a familiar landmark, a large statue in the middle of a square that stood out like a beacon from afar. From there, I quickly managed to regain my bearings and find my way back to my accommodation for the night.

Brazil had many customs but none more time honoured than its weather. Every afternoon the blue sky and scorching sun would disappear behind a thick mass of dark and ominous-looking clouds. They would appear upon the horizon and quickly race across the sky, turning day into night and sending everyone running for shelter. Their arrival would be announced by several loud claps of thunder that left your ears ringing, and heralded the impending storm, which would begin soon after. At first these would be just a few drops falling here and there, until suddenly, the great mains tap in the sky would be turned on full, and down would come the waters of the heavens, the ferocity of which I had never encountered before. Almost immediately the ground would be transformed into a colossal mud bath and my trousers would invariably develop an uneven coating of slimy mud.

The rainstorms had two immediate advantages, however: firstly they helped clean the streets of some of their detritus, and secondly, during their short, tempestuous lives, the hot, sticky atmosphere would be replaced by a cool, crisp freshness in the air which I found made it much easier to breathe. But alas, like all good things, once the storm had passed, the familiar humidity and heat of the tropics would once more descend upon the land and my body would immediately respond by perspiring like an upturned watering can recently filled to the brim.

***

São Paulo has the largest Japanese community outside Japan.

*

São Paulo has some of the world's worst traffic jams. According to Companhia de Engenharia de Tráfego, the city's traffic management agency, a congestion record was set on November 15, 2013, with a total of 309 kilometres (192 miles) of queues around the city during the evening rush hour.

*

130km away from Sao Paulo is the town of Americana set up by Confederate refugees emigrating from the southern states of America after the American civil war.

*

On October 2nd 1992, following a prison riot in a São Paulo jail, police opened fire and shot dead 111 unarmed and naked prisoners after they emerged from the buildings arms held high, having earlier agreed to surrender. Overall, Brazilian police kill four times as many people as they wound.

*

Sao Paulo has the second tallest Lego tower in the world, consisting of over 500,000 Lego bricks, which was constructed using a crane and stands at 31.2 metres tall.

*

Simon Bolivar is one of the greatest military and diplomatic figures in the history of South America, having led five countries - Bolivia, Colombia, Ecuador, Peru and Venezuela - to independence (along with Panama, in Central America) from their colonial powers.

*

On the 31st October 2018, the World Meteorological Organisation recorded the longest ever single flash of lightning, setting a new distance record of over 709km (440 miles). The 'megaflash' stretched from North Eastern Argentina, across Southern Brazil and ended over the Atlantic Ocean.

*

Divorce was only legalised in Chile in 2005.

*

Fishermen in Laguna, in the southeast of Brazil, have a novel way of catching fish by using dolphins as a type of water-based sheepdog to herd the fish towards their waiting nets. This practice has been going on for generations and at the end of each successful catch, the dolphins receive a share of the bounty.

*

Pistol duelling in Paraguay is legal as long as both parties are registered blood donors.

*

In 1992 it was estimated that there were over 2.7 million slum dwellers living in over 600 favelas or shanty towns around the city of Rio de Janeiro.

*

Sao Paulo, like most South American cities, had an appalling record of road accidents, and in 1987 the statistical average stood at one road death every three hours and an accident every four minutes.

Day 12

February 6, 1981

I awoke at 04:30 thanks to my trusty alarm clock and, having bought some fresh fruit from a nearby local stall, caught the early morning train to Santos. The journey was supposed to pass through some interesting scenery but, once outside São Paulo, the train ran into a thick blanket of drifting fog, which followed us all the way there. Consequently, I sat staring through the window into a blank void of emptiness and little else. Occasionally the remnants of a decaying tree would loom through the misty veil at me, before being engulfed once more by the fog's insatiable hunger. At any given moment, I was half expecting to see a skull impaled upon a spear, a warning of impending doom to all who passed this way. While in the distance, I swore I could hear the slow, rhythmic beating of a drum. However this, as usual, was no more than my vivid imagination playing tricks on me to help pass the time.

The train slowly pulled into Santos around 08:00 and I immediately wished that I hadn't been on it. It was a wet, depressing place and I spent a long time walking the streets trying to find a suitable refuge, but every hotel I came across was as usual either full or out of my price range. By now I was convinced that Silfide had been right and that a sizeable proportion of the hotel proprietors were increasing the prices of their rooms as soon as they saw me coming: a gringo, therefore a rich foreigner. My suspicions were later confirmed when one local behind the front desk tried it on while standing next to the price list, displayed for all to see on the wall. Needless to say I was not amused, and having expressed my feelings, using a selection of descriptive and colourful language which was totally wasted as the manager couldn't understand English, I proceeded to leave.

I finally decided to have a break and temporarily postpone my search, by treating myself to a late breakfast. However, on entering a nearby bar, I suddenly lost my appetite. The place was infested with fat, bloated flies! Why do I always pick them? It seemed that I had discovered the rendezvous point and breeding ground for all the flies in the immediate vicinity, as they were literally crawling everywhere. I even had to ask several of them to move so I could sit down on one of the shabby-looking bar stools. In front of me, perched on the bar, was a dirty-looking food cabinet. I couldn't tell what type of cake was inside, but judging by the number of flies crawling all over it I guessed it was probably the bar's specialty: 'Egg Cake Surprise' (flies' eggs, that is). The floor was coated in a thick, congealed mass of chicken skin and bone, tissues, beer bottles, cake, assorted rubbish and spit (which my fellow diners seemed to partake in, with consistent regularity), and coated in a thick piled carpet of crawling flies. I quickly decided to play safe and ordered a wet breakfast, a beer drunk from the bottle, as I wouldn't trust the cleanliness of their glasses, plus a cigarette, after which I promptly left.

It was 10:40, still raining and I longed to be somewhere else (Santos has the highest rainfall in Brazil, averaging over 381 centimetres (150 inches) per year). I made my way to the bus station and bought a ticket for the afternoon coach to Utopia (or at least that's where I thought I was heading): Rio de Janeiro. Before leaving England, a friend of my brother who had spent some time living there and happened to be visiting friends in

London prior to my departure, had given me the names, addresses and telephone numbers of four contacts in Rio, three of which were women, and I was eager to sample some Brazilian hospitality!

The coach was luxurious and not only had a toilet, but also a small bath-shower, although there was one slight problem. It had been accidentally parked so that the toilet's air vent was positioned directly below a broken drainpipe from the bus station roof. Consequently, the rain water from the gutter had been continuously running down the walls of the toilet. By the time the coach left Santos there was an 8-10 centimetre pool of water on the floor and not a lifejacket in sight.

Upon reaching the coach station in Rio at 22:00, I immediately located the nearest telephone, bought some special telephone discs from a nearby kiosk, and proceeded to phone the first of my contacts. Unfortunately though, I received no reply to the first call; the person couldn't speak a word of English on the second; I managed to make out that the girl was away on holiday on the third, and I once again received no answer to the fourth. I flung the phone down in a rage, swung my rucksack over my shoulders and picked up the rest of my belongings. Then, barging my way through a babbling wall of taxi drivers who had miraculously appeared before me, I headed out into the night. I was furious with myself for being so naïve and stupid enough to believe that just because I had been given several telephone numbers and addresses, everything would automatically be all right. I had ignored two simple facts: one, they were not expecting me and two, it was the middle of the Brazilian holiday season, so many people would be away.

Once outside the confines of the station I stopped and asked several passers-by for directions to the city centre using one of the very few words of Portuguese I actually knew, 'centro', and went off in search of some cheap form of accommodation. The only trouble was, no one tried to warn me about the particular route that I was taking. Following directions, I turned right at the next junction and started walking along a road somewhere in the suburbs of Rio. The road was well over 3km long and stretched before me until it disappeared into the distance. On one side of me stood a four-metre-high wall, behind which lay several railway lines, while on the other side beyond the main road that I was walking alongside was a long jagged section of rock which, halfway along, fell quite steeply until it levelled out for several hundred metres before rising sharply up again.

It was here, upon this barren stretch of rock raised a couple of metres above the road, that between thirty-five to forty tiny corrugated iron huts were situated, huddled closely together, as if they would fall down if left to stand on their own. As I walked past, the inhabitants of these pitiful hovels all came out to watch me pass by. Clothed in rags, and wearing faces long since scarred by years of poverty, hunger and disease, they stood there, silently watching me, their eyes transfixed upon my sweating body. By this point, I was beginning to wish that I had never left England and had settled for two weeks at Southend-on-Sea instead! I was sweating buckets. In fact, I left a trail of them behind me: they made a terrible clatter as they hit the ground.

Then, a few minutes later and at first very faintly and far away in the distance, but gradually coming closer and closer, I could hear the sound of an engine. This engine sounded distinctly different to the noise of all the other cars that were screaming past me at speed. I quickly glanced behind to see a car slowly cruising along towards me, so I immediately increased everything: my pace, length of stride, pulse, production of adrenaline and sweat. The car slowly motored up alongside me and I glanced round and stared through the windscreen, only to find two black faces staring back. My eyelids opened so wide that I thought my eyeballs were going to fall out of their sockets. I could feel my muscles tensing up, my fingernails crawling back inside my skin and my tongue cowering at the back of my throat. I had been reduced to a quivering wreck of a human being, leaving a trail of sweat behind me, like a snail leaves its slime.

The car stopped and the passenger opened his door and slowly started to climb out, at which point I somehow managed to increase my pace even faster. I had by now practically reached the end of the road and didn't want to do anything sudden, which might have prompted them to rush straight at me. I was so heavily laden down with my rucksack and kitbag that I couldn't have run away, even if I had wanted to, and I definitely wanted to! My only consolation was that they obviously didn't realise this and were consequently being very careful themselves. I realised that control was the key to the problem and if I could master it, I would survive. Fear was no solution: just the signing of my own death-warrant.

I made it to the end of the road (although another five to ten metres and it might have been a different story!), and hurriedly turned the corner. A sudden wave of relief and ecstasy swept over my body, as the entrance to a large bus station appeared directly before me, which I immediately dived into and was now safe.

I reached into my pocket, and with trembling fingers, started fumbling for my cigarettes and lighter. I shivered uncontrollably and it was at this point that things started to fall into place as to why my potential muggers had been so slow to respond to such a golden opportunity. If I had screamed, I might well have attracted the attention of people in the bus station. The fact that at the time no one was at that end of the bus station and that I was too scared to even think of screaming was beside the point. They fortunately hadn't realised this and the good guy upstairs was working overtime.

After a few minutes' rest and a couple of cigarettes to calm my nerves, I felt sufficiently recovered to renew my search, and once more ventured out into the night. The area was not particularly to my liking and looked like the location for a disaster movie, with a number of burnt-out buildings and a police car with flashing lights and ear-piercing sirens screeching past. After several fruitless attempts, I found a hotel and checked into my room. By now I was prepared to accept anything, regardless of price or degree of habitation. I was just thankful for a roof over my head and a lock on my door. The furniture in the room seemed to suit the area, the bed was round and I surmised that people using these establishments liked to shave in bed. After all, why else would the ceiling be covered in mirrors?

I dumped my gear, locked the room and went out. What I needed was a few cold beers and a chaser or two to help me forget. Unfortunately, however, when I went to hand my key in, the desk clerk started waving his arms about as if throwing an epileptic fit, and shouting, "Nay, nay!" (*No, no!*). He then pointed to his heart and went, "Bang bang!" After a few more seconds of him babbling on in Portuguese, it dawned on me what he was trying to say. It seems that I had wandered into one of the city's favela (slum) areas: a no-go area for gringos especially at night-time, unless they wanted to be mugged, and here they tended to shoot first and rob later. Charming, I thought. If I'd have known that earlier, I would almost certainly have messed my undies. Even so, as I had noticed a bar across the street directly opposite the entrance to the hotel, I decided to risk it.

When I arrived there, I was viewed as something of a novelty by the locals. After all, I was probably the only white person in the whole area. Feeling uneasy under the scrutiny of everyone in the bar, who had immediately stopped talking when I entered and just stared at me, I quickly drank my beer, paid the bill and returned to the relative safety of my room, breathing a sigh of relief when I turned the key and locked the door behind myself.

That night, not unsurprisingly, I felt restless and couldn't sleep. Most people count sheep when they suffer from insomnia, but as I was in Brazil, I tried counting cockroaches instead. Funnily enough, however, this didn't seem to help. Perhaps I should have changed my name to Sally Mander first!

***

Santos is the busiest port in Brazil and handles over 40% of the country's imports and 50% of its exports. It is also the world's largest coffee port.

TALES FROM A SOUTH AMERICAN STORM DRAIN

*

There is an excellent air shuttle service between São Paulo and Rio de Janeiro (which only takes twenty minutes) that you don't have to book, simply turn up at the airport, catch the next available plane and pay on the way.

*

Off the coast of São Paulo is Ilha da Queimada Grande, also known as 'Snake Island'. It was estimated that at one time the island was home to over 430,000 snakes, and not just any snake but a unique species of pit viper: the golden lancehead. The lancehead genus of snakes are responsible for 90% of Brazilian snakebite-related fatalities, as they possess a powerful fast-acting poison that literally melts the flesh around the area where they bite.

The snakes feed on the many migratory birds that use the island as a resting point. Although it is now believed that the number of snakes has considerably diminished due to a combination of a lack of sufficient food all year long, inbreeding and wildlife smugglers, known as bio pirates, collecting specimens to be sold to collectors.

*

In the city of Santos, over ninety of the city's residential tower blocks lean in such a fashion that they stand anywhere from a few inches to several feet off-kilter. The issue arose after the buildings had been constructed. Due to lax building codes, the foundations of many of Santos' buildings were only built a few metres deep, on top of a layer of comparatively soft clay that was not able to handle the immense weight of the buildings, compacting in spots to create the leaning effect. They were South America's equivalent of the leaning tower of Pisa. Despite the creeping tilt, most of the buildings are still inhabited by tenants.

*

Rio de Janeiro when translated means River of January: so named, as it was discovered by Portuguese sailors in January 1502. However, it doesn't actually have a river, it's just that the Portuguese explorers who landed mistook the bay for the mouth of a river.

*

The San Alfonso del Mar resort, located about 100 km west of

Santiago, is home to the world's largest outdoor pool. The San Alfonso's pool is 1 kilometre long, covers an area of 7.7 hectares (19 acres) and holds over 250 million litres (66 million gallons) of seawater.

Day 13

February 7, 1981

In the morning, I quickly left the area and headed for a hostel that I had read about in my copy of the 'South America Handbook', while lying in bed. Although its exact location evaded me for most of the morning, I continued to doggedly persevere and finally arrived at its doorstep with a sense of achievement and satisfaction. This was regrettably followed by disappointment, as I and several other people who had arrived at the same time were informed that the hostel was full. Undeterred, however, and encouraged by the fact that one of the hostel representatives could actually speak English, I further enquired if there were any other hostels around and, having successfully obtained new directions, I was soon on the move again.

I caught a bus to Botafogo, a suburb of Rio, close to the city centre, from where I walked on to the university. Evidently, during the summer vacation that ran from February to April, a nearby hall of residence had been turned into a youth hostel for approximately 350 people and, for 200 cruzeiros a night, I procured the top half of a bunkbed. No bedding of course, just a mattress. After all, this could have restricted the movement of the bed bugs and I didn't want to be reported to the Brazilian equivalent of the R.S.P.C.A. for cruelty to insects.

The room offered the bare essentials but little else a wooden floor, four walls and a ceiling. It measured roughly 3.5 by 5 metres with a door at one end and a window at the other, and contained four wooden bunkbeds; two against each side wall but nothing else. I had seven roommates: a Frenchman called Gérard, a Swede called Roman, three Chileans and two Brazilians, one of whom was a confirmed revolutionary Marxist, with plenty of advice, leaflets and posters for everyone – at a modest price of course: *'after all, it was all for a good cause!'* For once I was glad that I couldn't speak either Portuguese or Spanish as, like most Brazilians, 'Karl Marx's' command of the English language was very limited. Consequently, he tended to reserve his sales patter exclusively for his other South American roommates.

The facilities available in the hostel were quite reasonable by South American standards, with shower and toilet facilities centrally located on each of its four floors. Furthermore, the view from the first-floor balcony was spectacular, as it overlooked the golden sands of Botafogo beach (the waters of which were unfortunately too polluted to bathe in), and beyond, across the bay, stood the famous Pão de Açúcar rock, otherwise known as the Sugar Loaf.

The name was originally coined by the Portuguese in the 16th century at the height of the sugar cane trade when blocks of sugar would be carefully placed inside conical moulds made of clay to protect them during their transportation back to Portugal. The shape of the moulds used was similar to that of the Pão de Açúcar rock and hence the name stuck. It was a massive 396-metre-high granite cone situated at the entrance of Guanabara Bay and is the highest peak of a low chain of mountains that surrounded Rio and together were shaped into the outline of a colossal reclining figure known as the 'Sleeping Giant'. The Sugar Loaf represented the giant's bent knee.

Yes, all in all I was well pleased with myself and let's face it, for US$10 a week, who could complain? In the evening, I went out for a stroll along the beach and for a long time stood gazing up at the magnificent Cristo monument, shining out in the distance. It was without doubt a real sight to behold.

***

Set on the top of Corcovado, a jagged peak some 740 metres high, and located in the Tijuca Forest national park, stood the awe-inspiring statue of Christ the Redeemer (recognised as one of the Seven Wonders of the Modern World). Carved out of white stone and weighing in at 1,145 tonnes, this symbolic figure stood some forty metres high with arms outstretched as it surveyed the city beneath its feet. At night-time the statue was lit up by hundreds of floodlights. Occasionally clouds would form at the base of the statue, obscuring these lights from view, so that when you looked up you saw the statue of Christ standing upon a cloud shining out in the night against a black sky. It was, without doubt, one of the most awe-inspiring wonders of the world and a memory that I would treasure for the rest of my life.

*

The National Museum in Rio exhibits the famous Bendegó meteorite which landed in the northern state of Bahia in 1888. It is the largest meteorite ever found, weighing over 5,360 kilograms. Two and a half thousand years earlier in Egypt, the pharaohs actually believed that meteorites were dribbles of semen from the gods that fell to the earth.

*

On the 4th July 1987, the Guardian newspaper reported the reappearance of death-squads in Rio. Between November 1986 and April 1987, over 1,135 people had been murdered in the city. The cost of assassination by the death-squads was US$250 for an adult and US$70 for a street-kid. On average two street-kids are murdered in Rio every day. Their mutilated bodies were dumped on the main streets as a warning to other children living on the streets to stay away from the *area.*

Day 14

February 8, 1981

Needless to say, things don't often turn out to be what they at first seem. The hall of residence I was staying in backed onto a hospital, and the window in my room was directly opposite that of the maternity wards. Consequently, every morning without fail, I would be torn out of my peaceful slumber by a chorus of little screams demanding breakfast, which ensured that I seldom got any chance of a lie in.

I spent a quiet day wandering around Botafogo and in the evening caught a bus into town with the rest of my bunkbed comrades for some light refreshments. The evening's entertainment got under way rather earlier than expected though, when a group of about twenty 'down and outs' performed their own interpretation of the siege of Troy, on the bus that everyone was travelling in.

The bus at the time was waiting by a set of traffic lights, when suddenly, this unruly mob of riffraff that were sitting under a palm tree close to the road, took exception to people looking at them and decided to make their feelings known by charging the side of the vehicle. After beating it with their fists, spitting and attempting to fling punches through the open windows, they then started to rock the bus over onto its side. After about four or five attempts the bus was beginning to feel unsafe, as each time it tilted over a little bit more. Fortunately for everyone on the bus though, they were beaten by the traffic lights before they could achieve their goal, which obligingly changed to green and the bus quickly moved off with its passengers a little bit shaken but otherwise none the worse for the experience, although several people later complained of feeling a little bit seasick.

Later on, even more live action occurred as my roommates and I were sitting down outside a bar in the centre of Rio, quietly sampling the local beer. The bar was one of several situated along a busy pedestrianised thoroughfare leading up to a large piazza and boxed in on either side by an assortment of shops, each with its own eye-catching displays and ever-welcoming open doors. It was a warm, tropical summer's evening with a cool breeze and long shadows. The beer was cold, the company good, and everyone was relaxing, lying back in their chairs, each lost in their own thoughts. Then, suddenly, along the road, sprinted a young guy of about seventeen years old, who was being hotly pursued by an unpleasant-looking gang of young thugs. They appeared to be under the leadership of a particularly nasty-looking yob, whose left leg had been amputated above the knee. It was amazing to watch him, for with the aid of a crutch he could actually run as fast as, if not faster than, the rest of the youths, although, I got the impression that this wasn't the only reason he was their leader.

The young lad who was being chased rushed straight past our table and headed for the comparative safety of the bar. However, before he could reach the doorway, the crutch-wielding yob flew past me at great speed before coming to an abrupt halt in front of a nearby, recently-vacated table, from which he grabbed an empty beer glass and hurled it at the boy. The glass missed its intended target and shattered against a nearby pillar instead, showering glass all over a group of people sitting close by. At this point the owner and several heavies appeared from inside the bar and chased them away.

Once all the commotion had died down, I was introduced to the Brazilian equivalent of meths: their local fire-water, called Cachaça (made from raw sugar cane). It had an immediate and noticeable effect upon me, as it hit the back of my mouth and slowly started burning its way down my throat, rather like molten lava flowing down a mountainside. I suddenly began to realise why these people were called hot-blooded Latin Americans. After all, they had to be to drink this sort of stuff!

**

There are well over 100 different brands of Cachaça, the taste and quality of which vary considerably. The cheapest varieties are reputed to burn a hole in your stomach lining if you drink too much at once, and probably double up as paint stripper!

*

In Santa Rita do Sapucia prison, on the outskirts of São Paulo, the authorities offer reduced sentences to inmates who exercise on stationary bicycles. When a prisoner pedals for 16 hours, their prison sentence is reduced by one day. This is because the bikes generate electricity that is then sent to a nearby town. Therefore, the benefit of this innovative act is double: both for the citizens and for the prisoners.

*

Around 75% of electricity used by homes and businesses in Paraguay comes from hydroelectric power stations

Day 15

February 9, 1981

The buildings around me started to shake and the ground began to shudder violently, as the sound of breaking glass and falling masonry filled the air. My heart started pumping like a pneumatic drill, my body perspiring like an industrial sprinkler system and my adrenaline flowed through my veins like a toboggan hurtling down the Cresta run. I was gaining first-hand experience of an earthquake of terrifying proportions and I didn't like it. Fortunately, however, I had mentally and physically prepared myself back in England for all eventualities, and so, without a moment's hesitation, I knew exactly what to do… Panic!

I began running around like a headless chicken, screaming obscenities and crying. Stumbling over debris, I was thrown this way and that, as I scrambled around on all fours like a whimpering dog. The whole area became a moving sea of turmoil, a kind of out of control merry-go-round, which had forgotten to break in the horses.

I tentatively opened one eye to realise I was dreaming and found one of my Brazilian roommates vigorously shaking me. Evidently, my presence was requested on the balcony for a group photo of everyone in the room.

I arose, bleary eyed and sleepy, and wandered off down the corridor to the bathroom for a wash. My respect for Cachaça had grown considerably overnight, as I found out from first-hand experience that it had a kick like a kangaroo the morning after. The sight that awaited me when I eventually caught sight of myself in the mirror was not a particularly pleasing one: I had decided to grow a beard and now possessed several days' growth. Fortunately, the mirror was rather dirty, so I missed the full effect of my stubble.

Still, the sun was shining, there was not a cloud in the sky and apart from my hangover, it felt good to be alive. Back in England, everyone would be huddling around their fires and donning jumpers in an attempt to keep warm, while over here I spent my days wearing a pair of shorts and little else. It was 10:30 local time and the temperature was already 30+ centigrade and soaring skywards.

Once the photo call had been completed, it was suggested that everyone should go to the beach, and an enjoyable day of swimming, sunbathing and ogling at bikini-clad women, not necessarily in that order, seemed in prospect. However, if there's one thing that Rio taught me, it was never to go anywhere or try to do anything with a group of Brazilian students, as we were joined before leaving the hostel by several of Walid's (one of my Brazilian roommates) friends. No sooner had we left the building than the Brazilian contingent of the party abruptly stopped on the pavement outside and a great debate arose as to where exactly on the beach, which stretched out before us on the other side of the road, we should all go to. This somewhat heated discussion quickly developed into a full-scale argument and with a liberal supply of raised voices and flapping arms thrown in for good measure, I was given an introductory lesson on the finer points of Brazilian swearing.

Unfortunately, the emotional festivities culminated with everyone walking off in different directions, myself included, as I didn't want to feel left out of it just because I couldn't speak the language. Consequently, I ended up having a somewhat quieter day than expected, with plenty of time on my hands. I decided to put the time to good use and spent most of the afternoon trying to locate the British Consulate in the hope that they would have some recent copies of English newspapers. However, my search was all to no avail, as upon entering the building, I was unable to find anyone who could speak English let alone read English newspapers.

That evening, I met the missing link, which I appropriately named the abominable 'Tropicman'. Yes, I thought, *Neanderthal man is alive and well and living in Rio. Who knows, he might even be sharing an apartment with Ronald Biggs.*[3]

There I was, sitting in a bar quietly enjoying a beer, when in walked a short, stockily built creature, with a protruding jaw, shallow forehead, long, dark, unkempt hair and an unpleasant pungent odour that emitted from his ragged clothes and person. I deduced it to be a male member of the species by his straggly looking beard and the way he sat down beside me, opened his legs and started spitting on the floor.

In-between spitting, strange grunting noises permeated from between his cracked lips and yellow teeth which seemed to be mainly aimed at the barman.

Initially the barman ignored his verbal barrage, avoided his stare and tried to make himself look extremely busy, so that he would hopefully forego the pleasures of serving him. However, after a few minutes the apeman began to get rather agitated and started banging the bar with his hairy fist, at which point the barman must have reached the inevitable conclusion that if ignored he probably wouldn't go away. Consequently, he obligingly came over and placed a large mat in front of him, onto which was shortly afterwards placed a dish of thick oily-looking soup. Apeman immediately responded by grabbing the spoon in front of him and holding it clumsily in his fist.

He then started greedily shovelling the contents of the bowl

[3] *Member of the Great Train robbery gang who robbed a Royal Mail train in 1963 of £2.6 million (equivalent to £54 million today). He escaped from Wandsworth Prison in 1965 and lived in Rio de Janeiro for thirty-one years before returning home voluntarily to serve out the rest of his sentence.*

into his mouth, or at least trying to, as most of it went onto the mat, the floor or became tangled up in his beard. He seemed to enjoy dropping things between his legs. *Maybe he's retiring to the floor later on for dessert,* I thought. The idea sent a shudder through my body and I felt a strong revulsion towards my dining partner, so I hurriedly finished off my beer and left.

**

On April 12th, 1976 in Rio de Janeiro, twenty-one people, including several cripples, were trampled to death when a large crowd rushed the narrow exit of a church in order to greet a renowned faith-healer.

*

During August 1981, special investigators of the state secretariat started using a novel method of interrogation in order to frighten and intimidate prisoners into confessing: a two-metre-long boa constrictor!

*

During the 1983 Mardi Gras carnival, twenty-eight prisoners took advantage of a reduction in the number of guards on duty by attempting to break out through the city's sewer which they had painstakingly dug down to reach, using only home-made implements. The only trouble was the particular manhole cover which they randomly selected to escape from, was situated directly in front of a police station. The occupants of which immediately rearrested the prisoners as they emerged from the manhole!

*

You were strongly advised in Brazil to take care whenever you used an electric shower unit, as it seemed a large number of them hadn't been properly earthed when installed and could consequently deliver a dangerously high electric shock to potential users at any time and without warning!

Day 16

February 10, 1981

I spent the day around Botafogo, devoting the morning to standing by a basin up to my arms in soap suds, washing clothes. I then tried to secure these sodden garments to a length of cord, which I had carefully brought from England, with my extensive collection of four clothes' pegs. I only wished I had thrown caution to the wind, ignored the extra weight factor and brought a few more pegs.

Realising that weight was of paramount importance, I had left England to tour the world for three years with the following wardrobe:

- One pair of cords,
- One pair of jeans,
- One pair of shorts,
- A Greek kaftan,
- Three pairs of undies,
- Six pairs of socks,
- Four T-shirts,
- Two short-sleeved shirts for those special occasions that I hoped to come across.

The trouble was, sooner or later they had to be washed and today was 'W' Day, although, luckily for me, I didn't usually wear that much due to the heat and would often be found clad in a pair of denim shorts and little else, so my dirty-washing bag tended to fill up very slowly. I felt that the only way of ensuring against getting mugged, especially as I spent much of my time walking through the backstreets, was to wear no jewellery and the minimum of clothing. In this way any potential robber could immediately see that I had nothing of any value to steal.

Upon completion of this task, the rest of the day was devoted to more leisurely pursuits: mainly sipping cold drinks while lounging in the shade.

As the evening drew near, I felt restless and went for a stroll along the bay to Ulca, a stretch of coastline that jutted out into the Atlantic like a gnarled finger. The view of Botafogo and its surrounding districts from here was spectacular, and as the sun set over Rio and the lights of the city burst into flame, I homed in upon a small bar tucked away under the trees close to the beach. Then, with beer bottle in hand, I leaned against the sloping trunk of a nearby palm tree and allowed my mind to slowly drift away into oblivion. A cool breeze gently rolled in from the Atlantic and the sound of children's laughter, as they played among the rockpools close by the water's edge, floated through the air. In the distance, the sparkling lights of Rio sent their reflections dancing across the moving waters, while high above and in all its glory stood the Christo monument, a suitable setting for such a vision of beauty.

It was moments like this that made everything worthwhile: the endless days of lugging a rucksack from place to place, wandering around looking lost and feeling afraid, spending hour upon hour waiting around in coach stations and travelling on buses, wearing dirty clothes that hummed like a male voice choir. Yes, all this and more seemed a small enough price to pay for moments such as this.

I closed my eyes and breathed in deeply. I felt good, relaxed and at ease with the world, as if I had just shaken off all of the problems and discomforts of the last sixteen days.

Consequently, it was with some reluctance that I left this sanctuary of peace and tranquillity and slowly headed back to the hostel. Upon reaching the road, I was quickly brought back to reality by the flashing lights and screeching brakes of the Brazilians' equivalent of Russian roulette: it's called 'driving' and the contestants in this precarious game are called 'pedestrians'!

The typical Brazilian motorist was a complete and utter maniac and would have made the average boy racer back home look like a paraplegic pensioner driving around in an electric milk float with a half-drained battery. They were a law unto themselves and seemed to be under the illusion that the road went wherever their car took them. Whether that was on the road, grass, pavement or beach, their motto was simple: 'where there's a will there's always a way', and if anyone got in their way, well it was their own fault and they simply got what they deserved. After all, they shouldn't have been there in the first place!

***

In 1991 a grisly trade in human organs was uncovered when a doctor became suspicious of a spate of hit-and-run accidents occurring on the same stretch of road outside his hospital every Saturday night, when only a minimum of staff were on duty. Investigations revealed that people, especially homeless children, were regularly being run over, only to be rushed into the hospital and then have vital organs such as their heart, kidneys and corneas harvested. These were then being frozen and later sold to clinics in America. Most of the injured children either died from the traffic accident itself or the operation shortly afterwards. The normal rate of payment for a kidney in 1991 was US$25,000 and twice that for a liver.

*

Bangu is a neighbourhood in the West Zone of Rio de Janeiro. A densely populated lower-middle-class area of mainly office workers and surprisingly the location of a little-known sculpture by the famous French artist Frederic Bartholdi. The sculptor is the designer of the famous Statue of Liberty in New York City, and was commissioned to build a similar sculpture to celebrate the tenth anniversary of Brazil's independence. The downsized version of the statue is made of nickel instead of copper, but still retains the original's green hue.

*

Rio de Janeiro continues to be a dangerous place: 10 soldiers recently riddled a family car with 80 bullets as it drove by, killing the driver and injuring a passenger. The family inside were driving to a baby shower celebration and the patrol mistook their car for one of the same colour being driven by gang members.

*

The former governor of Rio de Janeiro recently admitted in court that he had paid $2 million to buy votes to ensure the city was selected to host the 2016 Olympic games.

*

The North Yungas Road , is a two-way, 3.5 - 4 metre wide (10-12 foot) path that was cut into the side of the Cordillera Oriental Mountain chain in the 1930s and is ominously known as the "Death Road" . Connecting Bolivia's capital, La Paz, to the town of Coroico, it is littered with hairpin bends which can be extremely dangerous due to fog, landslides, oncoming traffic and vertical drops of over 2,000 feet (610 meters). On average approximately 300 people were killed every year up until 1994 when the government started a long overdue 20 year programme of road improvements.

*

On July 24, 1983, a bus veered off the Yungas Road and into a canyon, killing more than 100 passengers it was Bolivia's worst ever traffic accident.

Day 17

February 11, 1981

Today was 'let's be taken for a ride' day. At the time, I was walking down a side-street trying to locate an art gallery, when I was approached by a middle-aged man, casually dressed with a well-developed paunch, triple chin and receding hairline. He asked me for the time and upon establishing that I was English, proceeded to inform me that he was a captain in the Brazilian airforce and that his brother was the Brazilian ambassador to England.

Well, why not? I thought. After all, I had wined and dined with the ex-Uruguayan Consulate General's wife and daughter in Porto Alegre. The stranger continued by stating that he loved England and the British people, so would I like to join him for a drink?

My eyes lit up like two raging forest fires, and like a lamb to the slaughter I eagerly agreed. So, without further ado, we embarked upon a miniature pub crawl: drinking our way through several beers and Cachaça chasers, which my newly acquired drinking partner insisted on paying for.

He began to feed me an elaborate story of his life, and what's more, I even believed him (although by now the alcohol was doing most of the believing for me). Supposedly, the Brazilian had just returned from the Far East where he had been on official business, and as he had taken a liking to me, asked if I would like to join him tomorrow morning for a helicopter ride around the Christo monument and the Sugar Loaf Mountain. He elucidated further by informing me that he had dated two Japanese air hostesses during the return flight from Tokyo and had promised to show them the sights, so would I like to make up a foursome? My mouth opened so wide that the Brazilian could have climbed in! Everything seemed too good to be true and, unfortunately for me, it was.

We reached our fifth bar and once again the Brazilian obligingly ordered two beers, this time with double Cachaça chasers. However, as he reached for his money, a worried look quickly spread across his face, and so, he turned towards me explaining that he had found himself in a temporary financially embarrassing situation. It seemed he had not yet gone to the bank to change any of his travellers' cheques, and as they had drunk their way through what little cash he had with him, would I mind paying for the drinks? *Fair enough*, I thought, after all, the Brazilian had insisted on paying for all of the previous rounds so how could I refuse? Therefore, without further hesitation, I proceeded to settle the bill. As I pulled out a wad of notes and handed over the money, a broad smile lit up the Brazilian's face, and having slapped me on the back and called me a good fellow, he raised his glass of Cachaça to his lips, toasted my health and knocked it back in one, indicating afterwards that I should do likewise. Foolishly, I followed his advice and immediately felt the effects as it numbed my mouth and practically made me fall off the stool that I was sitting on at the time. I closed my eyes in the vain hope of trying to stop the room from spinning, but found it had had little success upon reopening them a few moments later.

I was as nissed as a pewt, and unfortunately for me, my newly found companion knew it only too well. This was the moment he had been waiting for and he immediately grabbed the opportunity by announcing that he must shortly go and phone the air hostesses as he had promised to meet them that afternoon. However, he must firstly buy some champagne for the occasion, as he wanted to ensure they would be in a fairly relaxed and receptive mood for the ensuing evening. So he asked me if I could lend him some money, which of course he would pay back later. He initially asked for 500 cruzeiros,

but then with his confidence increasing, along with my noticeably drunken stupidity, he asked if I could spare 1,000 cruzeiros, which I obligingly handed over without a second thought. The Brazilian then disappeared for a moment, under the pretence of phoning the two air hostesses, and never returned, leaving me about six quid lighter and feeling like a prize jerk.

Needless to say, once the realisation had dawned on me that I had just kissed goodbye to a thousand cruzeiros, I was extremely annoyed with myself! *Well, what's done is done*, I said to myself, *and you can't change the past, you can only change the future*, so I promptly left for my original destination and attempted to blot out this unfortunate episode by absorbing myself in famous Brazilian works of art. Although this turned out to be somewhat difficult, as having consumed five beers and six Cachaça chasers before eleven o'clock in the morning, I was having trouble focusing, let alone trying to walk in a straight line.

Later on, after having returned to the hostel with a sore head and unsteady feet, I went for a stroll, hoping that the fresh air would help clear my head. I headed in the opposite direction to Ulca and followed the path as it ran alongside the beach. The sand was hot to the touch and the water dazzling as it reflected the rays of the sun, and as I ambled along, a feeling of peace once more descended upon me, as my mind began to wander, and I temporarily forgot about the morning's unfortunate encounter.

Upon leaving the Botafogo area, the sand on the beach was replaced, initially by pebbles and then later by large rocks, while the path I was on became covered in a crawling mass of insects like a moving fine-piled carpet. These were ugly-looking creatures of anything up to six centimetres long. They had an oval shaped shell-like body, a mass of long hairy legs and a pair of large antennae sprouting out from their heads like two elongated C.B. aerials. They were a sort of shoreline equivalent to my usual roommates: cockroaches, and I viewed them with some fascination. As I walked forward, they would scatter before me in all directions, and I felt like I was re-enacting the biblical scene of Moses parting the waters of the Red Sea, or in this case, Michael Plummer parting an ocean of insects! No sooner had I lifted my foot off the ground, than they would sweep back in again to occupy the space that had just been vacated. I was literally surrounded by them, as they were everywhere I looked, and this carried on for several hundred metres. Using pen and paper, I later estimated that there must have been well over thirty-seven million of them: an insect eater's paradise!

On the other hand, the rocks themselves situated by the water's edge were inhabited by a more menacing sight: rats. They came in all sizes, ranging from tiny little ones through to huge, great, big fat ones. They scurried about their business oblivious to my presence, searching for food or attempting to settle territorial disputes with their neighbours, which from the sound of it was not always amicably achieved.

Further along still, I came across a more sickening and pitiful sight, as the rats were replaced by people. Whole families were living in among the rocks, clothed in tattered rags and wearing hungry faces. These bedraggled members of the human race watched me walk past with empty, lifeless eyes. They sat there, huddled amongst the rocks, their only form of protection from the sun and rain being either a small rusty sheet of corrugated iron or a tattered piece of cloth stretched across two rocks and held in place by a collection of stones of various sizes.

As late afternoon turned to evening, I started heading back towards Botafogo, this time walking through a narrow stretch of public garden that separated the beach area from the road. It was here, much to my surprise, that I came across a number of burning candles carefully placed under various trees with an assortment of objects lying close besides them: for instance, a small bunch of red roses. I quickly decided that it was unlikely to be Rio's equivalent of Interflora, or a variation on the paperchase by the local league of arsonists, so upon reaching the hotel, I asked one of the Brazilian students on the front desk who could speak some English for an explanation. It turned out that they were a form of worship to one of the local saints, which somewhat relieved me, as the thought had occurred that they might have been some form of voodoo.

***

There were 170 cruzeiros to the pound and denominations went as low as a one cruzeiro note being worth 0.6p.

Furthermore, one cruzeiro = 100 centimos, and you could get 50, 20 and 10 centimo coins, which were worth approximately 0.3, 0.12 and 0.06 of a one pence piece, respectively. Inflation was running at 120% and the economy was in a mess. However, things could have been worse: in Germany in 1923, prices rose by a staggering 60,000,000,000%. That's the equivalent of saying that a sweet costing a mere 1p at one minute past midnight on January 1st would cost £6,000,000 at one minute to midnight on December 31st of the same year! Money became practically worthless and was eventually replaced by cigarettes. There was even a well-documented case of a man on his way to the shops pushing a wheelbarrow full of paper money hoping to buy some food, when he got mugged. The muggers tipped the money out onto the road and ran off with the wheelbarrow!

*

Due to the blunderings of successive leaders who implemented erratic hair-brained policies as they searched for economic growth like an old man chasing the secret of eternal youth, the country's national debt had risen from US$10 billion in 1973 to US$47 billion in 1979 and a staggering US$90 billion in 1982.

On the 17th March 2019, the exchange rate was £1 = 13,984 cruzeiros.

Day 18

February 12, 1981

By now the room had become a European stronghold with two Germans, a Frenchman, an Italian, a Swede and myself, representing good ol' England. Six out of eight wasn't too bad, especially considering we were all well over 9,000 kilometres away from home. It seemed that the student authorities in Botafogo had wrongly translated an old English proverb, so that it now read: "Best to put all your bad eggs into one basket!"

I spent the morning carefully retracing my steps from the previous day, in the vainest of hopes that my con-artist-cum-drinking-partner-companion of yesterday would turn out to be a creature of habit. Unfortunately for me, however, the Brazilian was nowhere to be found, and I eventually left the area empty-handed and disappointed. I had reached the inevitable conclusion that I was not, after all, the world's 20th-century equivalent to Sherlock Holmes. Grudgingly, I decided the only possible course of action left open to me was to try to completely forget the whole regrettable incident and put it down to experience. Consequently, I treated myself to a cold beer and sandwich lunch, and then made my way to the foot of Corcovado Mountain. From there, I joined the throng of people queuing up outside the entrance booth.

After making slow progress for the best part of an hour, I finally paid my entrance fee and was directed onto a strange contraption called a cog-train, which slowly crawled up the side of the mountain like a limpet climbing a rock. It consisted of an elongated rectangular-shaped carriage, with windows on all four sides, into which were herded approximately 35-40 people. The inside was devoid of all furnishings, apart from a few strategically positioned poles in the centre to hold on to, and a series of handrails situated beneath the windows. The underneath of the cog-train was attached to a long chain which ran the length of the mountain and slowly hauled it up a narrow gauge rail. The angle of ascent was well over sixty degrees and throughout the journey, which took approximately twenty minutes, the train creaked and groaned painfully. On the way up, we passed a similar device coming down containing a tribe of camera-clicking tourists, whose sole aim appeared to be to take the maximum number of photos in the shortest time possible.

Upon completion of its task, I alighted from the machine and quickly followed the path to gaze at Rio's crowning glory, the Cristo Redentor (Christ the Redeemer) monument: carved out of white stone with a powerful aura about it that left one feeling humble and speechless.

I was surprised at the simplicity of its design, yet for a long time I stood in its shadow, overwhelmed by its magnificent beauty and dwarfed by its sheer size and magnitude, as it towered some forty metres above me. It was colossal, and weighed 1,145 tons; in fact, the base of the statue was so large that it even had a small chapel built inside it where mass was held every Sunday morning.

Corcovado itself, a 710-metre-high jagged peak, otherwise known as the Hunchback, was the highest mountain around Rio, and the view of the city from this particular vantage point was quite spectacular. Rio de Janeiro lies at the mouth of Guanabara Bay, and in the distance across the water I could see the town of Niterio and the rest of the rugged coastline of Ponta de Fota. A number of small islands lay dotted around the entrance to the bay, acting like natural wave-breaks to the waters of the Atlantic that constantly pounded and crashed against these barren and desolate rocks.

In the evening, my suspicions that Brazilian students were unable to organise anything were confirmed when a group of friends and I, several of whom were Brazilian, decided to visit Copacabana Beach for a drink. However, two bus journeys later, and after being dragged around for a couple of hours past numerous bars, none of which we stopped at I might add, the Brazilian contingent finally decided they should all catch a bus into the city centre for a drink instead.

***

The Christ the Redeemer statue was the brainchild of Carlos Oswaldo who initially envisaged it being a figure carrying a cross. However, the engineer (Heitor da Silva Costa) and sculptor (Paul Landowski from Poland) changed the design to omit the cross. It is made of reinforced concrete covered with well over six million soapstone tiles. This metamorphic rock was used as it was considered to be both durable and resistant to harmful damage from the elements (wind, rain) and pollution. It was sculpted in France and took over nine years to complete and construct. The statue was finally inaugurated in October 1931, and is owned by the Catholic Church.

*

Copacabana is built on a narrow strip of land between the mountains and the sea. It is only four square kilometres in size but has one of the highest densities of population in the world with over 62,000 people per square kilometre.

*

Rod Stewart played to an estimated audience of three and a half million people on Copacabana Beach in 1994.

*

Undoubtedly one of the strangest sights to witness in Brazil takes place every New Year's Eve on Copacabana Beach. For it is here that over a million voodoo followers from all over Brazil congregate to worship Lemanja, the goddess of the sea.

As the night progresses, drummers up and down the beach start banging out a rhythmic pulsating drum beat, while multitudes of candles are lit and countless revellers swirl around elaborately made sand altars dancing.

Meanwhile older men and women alike sit around puffing cheap cigars and pipes stuffed with old-fashioned black coil tobacco while passing around bottles of sugar-cane rum.

At the first stroke of midnight everyone rushes into the water carrying offerings of flowers or other gifts suitable for a woman, such as combs, mirrors, ribbons, make-up, perfume and wine.

If the water takes their gifts out to sea, the worshippers can go home happy in the belief that the goddess has accepted their gifts and will grant all of their wishes. However, if the ocean throws the offerings back onto the beach, it is a sign of impending misfortune and bad luck.

Upon hearing this story, I was left to wonder how, with a million people crammed onto such a small sandy beach, could anyone decide whose comb, lipstick or mirror etc. had been accepted and whose had been thrown back?

Everyone wears white, the colour of Iemanja, although tradition states that it is also lucky for women to wear pink panties.

*

There are over thirty million followers of voodoo worldwide today.

*

Ecuador is the world's largest exporter of bananas in the world.

*

It is considered rude to say 'no' in Paraguay. So instead, they will say 'thank you' or 'another day'.

Day 19

February 13, 1981

I awoke to a new roommate moving into the bottom half of my bunkbed. He was a Bolivian called Tito and the mere sight of him made my legs tremble and persuaded my kneecaps to apply for a one-way exit visa out of my body. He was a huge modern-day Goliath, standing well over two metres tall, with broad shoulders and muscles that made Sylvester Stallone look like he was suffering from anorexia nervosa. He had dark tanned leathery skin, a broken nose, protruding jaw and low cheekbones that altogether made him look all the more menacing. He had trained as a journalist, and I was convinced that he would be very successful in his chosen career: after all, who in their right mind would have dared refuse him an interview?

Tito looked like the type of guy that if he asked you for the time you'd give him your watch, and then politely ask for your wrist back. Fortunately for everyone in the room though, he turned out to be one of the good guys, the original gentle green giant, with a little less of the green.

The day was spent strolling around the city and in the afternoon I attempted to visit the Museu de Caca e Pesca

(Museum of Hunting and Fishing). Although unknown to me at the time, it had recently been moved, and its new location unfortunately remained an unsolved mystery and so instead, I ended up visiting the Maracanã football stadium. It's one of the largest and most famous stadiums in the world and has a total seating capacity of well over 200,000 people. When Frank Sinatra held a concert there, the promoters had to sell the tickets for a mere US$2 apiece just to try and ensure that the place would be filled to capacity.

During football matches which are regularly held every weekend, the fanatical fans of the home team often bombard the opposition players with toilet paper, beer bottles and, believe it or not, dead chickens!

By early evening, I was becoming extremely fidgety and restless due to the high level of humidity, and decided, in a momentary fit of madness, that the best solution to this uncomfortable condition was to go out circuit-training and burn off some excess energy. So, without further ado, I changed out of my sandals, ran out of the hostel, crossed the road and followed the path alongside the beach; head held high and chest stuck out, looking like an oven-ready turkey wearing shorts and plimsoles.

This is the life, I thought as I jogged along happily, stopping every few hundred metres or so to do a series of sit-ups and press-ups. However, it was quite a different story when I crawled back into my room an hour or so later, feeling sick and suffering from a bad case of dehydration.

Dehydration was a major problem for me, due to the high percentage of humidity, and the nearer I got to the Equator the more I perspired. Consequently, no sooner had I regained my breath, taken a shower and donned a clean set of clothes, than I was off again, this time with several friends to the nearest bar. Once there, I gracefully retired for the rest of the evening to sink ever-increasing quantities of beer to help top up the liquid levels of my body. Although, this time without the customary Cachaça chasers.

***

Ipanema Beach, along the coast from Copacabana, was regarded as Rio's richest, and the most fashionable beach to be seen on. The problem was "Ipanema" is Indian for "place of dangerous sea", and the waters around the beach have a dangerous undertow which is often very strong and has dragged many unwary swimmers down to an early watery grave.

*

<u>On all of Rio's twenty-three beaches, you are strongly advised to take a towel or mat to lie on to help protect you from the hordes of small biting sand insects that frequent the beaches.</u>

*

Sept 6th 1990, Rio de Janeiro. After being picked up by police on suspicion of breaking into a shop, thirteen-year-old Leandro Cardosa da Sila and two friends (aged nine and fifteen) were driven to waste ground where they were forced to play Russian roulette with a loaded revolver. Leandro lost and his body was later dumped up a side-alley behind a hotel as a warning to other children. In Rio alone, on average two children a day end up like this.

*

On 28th March 1992, Rio de Janeiro police confirmed that a heavily pregnant woman had been kidnapped by three men who induced her into labour and then stole her baby. It was believed that the child had been taken by baby traffickers who would have sold the infant to a childless couple overseas for a considerable sum of money.

Day 20

February 14, 1981

It was an extremely hot day, in fact it topped 40ºC (105ºF), and I was glad that Rio was blessed with cool trade-winds which regularly swept in across the bay keeping the humidity down to a reasonable level, and bringing a welcome breath of fresh air to my often tired and somewhat lethargic body. The humidity seemed to drain away all of my strength, and at times even the simplest of tasks became difficult to perform. Days like this were meant for sitting in the shade, sipping cold beers and taking the occasional cool shower but little else, least of all any form of physical exertion. Due to the high humidity of the tropics, you were always strongly advised to drink as much fluid and take as much salt as possible, to help counteract dehydration. The hustle and bustle of English life seemed a world away and I revelled in this strange environment that I now found myself in.

That evening, I left Rio and caught the overnight coach to Ouro Preto with one of my roommates who happened to be travelling in the same direction, Roman Kurrowski. Roman was an amazing guy: born in Sweden, of Polish parentage, he had worked his way through university and then formed a highly successful jazz agency in Stockholm. From there, he had toured Europe as the road manager for some of the greatest names in jazz; Count Baisie, Duke Ellington, Ella Fitzgerald and Benny Goodman, to name but a few. By the time I had met him, he had backpacked his way across Europe, the Far East, North America and most of South America. Furthermore, he could speak fluent Swedish, Polish, German and English, and converse in several other languages, including Portuguese, Spanish and French, which, needless to say, in South America became extremely useful.

The journey was an uncomfortable one for me, as the bus seemed more suited to a museum than the open road. I was convinced it had either been built prior to the introduction of suspension or was being driven by an ex-rodeo champion who was attempting to relive old memories with the aid of the bus and any available pot-holes that he could find on or near the road.

***

During the gold rush in the 18th century, an entire tribe, including its king and members of the royal family, were captured in the Congo, central Africa, placed in chains and transported to Brazil, where they were sold 'en masse' to the owner of several gold mines around Minas Gerais.

Chico-Rei, the African tribal king, was immediately appointed by the mine owner to become the mine's foreman due to his established position among the tribe; for which he received a small wage. Working seven days a week, fifty-two weeks a year, he eventually saved up sufficient money to buy his own freedom and that of his sons. Together, they then continued to work away, saving every cruzeiro they could until they had eventually bought the freedom of the whole tribe.

The tribe then continued to work, this time for pay, until they had saved up enough money to buy their own gold mine, 'Encardideira' in Vila Rica (modern-day Ouro Preto), which they then proceeded to work in. The mine turned out to be fabulously rich in gold deposits which were used to buy huge tracts of land and it was upon this land that Chico-Rei was finally able to build himself a palace, whereupon he once more took his rightful place holding court and ruling over his subjects.

*

In the leafy suburbs of Belo Horizonte lies an unusual street called Rua Professor Otávio Coelho de Magalhães. This is because if you stop your car and forget to apply your emergency brake, it will slowly begin to roll uphill, gaining speed as it goes. There are lots of local explanations, including that the hill is haunted or that a massive deposit of iron ore lies beneath the street, drawing vehicles up with its magnetic pull. But in reality, the phenomenon is apparently an optical illusion. Though the street appears to be on a steep incline, there is actually a slight dip in the road. Although the cars appear to be rolling uphill they are actually rolling downhill.

*

In August 2019 Clauvino da Silva, the 42 year old leader of the notorious Red Command gang was caught trying to escape prison wearing his teenage daughter's skinny jeans and pink t-shirt, along with a wig and silicone mask of her face.

He was spotted by guards as he attempted to walk out of the jail pretending to be his daughter at the end of visiting hours along with a group of other visiting women.

The drug lord, was serving a 73-year sentence at Gericino prison in Rio de Janeiro. He was subsequently moved into solitary confinement as punishment and three days later committed suicide.

*

Instead of ringing a doorbell when visiting someone's home, the people of Paraguay always clap before entering.

Day 21

February 15, 1981

Ouro Preto, which means black gold (so called because the concentrated deposits of iron oxide in the surrounding soil caused the gold to turn black), was a sleepy little town that looked more suited to the pages of a Brazilian history book than the 20th century. This was due to the fact that in 1933 the Brazilian government placed a preservation order on the whole area to ensure that everything remained undisturbed, as a monument to Brazilian architecture from a bygone age. It was built on a series of undulating hills and included, among other things, a large number of red-tiled houses, several lavishly decorated churches and the town's centrepiece, a fountain which, needless to say, did not work!

The bus terminus was situated on the edge of town and consisted of a small muddy square of uneven ground with a dilapidated wooden shack which acted as a ticket-office-cum-waiting-room. It was here, that Roman and I started talking to another couple of backpackers, and as a group, we proceeded to walk into Ouro Preto.

Evidently, the road we were on was notorious for thieves who made a living by preying upon unsuspecting tourists that happened to be passing through. On one side of the road was a gently sloping hill where a gang of reprobates would often sit watching and waiting for suitable victims. When one or more appeared, they would carefully manoeuvre themselves into position, and at an appointed place or time, race down the hill and run past their pre-selected victim, snatching anything of value in the process. Fortunately for everyone, on this occasion it was either a case of safety in numbers or the snatch squad were having a siesta, as the hordes never appeared.

Upon reaching the fountain, it was agreed that we would split up to try and search for some suitable accommodation and meet up again later, but it was all to no avail as everyone fruitlessly wandered up and down the cobblestoned streets only to return tired and empty-handed. It seemed the town had little to offer as far as accommodation was concerned and so, after a brief discussion, we all agreed to settle for a bread roll, bottle of beer and a one-way ticket to Belo Horizonte instead.

However, the morning had not been wasted, as I was provisionally offered a job in Lima, Peru, by one of my fellow travellers. She was teaching at a private school in Lima for European children and was currently on holiday visiting Brazil for the Mardi Gras. It appeared the school was invariably on the lookout for experienced, well-motivated teachers, and the present time was no exception. I provided her with a miniature photo of myself (*I later asked myself if this was a wise idea*) and wrote out a quick curriculum vitae. All being well, there would be an important letter awaiting my arrival at the British Consulate in Manaus. This would hopefully offer me a job and an opportunity to see the west coast of South America, along with some of its breathtaking sights such as: Machu-Picchu (the lost city of the Incas), Lake Titicaca and the Galapagos Islands, to name but a few.

The journey to Belo Horizonte was largely uneventful, and

by 15:00 we had reached our destination, located a suitable hotel and checked in. It was then, after a quick shower and change of clothing that we got down to more serious business. While waiting for a connection at São Paulo central bus station a couple of weeks back, Roman had met three Brazilian students (all female), one of whom had given him her telephone number, saying that if he was ever in Belo Horizonte, he should give her a ring and she'd show him around. So he did, and it was arranged that she would meet us, hopefully with a friend, at our hotel later on that evening. In the meantime, Roman and I spent the rest of the afternoon wandering around the local market, before adjourning to a nearby bar to have something to eat and drink.

It was here, much to the amusement of Roman and everyone else in the bar, that I experienced my first close encounter with a prostitute. At the time, I was innocently sitting by the bar sipping on a cold beer, when a hand suddenly appeared over my shoulder and started slowly burrowing its way down into the dark recesses of my open-necked shirt. Deeper and deeper it travelled until it could venture no more, whereupon its owner emerged from behind my shoulder with the announcement, 'Ello, you want buy me drink?'

Somewhat taken aback by this young lady's unusual approach, I blurted out in Portuguese, 'Desculpe, não cruzeiro.' (Sorry, no money.) She carefully eyed me up and down then once again stated her request, to which this time I replied, 'Não compreendo Português!' (I do not understand Portuguese.)

Undeterred, she stood looking at me with pouting lips and sultry eyes, until a smile gradually spread across her face and she whispered, 'You like me!'

By now, Roman was nearly falling off his stool trying to keep back the laughter and there was deadly silence in the bar as all eyes were turned to witness this strange encounter. 'Sim, sim,' (Yes, yes,) I replied, trying to keep a straight face. She immediately responded by moving in closer with renewed confidence and determination, convinced that she had won me over. Her face broke into another smile, as she seductively ran her tongue lightly over her lips, and then reaching out, slowly stroked part of my anatomy.

Her expert fingers delicately traced the bulge in my trousers, applying just the right amount of pressure to ensure a reaction. Then, satisfied that she had secured my full attention, she withdrew her hand and pointed between her legs, whispering softly, 'You want?'

I could control myself no longer and burst out laughing saying, 'Não compreendo!' (I do not understand!) Her eyes flashed and lips parted, as she once more reached out to slowly stroke my manhood, then with a sigh and wave of her hand, she swung round, blowing a kiss in my direction and walked out into the night, slowly moving her hips from side to side. Roman and I looked at each other in total disbelief and then spontaneously broke out into fits of uncontrollable laughter. Our drinks finished, we returned to the hotel and awaited the arrival of Roman's contact. We were in a jovial mood and a promising evening seemed in store.

When she eventually arrived, however, I was disappointed to see that she was on her own, and I embarked upon the guided tour of the city feeling a little disheartened and let down. The rest of the evening passed off fairly quietly, and for me at least ended on a note of anti-climax, especially after it had begun on such an amusing one.

Without doubt, the highlight of the evening was watching a performance by two street-fighters/dancers of 'Capoeira': a ceremonial dance based upon the traditional foot-fighting techniques introduced to Brazil by Angolan slaves brought over during the 19th century, to work on the sugar plantations of rich colonials. 'Capoeira' is a fusion of religious, rhythmic and social dance influences, blended with urban combat. The fighting part was eventually banned, as the contestants invariably carried on until one of them was either killed or maimed for life. So it had since been developed into a form of dance and resembled a ferocious display of martial art fighting, in which the two performers attacked and counter-attacked each other with numerous kicks from every conceivable direction and angle, each one of which came within a hair's breadth of making contact with its opponent. The fight sequence was performed to music, played on a one-stringed African instrument, and as the dance progressed, the beat and consequently the sparring, became faster. It was a fascinating sight to watch and one that I, had I remained in Belo Horizonte for any length of time, would have endeavoured to study.[4]

We ended the night in a bar near the hotel and I quickly finished my drink, made my apologies and left, sensing that my presence might have been impeding Roman's potential conquest. However, unfortunately for Roman, it seemed this was not to be as he returned to the hotel shortly afterwards.

Our room was clean and reasonably priced, but I couldn't help noticing that, once again, I was staying in one of the more colourful parts of yet another city. Our window was directly opposite a whore-house, with women, in various stages of undress, situated in every available door and window, trying to entice any potential passing custom into their den of iniquity.

***

Unbeknownst to me at the time I visited, one of Ouro Preto's most renowned attractions was the church of São Francisco, the inside of which was adorned with a large collection of wooden and stone carvings by a famous Brazilian sculptor called Aleijadinho. He was a crippled mulatto (someone of mixed parentage), whose face and body were so badly deformed by arthritis that he used to wear a sack over his head so as not to frighten people. Towards the end of his life, his assistants used to tie his hammer and chisel to his wrists with leather thongs, as his fingers had become so gnarled. This way he managed to continue working right up until the time of his death.

*

---

[4] *Before leaving Birmingham I had put myself through a rigorous programme of weight lifting and karate, training five nights a week for several months at the Birmingham Shukokia Karate Centre under the watchful eye of the legendary Shihan 'Eddie Daniels', black belt, ninth dan (KSI Joint World Chief Instructor).*

There are 10 million alpacas in the world and three-quarters of them live in Peru. *

Ouro Preto also contains the Church of Santa Efigenioa dos Pretos. It was financed by gold from Chico-Rei's mine and built by the slave community for their own use in the 1740s. The slaves contributed what they could towards its upkeep by regularly washing their gold-flaked hair in the baptismal font and smuggling gold powder under their fingernails and inside tooth cavities.

*

The Hand of the Desert (Mano del Desierto) in the Atacama Desert in Chile is a 36 feet high sculpture which attracts thousands of tourists every year even though it is 75 km away from the nearest town (Antofagasta).

*

90% of people in South America identify themselves as Christians.

*

In July 1981 an Argentinian football referee was arrested on charges of threatening players!

*

Brazil is the only country in the world where the death penalty applies to children as well as adults.

*

If you hated queuing in Brazil, you could always pay a Guadacolas (professional queuer) to queue for you.

*

Rio's newspapers print daily beach reports on their E.coli counts, which indicate the expected degree of faecal contamination on each beach for that day.

Day 22

February 16, 1981

Over breakfast, we agreed that Belo Horizonte had little to offer us and that it was time to move on to pastures new. Furthermore, it was also decided that, for the time being at least, we should go our own separate ways and then meet up again at a later date for the Mardi Gras. Consequently, Roman bought a ticket on the overnight coach to Brasilia, capital of Brazil, while I bought a ticket on the overnight coach to Victoria da Conquista. After which we both checked our rucksacks into the left luggage office at the coach station and then spent the rest of the day deep in conversation, discussing our lives to date, and our hopes and aspirations for the future. It seemed that the more we talked, the more we found we had in common: we were both fairly young and career-minded, with a fanatical love for life and a distinct weakness for women, although for the time being at least we were both confirmed bachelors. We both enjoyed backpacking, had an aversion towards package-tour holidays and had a similar weird sense of humour.

That evening at the coach station, Roman and I were somewhat surprised to be met by Maria (Roman's contact), and what's more, this time she had bought a friend along with her. Her friend was pleasantly attractive, could speak some English and seemed to find me totally irresistible, to the point that she could not keep her eyes off me. *Just my luck*, I thought, *just as the coach is about to leave, too!* But all was not yet lost, and with time running out, it was quickly agreed that we would all meet up again in Salvador for the Mardi Gras. I was already beginning to look forward to the forthcoming encounter, especially when Maria's friend, Serena, invited me to stay with her upon her return to university in April, and quickly proceeded to scribble down her address in Goiania, 202 kilometres southwest of Brasilia. There was no doubt about it, if my assessment of the situation was correct, she was very interested in embarking upon a voyage of carnal exploration.

My coach left at 6pm and it was not long before I realised that I had once more become the centre of attention. This time from a couple of young, vivacious girls, in their early twenties, who were sitting near the back of the coach.

By now, I was becoming totally mystified as to how, and indeed why, women should suddenly start finding me so attractive. *What have I been doing wrong all my life?* I kept asking myself over and over again. The answer, it seemed, was quite simple: *I, Mike Plummer, being a tall Caucasian with blue eyes, fair hair and a beard, was practically a freak of nature in Norther Brazil as most tourists only travel to Southern Brazil mainly Rio de Janeiro.* For here, most, if not all Brazilian men were small in stature, had dark-coloured skin, black hair, brown eyes and couldn't grow facial hair. In fact, I was assured by several Brazilian friends that if only I could have spoken Portuguese, I could have probably had any woman I wanted. Furthermore, I later found out that blue eyes worked as an aphrodisiac on Brazilian women, as it literally turned them on.

Who needs powdered rhino horn when you've got blue eyes! The Orientals believed rhino horn had aphrodisiac properties based upon the assumption that the rhino's tremendous strength was centred in its horn. The Chinese also believed that drinking the warm blood of certain species of snake straight from the still writhing and recently decapitated body was supposed to impart manliness and enhance their performance in bed![5]

At approximately nine o'clock, the coach stopped for a half-hour break, and while I was at the bar enjoying an ice-cold bottle of Choppie (a well-known Brazilian beer), I was approached by my two newly found admirers, who attempted to strike up a conversation. The only problem was, as was almost always the case, unfortunately I couldn't speak Portuguese and they couldn't speak English. This, needless to say, was a great pity as I would have loved to have known what they were saying or even proposing to do to me! However, due to the total breakdown in communications, they moved off whispering and giggling away amongst themselves and I had to settle for another beer and my weekly malaria tablet instead.

Malaria was quite common in South America, especially around the coastal and jungle areas, as these were the favoured habitats of its carrier, the Anopheles mosquito (only the female carries the organism), which carries the malaria parasites in its saliva, through which it enters the victim's bloodstream. It was at one time believed that malaria was caused by breathing in the foul-smelling air from the marshes, hence the Latin words "mal aria" meaning "bad air". But this was later disproved at the end of the 18th century when the true culprit was finally identified.

The malaria tablets must be taken one day before entering an area prone to malaria and continue to be taken six weeks after leaving the region. Most Europeans that catch malaria develop it upon their return home, having stopped taking their tablets before the recommended six weeks are up.

---

[5] *June 29th 1990. The South African government sanctioned the slaughter of 30,000 Cape fur seals in order to satisfy sexual appetites in the Far East. Their genitals were to be exported as aphrodisiacs, for which the South African Government was to be paid 5p a carcass. Luckily, this was postponed after worldwide protests. Thank goodness for the freedom of the press and public outrage!*

It has been estimated that, worldwide, up to two million people die and 100 million people suffer from malaria each year. No one knows where it originates from for it has been around for thousands of years. In fact, it was believed to have killed Alexander the Great in 323 BC in Babylon. Without doubt he was one of the greatest military leaders of ancient times. His most famous quote was, 'I am not afraid of an army of lions led by a sheep; I am afraid of an army of sheep led by a lion.'

***

Malaria kills more British tourists than any other tropical disease. In 1991, there were 2,342 reported cases of malaria in the UK, including thirteen deaths.

*

Some 5.7 million cases of malaria have been recorded in Burundi in 2019, AFP news agency quotes the UN's humanitarian agency as saying.   That's roughly half the population of the country.

*

From the nearby town of Diamantina, so named after the large quantity of diamonds extracted from the ground, comes the story of Chico da Silva: a mulatto (mixed-race) slave whom a local wealthy Portuguese mine owner, Joao Fernandes de Oliveira, fell hopelessly in love with. He showered her with gold and precious stones and built her a large palace to live in.

He then bought her a yacht and while it was being transported 400km overland from the coast, he set thousands of slaves to work digging a large hole and then diverted a nearby river to form a lake on which she could sail. They went on to have thirteen children and she became the most powerful woman in colonial Brazil.

*

In 2013 Paul McCartney was on stage at the Serra Dourada Stadium in Goiânia, in the neighbouring state of Goiás, when he was covered by a swarm of Esperança Grilo grasshoppers. One remained on his shoulder for the majority of the three-hour show.

*

The convent of Santo António in Divinópolis, contains the tomb of a Scottish soldier of fortune known as "Wild Jock of Sketater". During the Napoleonic wars he was appointed the first ever Commander-in-Chief of the Brazilian army.

*

Guarapari is a coastal town in the Brazilian state of Espírito Santo and is a popular tourist destination even though its beaches are highly radioactive due to the presence of a mineral called Monazite mixed in amongst its sand.

In the 1970s, Silva Mello, a well-known Brazilian physician, wrote a book within which he falsely claimed that the radioactive sands of Guarapari had curative properties when exposed to the sun's UV rays and could cure a variety of ailments including arthritis and cancer. Consequently, visitors flocked to the town and caked themselves with sand, hoping for a miracle cure.

However, nuclear energy experts in Brazil were utterly horrified by Dr. Mello's recommendations as the radioactive sands of Guarapari give off the same amount of radiation as a chest x-ray. To this day it remains a popular holiday destination for health conscious tourists looking for a miracle cure.

Day 23

February 17, 1981

The journey to Vitoria da Conquista took a painstakingly long fifteen hours, during which time I got little or no sleep as the bus was extremely uncomfortable and the roads were in bad need of repair.

From here I caught a connecting bus to Itabuna, which was, thankfully, my final destination, although in the process, I had to wave goodbye to my still giggling admirers, who it seemed were heading in a different direction. I settled into my seat and viewed the passing scenery with a nonchalant eye: I had only been out for some three weeks but had already seen more than my fair share of roadside scenery. Consequently, I showed little interest in the villages that we fleetingly drove past. Unfortunately for me, what I had mistakenly assumed to be a short bus ride down the road to Itabuna, turned out to be a gruelling six-hour sightseeing tour of all the surrounding villages, and by the time I eventually alighted from the confines of the bus, I was not only tired and weary, but ached everywhere and was extremely sore in specific places! I made a mental note to invest in a soft fluffy cushion at the earliest possible juncture.

The station, which was situated on the outskirts of town, was practically deserted with not a hotel in sight. I felt totally despondent and could have quite happily curled up on the floor where I stood and gone to sleep, except being in South America, I knew only too well that had I done so I would have probably woken up to find a knife held to my throat! Instead, I walked around the depot looking for a friendly face, but finding none, and in desperation, I tentatively approached the only people in sight: a small group of policemen who were standing close by, talking (the police in South America were not known for their patience and hospitality).

Using the total knowledge of my limited Portuguese vocabulary, I apologised for my intrusion and tried to explain that I was English, couldn't speak Portuguese and was looking for somewhere cheap to stay the night so could they possibly help? One of them smiled and beckoned me to follow him as he crossed over the road and headed towards the town for several hundred metres before turning up a side-street and stopping outside the front door of a private house. Once inside, he procured me a room for 250 cruzeiro. It wasn't much to look at, it was dark and dingy, had an unpleasant musty smell hanging around it, and an unimpressive view from the window of a three-metre-high wall that stood towering above me one metre away, but beggars can't be choosers and I gratefully accepted it.

With the comforting knowledge that I now at least had somewhere comparatively safe to sleep, I began to feel a little more relaxed, and after a much-needed wash and change of clothing I walked into town for a cold beer and bite to eat before returning home for an early night and a much-needed rest.

At first everything was fine and I quickly drifted off into the land of sleep until I was rudely awoken at 00:40. by the sound of a howling dog on the other side of the wall, outside my window. At which point it started: as dogs from all over the town seemed to join in the recital, and serenaded the night away. By 02:00 they were still at it and I was by now convinced that I was listening to a performance of the Beggars Opera by I.D.A.O.S. 'the Itabuna Dogs Amateur Operatic Society'.

Needless to say, they made a memorable impression upon me and I felt sure that they were really putting heart and soul into their performance. The fight scenes were particularly exciting, with plenty of snarling, biting and yelping being thrown in for good measure. The only trouble was too much time was being spent on the wretched crowd scenes with everyone barking at once, that at times, I had trouble following the plot.

By 03:30, they must have been into the closing scene as all was quiet, but for the instigator of the whole performance, still standing its ground on the other side of the wall outside my bedroom window, who carried on regardless. Like the playing of the last post on the bugle, the dog's barks echoed on and on into the night.

***

*

1,400km west of Belo Horizonte, on the borders of Bolivia and Paraguay, is the Mato Grosso region of the "Pantanal": the largest wetlands in the world. It is 230,000 square kilometres (nearly the same size as the UK), and although it's over 2,000km from the Atlantic Ocean, it is only 100 to 200 metres above sea level. It is the remains of an ancient inland sea called the "Xaraes" which began drying out sixty-five million years ago.

The Pantanal offers some of the best fishing in the world and Pantanal cowboys have been known to lasso 80kg fish as they leap out of the water! It is also an ornithologist's paradise with well over 600 species of bird and probably has the largest selection of wildlife that can be readily seen anywhere in South America, and this includes the capybara.

The capybara is the largest rodent in the world, looks a bit like a giant guinea pig and when fully grown can weigh up to 79kg and measure over 1.3 metres long. Both its eyes and nostrils are situated on top of its head, it is equally at home both on land and in water and can gallop as fast as a small horse.

Day 24

February 18, 1981

In the morning, I made my way back to the bus station and caught a rickety old bus to C.E.P.L.A.C. (Executive Commission for the Renewal of Cocoa Crop), a government-financed research centre on the outskirts of town, set up to investigate ways of increasing the quality and yield of Brazilian crops. I cautiously approached the armed guard at the entrance to the driveway and asked if he would ring inside so I could speak to one of the research assistants. This done, I waited apprehensively, until a few minutes later a car drove up to the gate and out stepped a somewhat surprised and bewildered Forbes Benton. I tentatively walked forward to meet him, explaining that Forbes had met my brother in Mexico the year before, or so I reminded him, as he couldn't actually remember the encounter. Fortunately for me though, Forbes was one of the good guys, and happy to see a fellow 'Brit', and immediately offered to put me up for a couple of nights.

Together, we drove back inside the establishment, where I was given a quick tour of the grounds, before joining him for an early lunch. The canteen was excellent and you could eat as much as you wanted for a subsidised set price of eighty cruzeiros, which I accordingly did, feasting myself on large quantities of meat and fresh vegetables to the point where I had trouble carrying the plate back to the table without some of it falling off. Meanwhile most of my fellow diners were a little more reserved merely settling for a simple salad. If nothing else, I had learnt one thing since leaving England: *'Never look a gift horse in the mouth!'*

Lunch finished, we drove back to Forbes' flat in Itabuna where I unloaded my rucksack, before being dropped off at the bus station, from where I caught a local bus on to the coastal town of Ilhéus.

Here I spent a pleasant afternoon exploring the town and some of its magnificent churches. I entered the Cathedral of São Sebastião by the sea shore, with its imposing stained-glass windows and lavishly decorated interior, which left me stunned with a feeling of reverence and awe, only to discover that my camera's flashgun had died on me, as the batteries had corroded in the humidity.

Further along the beach on the outskirts of town, I came across a seven-metre-high statue of Christ in the grounds of a derelict colonial mansion house which had long since been gutted by fire and now lay abandoned to the elements. It was here, under the gaze of this silent statue, wearing a face of serenity and compassion, with its arms stretched out as if to welcome the waters of the Atlantic, that I sat back on the ground and contentedly watched the waves crashing upon the beach that lay before me.

I later returned to Itabuna, where I spent a pleasant evening with Forbes in a local bar, supping pints and exchanging stories of South America. That night I slept soundly, not even a rousing recital by the London Philharmonic Orchestra accompanied by the I.D.A.O.S. cast of hundreds could have woken me.

***

It seemed that in Brazil, some hotel owners supplemented their income by sending a girl up to your room for the night and charging you for her services the next morning, regardless of whether you partook in her services or not.

*

Motel is the Brazilian term for a sex hotel, in which rooms are rented out by the hour.

*

When walking near the main tourist attractions in Peru with a rucksack on your back, you are advised to be on your guard. Evidently, it is not uncommon for a local to come up behind you while you're walking along, slice open your backpack with a razor-sharp machete and remove any valuable possessions within easy reach. This would all be performed with such precision that the backpacker would usually remain blissfully ignorant throughout the whole proceedings until at a later time he or she stopped and took off their rucksack.

*

Bernardo O'Higgins was a wealthy landowner of Basque-Spanish and Irish ancestry, who became the Chilean independence leader that freed the country from Spanish rule following the Chilean War of Independence. He became the country's first ever Chilean head of state, and in his honour the official name of the Chilean football team is the 'O'Higgins a Patriot of Chilean Rule' team.

*

Also known as the Peruvian giant yellow-leg centipede, the Amazonian giant centipede is the largest centipede species in the world with a length exceeding 40 centimetres.

It is found in various places throughout South America and the extreme south Caribbean, where it preys on a wide variety of animals including other sizable amphibians, mammals and reptiles. A bite from this venomous centipede can paralyse prey many times its own size.

Day 25

February 19, 1981

I was awake by 8am and, soon after, Forbes dropped me off at the coach station on his way to work. From here I once again caught a bus to Ilhéus.

I spent most of the day walking along the beach towards Iguape, passing several fishing villages on the way. The sky was clear and the sun beat down upon me, making it unpleasant to walk any faster than a slow methodical pace. Wearing only frayed denim shorts, a lightweight T-shirt and sandals, I could feel my back burning as if it were on fire. Fortunately, my camera, which I always kept with me, was as usual hidden in a kitbag slung over my shoulder. *Out of sight, out of temptation*, I thought. *Never display your valuables and thereby ask to be mugged.*[6]

As I walked on, the sights that I encountered were not particularly pleasing to the eye, but coupled with the squalor

---

[6] *It never ceased to amaze me how ignorant, people were when they travelled to 'third world' countries. They would wander around aimlessly, wearing expensive clothing and accessories dripping with gold and other precious jewellery, and then complain when someone mugged them. Considering some of them wore more money on a single finger than most of the local people could ever hope to legally earn in a year, could you really blame them for wanting to mug these 'well-off' walking cash points?*

that I had already witnessed on my travels, and the sights that lay in store for me in the weeks to follow, it brought home the vast differences between the rich industrialised nations and the poor, impoverished 'third world'. The small fishing villages that I came acrosswere dilapidated and the stench that permeated from the surrounding area caused my face to grimace long before I had even reached the confines of each village. The children, some up to the age of eight or nine played naked in the dirt. Up to this stage in their lives, they had probably seldom experienced the sensation of wearing clothes and showed no sign of embarrassment as I walked past.

The villagers watched me apprehensively from their rotting wooden shacks, perched against a raised mound of clay beneath a sparsely populated shoreline of trees. I began to realise just how fortunate the UK and its people were. Here was the reality I had feared so much on the plane back at Heathrow. It now seemed like a lifetime away, but in reality, was only a matter of three and a half weeks.

The pungent smell of death started clawing at my nostrils and I felt like retching as I came across the decaying carcass of a dog, half-eaten and rotting in the sand. The remains of its body were baked hard by the sun, lying where it had fallen in the final throes of death. Limbs stiff with rigor mortis, its empty eye sockets, pecked clean, peered out into oblivion.

Further along, I came across another corpse, of what though, I couldn't tell as it was obviously a recent casualty of life and was now covered in a thick chaotic layer of quivering black feathers, as between twenty to twenty-five American black vultures (*Coragyps atratus*) hungrily devoured their latest acquisition. I walked right up to them and watched with a grotesque fascination as they tore at the lifeless flesh with their blood-stained beaks. These scavengers of death were a particularly repugnant spectacle, each one consisting of a mass of black feathers from which sprouted a bald neck and head covered in folds of dry wrinkled skin. They ignored my presence and carried on insatiably devouring their bloody feast, knowing full well that if they didn't, others would. I turned away in revulsion, wanting to remove the scene from my memory, and took the first available path inland.

Along the road, I passed by a collection of pathetic hovels, and shortly afterwards stopped at a roadside shop to buy a Coke to help quench my thirst. Inside the gloomy wooden hut, I was viewed with suspicion, and upon re-emerging into the daylight again, found that a number of children had gathered outside to watch me walk by. As I did so, they showered me with handfuls of gravel, while others, including several adults, shouted abuse and spat in my direction. I was understandably afraid as to what might happen next and quickly moved off, heading back along the road to Ilhéus.

I felt no anger towards them, just shame and disgust at myself and the civilisation that, in their eyes, I represented. I was fortunate and could always return home whenever I wanted, to the safety and protection of an affluent society, where warm clothes, good food and pleasant surroundings would help wipe from my memory the pain and misery that was written on their faces. But these people were not so lucky: they were travelling along a dead-end street, facing the wrong way, and they couldn't turn back. There was no way out and they were doomed to exist from day to day, in a living nightmare from which their only release was death.

In 1981, the average life expectancy in the UK for a woman was seventy-seven and for a man it was seventy-two, whereas in Brazil it was fifty-six. Although the north east of the country was an anomaly, it covered 2.6 million sq. km (larger than Western Australia) and contained approximately one third of Brazil's total population. It had the highest birth rate throughout Brazil but over large areas, sixty percent of babies died before reaching their first birthday and the average life expectancy for this region was an alarming twenty-eight.

By seven o'clock, I was waiting outside Forbes' flat in the dark. There had been a power failure a few minutes earlier and I spent the time watching the electricity escaping from the power lines overhead. The authorities must have installed the cheapest materials possible that included cable that leaked electricity like a colander leaks water.

The constant hum of the current was frequently interrupted by sharp crackles as electricity shot out to momentarily light up its immediate surroundings, like the electrodes on the operating table in a Dr Frankenstein movie. I felt a tingling sensation all over my body, as if I had been hit by a stun gun, as the night air became alive with escaping electricity that seemed to bombard me from every conceivable direction.

Forbes' car appeared around the corner, headlights blazing as he slowly drove up the steep incline leading to his flat. Greetings exchanged, we carefully climbed the steps leading to his front door and went inside to wait in comfort till the power was restored, after which we had a quick meal and then left for a nearby bar.

While sitting outside the bar in the cool of the evening, Forbes informed me that the place had, a few days earlier, been the scene of a local bloodbath. It seemed that a crazy Brazilian with a chip on his shoulder had strolled up to the bar, pulled out a gun and started shooting, leaving three people dead and several others injured. Needless to say, at the mention of this we both became a little jumpy, especially as most of the locals walking around were armed with handguns and carried a customary machete dangling from their belts. The noticeable bullet holes in the windows and surrounding walls, along with the occasional splatter of blood that they had accidentally missed when cleaning up, didn't help either. Upon finishing our drinks, we quickly moved on to another bar where the atmosphere seemed a little more relaxed.

***

In January 1985, a local teenager aged eighteen shot dead his mother, father, two brothers and sister after an argument about the volume of his record player in the middle of the night.

*

According to figures published in 1990 by the National Institute of

Nutrition, 'Nanismo' or dwarfism is becoming more common due to a combination of low income and prevalent malnutrition. The World Health Organisation defines dwarves as being men below 1.64 metres and women below 1.52 metres. Twenty percent of Brazilians aged between twenty and twenty-five years old are classified as 'Nanico' (dwarves).

In the north east, thirty-eight percent of twenty to twenty-five-year-olds are Nanico and thirty percent of all babies born currently weigh less than 2.5 kilograms.

*

On January 4th, 1988, during a protest against safety conditions at Serra Pelada, fifty miners died in a clash with police.

*

On Tuesday 16th July 2019 a Colombian man was detained at Barcelona's international airport after half a kilo of cocaine was found hidden under his over-sized toupee.

*

A Brazilian man was arrested at Lisbon's international airport in 2018 after attempting to smuggle 1kg (2.2lb) of cocaine inside a pair of fake buttocks.

*

A Brazilian clown, Francisco Oliveira Silva or Tiririca, 'Grumpy', was elected to the Chamber of Deputies of the National Congress of Brazil in 2019, with more votes than any other candidate: 1,353,355 votes.

He started working in a circus at the age of eight in the impoverished North-eastern state of Ceara, later becoming a TV comedian.

He ran under various election slogans such as: 'it can't get any worse' and 'vote for the dummy'.

Day 26

February 20, 1981

By nine o'clock I was on the road once again, clocking up the kilometres and wishing I had located that elusive shop which sold soft cushions, to help relieve a reoccurring numb bum. My new destination was Salvador, and I hoped it would live up to my high expectations. Salvador was the capital of the north-eastern state of Bahia and was (so I had been reliably informed) home to some of the most beautiful women in South America. For it was here that a large number of colonials mixed and interbred with the slaves and native Indians of the north, producing a race of bronzed Bahian beauties. The women had firm sun-kissed bodies, long dark hair and faces that would have adorned the centre pages of Europe's finest magazines, had they only lived there, but best of all, as far as I was concerned, they really went crazy for men with blue eyes!

    I arrived at the coach station around 18:00 and soon caught a bus into the city centre to begin looking for somewhere to stay for the night. Roman had given me the address of a student hostel and I quickly homed in upon the area, only to find that the hostel didn't exist. I kept on walking around the immediate vicinity, occasionally stopping to show people the address, and then with a vacant facial expression and a spreading of the hands, indicate the question, *'where is it?'* but it was of little use as no one seemed to know, or at least that's how I interpreted their blank responses.

Fed up and with the light quickly fading, I returned to the main square where I was approached by an enterprising young local who asked me in broken English if I was looking for somewhere cheap to stay the night. I immediately accepted his help and was led down a dark side-alley and steered towards the neon sign of a hotel, or at least that's what the sign said. Lurking in the shadows stood the sardine shack, which I generously awarded 0.1 points for making me feel better – as I felt so much better when I left the place!

The manager of this prestigious residence was an obnoxious fat slob of a man who slouched behind his desk opposite the front entrance, breaking wind. Wearing a sweat-stained vest that advertised the culinary delights of some nearby restaurant, I watched the perspiration running down his forehead. An unpleasant veil of body odour hung over him and wafted out to make my acquaintance as I walked through the doorway. He sat there looking at me through two narrow slits that attempted to pass themselves off as eyes, only moving to partake in what seemed to be his favourite pastime, spitting. This he undertook at regular intervals onto the floor between his legs throughout my unpleasant encounter with him. He looked more suited to the interrogation room of an S.S. headquarters than the foyer of a hotel and I shuffled uneasily under his threatening gaze.

Eventually, he grew tired of giving me the evil eye and crudely barked out, 'Passport!' which I accordingly handed over. The slob produced a registration card from under the desk and slowly began filling it in, holding the pen awkwardly between his grimy fingers. However, he seemed to have some difficulty in achieving this, as he paused after every word as if to take a breather before re-engaging his brain back into activity. By the time he had finished I felt like awarding him a merit badge, so I paid my 250 cruzeiros and, upon receipt of my key, swiftly disappeared upstairs.

At the top of the stairs stood a line of doors all closely huddled together as if they were afraid to be left on their own. I walked along the corridor until I found the door with my number on and unlocked it. Inside, the room was not much to look at: an overgrown shoe box measuring roughly three metres by two immediately sprung into my mind. It comprised of four walls (no window), three of which were made of cheap plaster board and didn't even reach the ceiling, an old squeaky iron bed and a rectangular box standing on one end which my vivid imagination assumed to be a wardrobe, although inside there were no coat hangers, just a piece of limp string running from one side to the other. The thought of, *'Oh for the simple things in life,'* began echoing through my mind as I unloaded my belongings and then chained and padlocked them to my bed, before heading outside. I always carried a padlock and chain around with me, as you could never be too careful in these places, especially as the locks fitted to the doors were often extremely crude and could easily be picked, or as in this case, someone could have simply climbed over the wall from an adjoining room, that is, providing the wall could have taken their weight!

The city was by far the most poverty-stricken that I had yet come across and it had a marked effect upon me. During the day the streets were covered with beggars, young and old, men, women and children, crippled, diseased or just plain starving. If they didn't beg they would die and even if they did, it wouldn't automatically ensure their survival. Out here there were no government handouts.

A high proportion of the beggars were paralysed from the waist down, and spent their days kneeling on their lifeless stick-like legs begging from an endless sea of passers-by. It was a pitiful sight to watch them dragging themselves about whenever they wanted to move from one place to another. The lucky ones would have strips of old car tyre tied around their legs with odd bits of string, and whenever they wanted to move, they would stretch out their arms, dig their fingers into the ground and physically drag themselves forward. The others just had rags. It was a painfully slow process and one that required patience, courage and an unbreakable will to survive.

In all my travels, I never saw a wheelchair, and on only one occasion saw a pair of crutches. This occurred one day as I was walking through the back streets close to the main square, when I heard a tapping sound close behind me. Out of curiosity I turned around, but couldn't see where it was coming from, until I looked down to be confronted by a man whose legs had been amputated some fifteen to twenty centimetres above the knee. He had pieces of tyre tied around the base of his stumps and was walking with the aid of a pair of miniature crutches. The sight of such abject poverty and deprivation turned my stomach and I quickly left the area distressed by the harsh reality of the pain and suffering people that these people endured.

After dark, the streets became littered with sleeping bodies while the shadows and dark passageways became the nocturnal haunts of prostitutes. For these women prostitution was not a choice. Here, if they couldn't find a job or a husband to support them, then their only other means of survival was to either sell their bodies or beg, and prostitution usually paid better. Few, if any, could speak English but they all knew one phrase, and as I walked through the streets at night-time, the frequent shouts of, 'Hey luvelley boy, you want good time?' would echo from the shadows, where one could make out the silhouette of a woman standing in the gloom, ready and willing to earn her daily bread. The older they became the deeper in the shadows they stood and the rougher the area they would hang around in. It was a sort of relegation in the pecking order of street prostitution, which sorted out the young and beautiful from the old and ugly.

I turned up a side street that I hoped would lead back to the main square and nearly stumbled over a young woman sitting on a doorstep, urinating into the gutter. These houses had no running water or toilets, so the people used to defecate in the streets.

The city of Salvador was divided into two parts: one half was built on a plateau, the Upper Town (Cidade Alta), while the other, the Lower Town (Cidade Baixa), was situated eighty-five metres below. They were connected by a vertical lift. It was close to this lift that I sat on a wall, feet dangling over the edge, watching the lights of the old port situated below, when I was approached by a young Brazilian student who was evidently learning English at university. The student turned out to be gay and wanted me to go home with him and his friend, who was hovering nervously close by, for a good time! *Where have I heard that one before?* I thought to myself. So I proceeded to quickly inform him, in the nicest possible way, that I wasn't that way inclined but thanks all the same. You tend to be very careful not to offend people when you're sitting on a wall, precariously perched over an eighty-five-metre drop.

Undeterred, the student remained where he sat and tried to start up a conversation by changing the subject. He bought me a cup of black coffee, which I cautiously accepted, from a passing street vendor who carried a large rectangular-shaped flask of coffee slung around his shoulder. This flask resembled an overgrown wine box, and he carried a collection of small paper cups in his hand. Then before leaving, the student advised me to beware of the back streets at night-time as they were full of muggers. It transpired that four days previously, this very student had been robbed of everything, and he meant literally everything, as they took his watch, chain, shoes and clothes, and that even included his underpants!

Now that would call for some explaining, I thought to myself, as I imagined trying to explain to the police if I'd had been found wandering through the streets in the early hours of the morning stark naked. Well at least he spoke the language.

I returned to my hotel room to be once more confronted by my friendly host, still sitting in the same chair, behind the same desk and spitting at the same place. I slept uneasily and awoke at 04:00 to the patter of tiny feet. No wonder my room had no cockroaches, as they had evidently been replaced by mice, and sure enough, in the morning I found the tell-tale signs of mouse droppings in my rucksack. My little visitor had left its calling card!

***

In 1596, Sir John Harrington developed the first ever flushing toilet which he built in his house in Kelston near Bath. While visiting him, his godmother, Queen Elizabeth I, used the toilet and was so impressed that she arranged for him to install one at Richmond Palace.

Harington later wrote of his contraption: "If water be plenty, the oftener it is used and opened, the sweeter, but if water was scarce, once a day is enough, for a need, though twenty persons should use it." Unfortunately after his death the toilet at Richmond Palace was demolished and it was nearly 200 years before the flushable toilet was reinvented by Alexander Cummings of London who patented a similar device in 1775.

*

Celebrations have recently taken place in the Bavarian village of Fuchstal after finally running out of toilet paper! Back in 2006 a clerical error occurred in the town hall which resulted in them accidentally ordering two truckloads of toilet paper. The mistake only came to light when the first truck arrived. Fortunately they managed to cancel the second truckload before it arrived but it has still taken the village twelve years to wipe away its mistake!

*

Sumatran orangutans have been observed in the wild using leaves to wipe their backsides.

*

In 1989, official Brazilian statistics estimated over seven million children slept rough on the streets of Brazil. They were collectively known as 'Abandonados', literarily translated as 'the abandoned ones', without parents or a home. The lucky ones could be seen carrying around their bedding, a sheet of cardboard to lie on. They survived through a combination of begging and stealing, which caused much resentment between them and local shopkeepers who referred to them as 'Piretes', meaning 'little farts'.

Local businessmen regularly paid off-duty policemen to kill the street kids, who, they believed, drove away tourists from the area. One businessman was interviewed on the radio saying: 'What is being killed is not a child – it's vermin. Killing them is doing society a favour.' Over one hundred children are abandoned in doorways or left in hospitals each month in Rio de Janeiro alone.

*

The sturdy walls of the Forte de Santo Antônio da Barra in Bahia, encircle South America's oldest lighthouse which overlooks the Bay of All Saints and has guided ships of all sizes for over 300 years.

*

The North Yungas Road, is a two-way, 3.5 - 4 metre wide (10-12 foot) path that was cut into the side of the Cordillera Oriental Mountain chain in the 1930s and is ominously known as the "Death Road". Connecting Bolivia's capital, La Paz, to the town of Coroico, it is littered with hairpin bends which can be extremely dangerous due to fog, landslides, oncoming traffic and vertical drops of over 2,000 feet (610 meters).

On average approximately 300 people were killed every year up until 1994 when the government started a long overdue 20 year programme of road improvements.

On July 24, 1983, a bus veered off the Yungas Road and into a canyon, killing more than 100 passengers, it was Bolivia's worst ever traffic accident.

*

In 2018 the British Foreign office in Buenos Aires received a call from a British national asking if they could supply him with a list of Argentinian women whom he might be able to marry.

*

All of Vitoria da Conquista schoolchildren between the ages of four to fourteen wear T-shirts as part of their school uniform, fitted with special locator chips under the school's crest to help alert parents to truancy or arriving late for class.

Day 27

February 21, 1981

The next morning I left the Sardine Shack with its gloomy claustrophobic rooms, and began trying to locate Roman, who I assumed would be staying at one of the other hostels in my South American Handbook. Having notched up a couple of kilometres of shoe leather and stopped several passers-by, preferably attractive young female ones, I found the hostel I was looking for and quickly moved in. It felt like luxury, with only six people to a room and not a screaming baby within earshot.

Before long I had met up with Roman who had arrived the day before, and we were soon exchanging stories about what had happened since leaving Belo Horizonte over a few cold beers.

It turned out that Brasilia, which was built in its entirety in only three years at the cost of US$10 billion was an ultra-modern city with a large number of architecturally impressive buildings (including the federal buildings made of white marble). It was designed in the shape of an airplane with the government buildings, communications and transportation centres located in its fuselage, and on either side of it, spreading outwards like the wings of a plane, were situated the commercial and residential areas.

Unfortunately though, it was extremely expensive and a pedestrian's nightmare. Everyone drove everywhere and there were hardly any pavements to walk along! Consequently, on average six people were killed every day while trying to cross the roads.

I spent the afternoon wandering through part of the old city before returning to the hostel in time to join Roman for dinner and plan our course of action for the evening. It turned out that Roman had an unusual South American guidebook, which at the end of each section on a city listed the local tourist attractions that all other guidebooks missed out, placing them under the dubious title of 'Sins of the city'. It seemed that Salvador had two sins, and that night we decided to visit one of them: a club called 'Holiday'. The book informed us that it was frequented by semi-professional and amateur prostitutes, and as neither of us had any intention of paying for the favours of a young lady, we felt sure that we wouldn't be bothered for long. After all, it would make an amusing change from our usual evenings of quietly sitting in a bar.

The entrance fee cost approximately £1.50, but as this included two free drinks, and the barman was very generous with his measures, neither of us was complaining. The club was different to how I had imagined it would be: it was small and consisted of little more than a dance floor surrounded by a number of tables and chairs with a bar situated in one corner and a toilet in another. There were no semi-naked women on raised platforms flaunting their bodies about, under a number of strategically positioned spotlights. There weren't even any well-endowed waitresses revealing all to the eye and leaving nothing to the imagination as they leant across the table to place our drinks before us. But there were women: in fact the place was full of them, and it soon became fairly obvious that these beautiful, nubile young ladies of the night could hardly be called semi-professional, let alone amateurs.

The only other men in the place were a group of three fat, middle-aged businessmen, dressed in expensive suits and wearing flamboyant ties, unlike our tatty old jeans and open-necked, short-sleeved shirts, they sat in the shadows engrossed with their newfound companions, oblivious to all that was going on around them.

No sooner had Roman and I sat down, than women started moving in from all directions, encircling us like a shoal of piranha fish slowly moving in for the kill. At first I couldn't believe what was happening as they began caressing me and rubbing parts of their anatomy along my back and against any other part of my body that was within reach, as they slithered past, one by one.

Then, after several tantalising minutes, one of them sat down beside me and began whispering something into my ear which was probably both complementary and erotically suggestive. But alas, with my limited command of the Portuguese language I might as well have been listening to a Brazilian party political broadcast or she could have been reading extracts from the Bahian telephone directory. Whenever she spoke I simply responded with my usual, 'Sorry, I don't understand Portuguese,' and, 'No money,' and after fifteen to twenty minutes she finally got the message and went away.

Meanwhile, Roman was deep in conversation with a young girl sitting close by, so I decided not to intrude. I looked up across the table to see three long-legged, smiling females peering back at me. My eyes began carefully examining their pleasing curves and sensuous smiles, until one of them caught my attention by rubbing her chin and then pointing to my beard. She then withdrew her extended finger and pointed between her legs, shaking her head from side to side. It seemed that, unlike me, this young lady regularly shaved and she didn't mean her armpits. I burst out laughing and she joined in with fits of uncontrollable giggles, before following up her somewhat unusual introduction by slowly walking around the table and sitting down next to me while placing her hand on my leg and gently moving it towards my manhood. She began talking to me in a deep but sexy voice which I once again could not understand a word of, so to every question I simply answered, 'I do not understand.' Frustrated, she reached out and shared my last cigarette and then went away.

Within a couple of minutes she had been replaced by yet another 'femme fatale' trying her luck at playing on my heart strings, in the vain hope that it would later enable her to play with my wallet, only to disappointedly leave shortly afterwards, unrewarded.

By now the rumours were obviously circulating that I was no good, as I had no money and the endless line of ladies temporarily dried up. So, I drained my glass and ordered my second complimentary drink, a glass of rum with a dash of Coke. *Were they trying to get me drunk?* I had been having such an interesting and unusual time that I had forgotten all about my first drink that had previously been sat in front of me for well over an hour, untouched. It seemed the management wasn't going to make much profit on drink sales as far as I was concerned. I looked over to Roman, who was still deep in conversation with the same young lady who had joined him when we first came in. Obviously she was having more success with Roman than the rest of the girls put together were having with me.

I felt a hand rest upon my thigh and turned around to find 'Miss Lady Shave 1981' once more sitting beside me. She sat looking deep into my eyes, while her well-trained hand once more moved towards my manhood. Upon reaching its destination, her deft fingers located my zipper, undid it and slid inside. It was a tight fit but I wasn't complaining. I felt myself blush, but in the dim lights no one could tell. Obviously she was trying a new ploy: body language. At least I understood that better than Portuguese. Reaching for my drink, I took a large gulp and, realising that it was unlikely anyone else could see what was happening due to the position of the table, I decided to sit back, close my eyes and enjoy the experience. The trouble was, she shortly afterwards relinquished her hold and withdrew her hand. I felt like reaching out and shoving it back in again but was too much of a gentleman, so I decided not to interfere with the proceedings.

She offered me a cigarette, then reached out and took a sip of my drink, before launching into another barrage of one-way communication. Several minutes later, though, she frustratedly gave up and, pointing to the empty dance floor, indicated if I would like to dance. I nodded and followed her onto the dance floor, fortunately remembering to adjust my zipper before leaving the table. The music was slow, the lights were dim and she fell into my arms, wrapping hers around me like the tentacles of an octopus. She raised her lips to meet mine and began grinding her thighs into my body, all the while digging her fingers deep into my buttocks. She had a vice-like grip for one so small and definitely knew exactly what she was doing.

At the end of a couple of dances, she released me from her grip and abruptly walked off, leaving me somewhat confused and momentarily lost on the dance floor. I regained my senses, and without further ado, returned to the comparative safety of my seat, where I retrieved my drink and took a large swig. Things seemed to be happening around me thick and fast as several girls formed a small group around 'Lady Shave', and were looking in my direction. *What have I done*, I thought to myself. *Surely it can't be anything I said?* My thoughts were suddenly distracted, as I looked up to see 'Lady Shave' lean across the table and speak to Roman.

Roman being the man of the moment, always there when I needed him, leant over and translated, 'Tell Mike, money no problem, if he likes me, he can come home!' Well, naturally being a gentleman, and realising that if I didn't go back with this bronzed Bahian beauty she would have to walk home in the dark all by herself, I graciously accepted the invitation.

It turned out that she only lived around the corner in an apartment block, and we were soon getting to know each other a little better in the privacy of her own small apartment over a bottle of wine. That night, I sampled the delights of my first coloured woman and was suitably impressed. After all, they don't call Latin Americans hot-blooded for nothing!

Unfortunately for me though, I did not think she was very impressed with me, as I kept on forgetting her name. She kept on pointing to herself and telling me and I kept on forgetting it whenever she asked me to repeat it a few minutes later.

The wine finished, we adjourned to the bedroom where she tantalisingly, slowly undressed me, before I obligingly returned the compliment, gradually revealing her amply proportioned body to my hungry eyes and adventurous hands. We lay back on the creaking double bed, watching each other carefully until I reached out and delicately covered the mounds of her heaving breasts with my hands. My nimble fingers began cupping and squeezing, while my tongue began to slowly move across her body on a voyage of discovery. The room began to fill with her gentle cries of pleasure as we both had a jolly nice time!

Our nocturnal exercises finished, we contentedly lay in each other's arms, both of us drained of energy, breathless and panting, as the perspiration glistened on our bodies. Realising how dry my throat was, I softly asked, without thinking, for a drink to quench my thirst. It seemed, however, that at that time it wasn't the most tactful thing to say, as she immediately reared up like a tigress, her eyes flashing like two red hot coals as she stormed out of the room, only to return a few seconds later and practically throw a cold cup of coffee at me. She then careered once more out of the bedroom, obviously in one hell of a temper and went to sleep on the settee. I laid back to try and sort out what I had done wrong and what I should do next, but immediately fell asleep. It was gone four o'clock in the morning and I was physically and mentally shattered.

Sometime later, I came to and got dressed. Outside, 'Lady Shave' was cooking breakfast, but not for me it seems, for as I walked up to her and romantically put my arms around her waist, she scornfully rebuked my advances. She was cold in her manner and very businesslike. It also seemed that she could speak English after all, as she turned around and told me to 'piss off'!

Looking back on the events of that evening, I realised that she had probably felt that she was paying me for my services. After all, she had supplied the apartment, cigarettes, alcohol and dare I say it, coffee, and it seems she did not approve of the arrangement!

***

Situated in the South of Bolivia is the Cerro Rico (rich mountain), in Potosí. This 500-year-old mine produced vast quantities of silver and tin that funded a large portion of Spain's colonization of the new world. In fact it has been estimated that the conquistadors extracted over 56,699 metric tonnes of silver from the mountain.

However, this rich bounty came at a huge cost as hundreds of thousands of indigenous Indians died working the mines which became known as 'The mountain that eats men'. For it is here that miners lived in constant fear of rockslides, endless clouds of rock dust which invariably led to silicosis and toxic gas emissions.

To counteract these fears, the miners created their own form of religious cult seeking to enlist the devil as an ally. They nicknamed him 'El Tio' (meaning uncle), believing that he controlled the rich veins of ore, revealing them only to those who made ceremonial offerings to him of cocoa leaves, alcohol and cigarettes which are to this day regularly placed alongside one of the many shrines that occur throughout the mineshaft.

The mountain is riddled with tunnels and over 15,000 miners work still work in the mountain. On average fourteen miners die every month and the average life expectancy of someone working in the mountain is forty years.

*

Salvador, Recife and several other north-eastern cities received their electricity from a power station built at the Paulo Alfonso Falls. Once regarded as one of the great falls of the world (the São Francisco River drains an immense valley three times the size of Great Britain), the power station has now regrettably diminished the river's magnitude considerably.

Day 28

February 22, 1981

I am embarrassed to admit it, but today my attempts to visit a nudist beach were thwarted by, of all things, an enormous cane toad. In the morning, I returned to the hostel, and while talking to one of my roommates, a Brazilian who had recently arrived in Salvador for the Mardi Gras, was informed that the path behind the hostel led to a secluded beach, where nude bathing was the accepted norm. The Brazilian continued by saying that if I wanted to see Brazilian women the likes of whom I had never seen before, I should take a stroll down there sometime.

Well, I had always been interested in local scenery, and so, without further ado, grabbed a towel and started off down the path. The trouble was, I hadn't gone more than twenty metres before turning a sharp corner and coming to an abrupt halt as I caught sight of a gigantic toad sitting on the path a couple of metres in front of me. It looked the size of an overgrown cat and contentedly sat there blocking my way, occasionally croaking, looking as if it owned the place, and I was in no rush to dispute its authority.[7]

I had heard of bouncers stopping people from entering nightclubs before, but never muscle-bulging toads barring the way to a nudist beach. The path was narrow and overgrown on either side with a thick mass of vegetation, so I could hardly go around it, and even if I had tried, heaven knows what I might have found lurking in there. After all, this was the tropics, where snakes, spiders and scorpions were prolific. I momentarily considered stepping over it, but the horrific thought of it jumping up and biting those parts that don't like to be bitten made me shudder and cross my legs. Visions of the throat-biting, fluffy white bunny rabbit from 'Monty Python and the Holy Grail' kept permeating through my brain.

I was faced with the daunting prospect of either giving up or somehow making this creature from the black lagoon move out of my way. I carefully considered the dilemma that faced me and came to the conclusion that as the vegetation was so dense, the toad could only move in one of two directions:

1. Backwards, in which case it would still be between me and the beach, and I didn't really want to arrive on the beach with Timothy toad. After all, the girls might not be too impressed with Timmy's appearance, and you know what they say, '*You can always tell a lot about someone by the friends they keep.*'
2. Or forwards, and that was where I was standing!

I looked up towards the hostel, scouring the windows, worried that people might be watching me, but fortunately couldn't see anyone. The last thing I wanted, was to gain the reputation of being such a coward that I couldn't overcome a simple problem like dealing with a harmless toad. I turned back

---

[7] *The cane toad is a large, stocky amphibian with dry, warty skin that has few predators. This is largely due to the poisonous glands situated on each shoulder which secrete poison whenever it feels threatened. If ingested, this venom can cause rapid heartbeat, convulsions and paralysis and will often result in death for any native animal feeling peckish.*

to face my opponent with renewed determination and began waving my arms and towel in the air while shouting, but my efforts were met with little success, as the toad continued to contentedly sit there croaking. I was convinced that it was perfectly harmless, but was averse to going any nearer to put my beliefs to the test. I turned around to check if there were any more of them lurking about, ready to appear behind me and cut off my retreat should the monster decide to start leaping towards me, but fortunately couldn't see any. Probably just as well: after all, who would have believed me if I had told them that I had just been attacked by a gang of marauding cane toads?

I was placed in the precarious position of attack or withdrawal, and it was make-your-mind-up time, so I reluctantly conceded defeat, turned tail and walked back to the hostel. It was a sad day for England, as I tried to convince myself on the way that I didn't really want to visit a nudist beach.

I mean, I thought to myself, *what was there to do other than swim, sunbathe and ogle countless hordes of beautiful women with firm naked bodies, watching their tanned breasts rise and fall to the sound of the ocean, gently lapping on the beach?* No, I decided I would much rather do something else!

Back once more in the hostel, I bumped into Roman who had been out having breakfast, and quickly decided to keep the 'close encounters of a toad kind' incident to myself. We discussed the previous night's activities and decided to spend the rest of the day on a crowded beach further along the coast. I never did visit that nudist beach, and to this day I do not know whether or not it was real or merely a Brazilian fantasy.

At the beach, I went in for a dip and fleetingly toyed with the idea of swimming along the coast to the nudist beach, but decided that my dog paddle wasn't quite strong enough to get me there and back. Anyway, it was a beautiful day, the water was warm, the sand hot and the sky clear: it was the perfect day for lying around and doing nothing. What's more, I noticed that I was either beginning to develop a deep tan or should start seriously considering changing my brand of soap.

In the evening, flushed with the success of my previous night's escapades, we decided to see if my luck would continue and Roman's improve.

Before leaving Los Angeles, where he was studying for his second Master's degree at UCLA, a friend of Roman's had told him that if he ever passed through Salvador he should not miss a visit to the infamous 'Café Zeh Zeh'. The place where anything and everything invariably happened! Well, we both felt a little apprehensive about this particular sin spot, as we didn't know what we might be letting ourselves in for.

Roman had been told some really wild stories about naked women swinging upside down on chandeliers doing strange things with candles, scantily clad snake-dancers performing some totally mind-boggling feats with their equipment and a collection of other weirdos. So we weren't too disappointed when we couldn't find a taxi driver who had even heard of the place, let alone knew where it was.

Later on over a beer, it was agreed that it probably only existed in Roman's friends' vivid imagination, and the subject was closed with Roman promising that if he ever became rich, he would return to Salvador and build a 'Café Zeh Zeh'. After all, he had spent four months travelling around South America waiting to verify its authenticity. I asked if he intended to use electricity or candles?

Still, the night was yet young, and we decided to visit the only alternative open to us, Salvador's other sin. After all, I had effectively made Club Holiday a no-go area for us, and it was agreed that if we ever set foot in there again, I would probably get lynched by 'Lady Shave' and her compatriots.

This other club was situated in the lower part of the city near the docks, and with this in mind, we proceeded to make our way to the vertical lift. At the bottom, we got out and started walking along the main street, when our conversation was rudely interrupted by two prostitutes shouting the usual 'come on' from across the busy road. We ignored their offers of friendly assistance and carried on walking, until a couple of hundred metres later the prostitutes suddenly re-appeared in front of us, breathless and panting, having run on and crossed the road ahead of us.

The tall skinny one walked up to Roman, while lucky me got the short, fat, ugly one. She was roughly 1.5 metre tall and at least eight and a half months pregnant. I didn't know what she was expecting to give birth to, but by the enormous size of her, it must have either been quadruplets or a pygmy hippo because she was so huge! She literally waddled up to me, smiling like a Cheshire cat, but not as good-looking, and having slapped her hands around the back of my trousers to attain a firm grip on my buttocks, began thrusting part of her enormous anatomy repeatedly against mine, saying she wanted to do things with me, not for money of course, just for fun. *Fun?* The thought made me shudder. *I could find more excitement in a sick bag!* She continued her 'let's not beat around the bush' approach for what seemed like an eternity, and all the time I stood there totally stunned. My mouth kept opening and closing like a goldfish, but nothing came out. For the first time on my travels, I was completely dumbstruck.

After a couple of minutes, she eventually relinquished her hold upon my body saying, 'You no want good time? OK,' and slowly began walking away with her friend, wolf-whistling and shouting, what I could only presume were crude insinuations. As a result of what had just transpired, I proposed that we forgo the pleasures of visiting another club and simply go for a drink instead. Roman agreed, after noticing that I was looking decidedly pale and shaken, so we returned to the lift, and once back on top immediately headed for the nearest bar. What I needed was an ice-cold beer with a large Cachaça chaser, and promptly ordered the same for Roman as it was my shout. However, when I went to pay for it, I found out that I had been robbed. It seems that while 'Miss Mobile Maternity Unit 1981' had been thumping her body parts against mine, she had gone through my back pockets and lifted me clean!

I lost approximately 305 cruzeiros which was only about £1.80, but was thankful for small mercies, as I had earlier that evening taken a 500-cruzeiro note out of my back pocket and put it in the security pocket of my trouser leg.

The twelve-centimetre turn-up on one of my trouser legs was completely stitched up except for a small gap, and it was here that I used to hide any notes of large denomination that I happened to be carrying around with me, for safe keeping. Even if I had been frisked by a mugger, it was unlikely anyone would have located it. I believed that, when travelling through third-world countries, it was always advisable to carry a reserve on you, for if you were ever mugged and had nothing to offer your attacker, they might have given you a shave a little too close for comfort across the neck for wasting their time.

**

By the middle of the 18th century, Salvador had become a thriving hub of entrepreneurial fervour and the Portuguese empire's second city after Lisbon. It was also renowned for its sensuality and decadence and the 'Bay of All Saints' became better known as the 'Bay of All Saints and nearly All Sins'.

*

Salvador is built along part of the Bay of Todos os Santos (All Saints), which is so large (1,052 sq. km) that it has been estimated that it could hold all of the ships of the world

*

The Pinocchio lizard (anolis proboscis) has to be one of the most bizarre looking lizards on the planet. First discovered in Ecuador in 1953, it was thought to be extinct until it was rediscovered in 2015. As the name implies the male of the species has an elongated nose which plays an important role in sexual selection, not only attracting females but also in fighting off other males..

Day 29

February 23, 1981

Roman and I spent the morning changing hostels, and once settled into our new residence, we both agreed that it was a vast improvement on its predecessor. It was not only cheaper and smaller in size, but had a friendlier and more relaxed atmosphere. There were ample showers and washing facilities available along the corridor and what's more, there was even a communal kitchen with an assortment of saucepans, crockery and cutlery. Our bedroom was large and spacious, which was just as well considering there were twelve people sharing six bunkbeds in it, and was situated at one end of the hostel. This meant that unlike the other smaller rooms, it had windows on three sides of the bedroom, assuring the maximum amount of ventilation possible, which was much appreciated by those roommates such as myself that were still unfamiliar with the humid conditions of the tropics.

Each room was also equipped with a security lock, although there were no keys, so instead you opened the door by thumping one of the side-panels which would jump the lock accordingly.

The rest of the day was spent sunbathing, although I

disappeared for part of the afternoon in search of a home from home. It seemed that Salvador had its own British Bahia club, and the thought of sinking a few pints with some expatriates and reading the occasional copy of an English newspaper to catch up on what was happening back home, put an extra spring in my step. The trouble was, when I arrived there, it all seemed like an anti-climax as the staff were all Brazilian and, as I found out later, so were all of its members. In fact, the majority of them couldn't even speak English. I left feeling disappointed but determined to return later that evening with Roman to act as an interpreter and find out why it was called the British Bahia Club.

That night, after I had cooked a disastrous meal which was largely consumed by the dustbin, we left for the B.B.C. The arrival of two white strangers in the bar was viewed with great interest by the club's members, and the President quickly came over to introduce himself and investigate further as he could speak fluent English. He asked if he could help us, and upon finding out that I was British, flung his arms in the air with a gesture of sheer delight and cried out aloud. He then led us to an empty table, sat us down and called several friends over so that they could be introduced to me. It turned out that the club had never had a British member and that I was only the third Brit to ever enter the club. Consequently, I was treated as a guest of honour. The President called over one of the waiters and before long, two large plates of food were brought to the table and placed before Roman and myself. This was accompanied by several bottomless glasses of beer and Cachaça, and right through to the early hours of the morning we ate, drank and talked to our newfound friends; who generously insisted on paying for everything. It seemed that the place was an exclusive businessmen's club run on similar lines to the British gentlemen's clubs of old, hence the name. At the front door sat a doorman who refused entry to any of the member's wives, while the members regularly bought their respective lovers in through the back door, leading from the car park. The club had a restaurant and bar where members could wine and dine themselves and their guests and there were several bedrooms for use of upstairs.

By the end of the evening, the place was empty but for a hardcore group of five: myself, Roman, the President, who was a lawyer, and two members: a circuit court judge and a paediatric surgeon. At one point the President even announced that what the club really needed was a British President and jokingly offered me the position, to which Roman, who had by now practically become my agent, piped up saying that I had mentioned about trying to get a job in Bahia (an outright lie but it sounded good at the time). Roman was a born businessman and always on the lookout for potential money-making ideas, for you never knew what might result from chance meetings.

We finally stumbled out of the bar at 02:30, much to the relief of the staff who had been waiting to lock up since a little after midnight, and made our way down to the car park.

Roman and I were then slowly driven home by a somewhat inebriated judge, who on the way managed to perform his own version of the conga, by steering his car from one side of the road to the other and then back again, only to start the whole process all over once more. Needless to say, that night everyone slept like the contents of a lumberjack's warehouse.

***

South west of Brasilia is the Emas National Park in the state of Goiás where you can witness some of the largest termite mounds on the planet. These mounds, which can grow up to thirty metres in diameter and over seven metres high, not only house several million termites, but they are also used as nesting sites for the Buff-Breasted Paradise Kingfisher and as home to hundreds of glowing Pyrophorus beetle larvae. At night-time the termite mounds look like they're wrapped in Christmas tree-lights.

*

Termites have the sharpest mandibles in the world.

Day 30

February 24, 1981

Roman was becoming increasingly irritated in the mornings whenever he went out for breakfast. There he was in the middle of Brazil, the major coffee-producing country in the world, yet he actually had difficulty in finding anywhere that sold it. He used to trek through the streets enquiring at each café as he went by, until he would eventually find one that actually sold coffee, and even then it would usually stop serving it after 10 or 11am. The trouble was that even when he did find somewhere that sold coffee one day, it didn't automatically mean it would be selling coffee the next day. Unfortunately though, he couldn't even consider facing the new day until he had consumed his daily dose of caffeine.

It got so bad, that anyone would have thought he was trying to break the law. In fact I, who invariably accompanied him on these treks, could just imagine Roman having to walk through the back streets of some sordid part of the city, until out of the darkness a ghostly voice would call, '*You wanna fix, man?*'

A figure would emerge from the shadows wearing a long trench coat, dark glasses and hat and for a small fee would agree to take Roman along to an illegal coffee house. Outside, the sign 'Opium Den' had been changed to 'Caffeine Den'. It was the same all over the city, the drug barons were being squeezed out by the coffee plantation owners.

The hypnotic sound of a bubbling percolator would welcome our arrival, as we would step through the doorway into a dark and secluded room. Roman would stand there, momentarily swaying from side to side, breathing in its familiar aroma before stumbling forward and sinking into a vacant seat by the counter. He would reach out to pour himself a cup of black coffee but his hands, clammy with nervous anticipation would often start shaking, until they got so bad that he would have to put down the percolator for fear of spilling the precious liquid. The shakes gone, he would once more reach out and try again. Then, cradling the hot liquid carefully between his hands, he would sit back and begin drinking in great gulps to quench his insatiable thirst. But I was merely daydreaming, after all who would wear a trench coat in the humid climate of South America?

I had an interesting morning: over breakfast Roman explained that for all their sexual liberation, Swedish people in general tended to be rather introverted and lonely, usually having only a small group of friends to socialise with, but little or no one else. He continued by stating that Sweden had the highest suicide rate in the world, even higher than Japan.

As if to reinforce this surprising revelation, he then quoted the case of a forty-five-year-old Polish taxi driver that he knew of back in Warsaw. It seemed that he too was lonely and desperately wanted a wife, so he placed an advert in a Swedish newspaper and received well over fifty replies! My mind immediately broke into overdrive at this surprising fact, and before long had devised an unusual method of travelling Scandinavia on the cheap, which I made a mental note of, for the future.

Some years later in fact, while planning a backpacking trip through Scandinavia, I actually wrote to an old school friend living in Stockholm, Sweden, asking him to place the following ad in a well-known national paper:

'Young (28) English college lecturer, planning to travel through Sweden this Summer. Would be interested in hearing from any young

ladies who could offer him temporary accommodation and show him local scenery and customs.'

Regrettably, my friend, Pete, didn't take me seriously and, therefore, didn't place the advert. Consequently, I never did try out my master plan on how to bed around the world, and as far as I know, it remains to this day untried and tested.

Later that morning while queueing up to change some travellers' cheques, I started talking to a French guy who informed me that he had spent the last six years travelling through South America during the winter months. He continued by explaining that he financed each trip by buying numerous local 'knickknacks' and semi-precious stones which he took home each summer to sell for a huge profit on the Parisian streets. This profit would then be used to finance his next trip out.

The rest of the day as usual, was spent slaving away on the beach working on a suntan, occasionally turning this way or that to fully appreciate the noticeable qualities of one of the many beautiful women strolling by. After all, some of them were so hot, they could melt an ice cream at fifteen paces. The fashionable bikinis among the young and trendy came from a chain of boutiques called 'Bum Bum'. They consisted of a piece of coloured string with barely enough fabric to cover their pubic hairs. That is, as long as the young ladies in question trimmed them back a little! The bikinis were referred to as Fio Dental, which translated literally means 'Dental Floss'

That evening, I went to a folk concert held in the grounds of the hostel. However, I left soon afterwards, suddenly beginning to appreciate just why European music was so popular in Brazil.

***

With eighty-two percent of its population tracing their ancestry back to the days of slavery, Salvador is described as 'the biggest African city outside Africa'.

Day 31

February 25, 1981

I awoke as a shaft of sunlight slowly edged its way across my face. Outside, the clear blue sky smiled down upon this rich and lush part of the tropics, and the tall palm trees stood towering majestically over the green foliage that lay around in an abundance. From a bathroom window, I watched with fascination as a tiny hummingbird flitted among the blooms of a giant honeysuckle bush just outside the window, feasting upon the rich stores of nectar hidden deep inside each colourful bloom. *Yes, this is the life*, I thought. Mornings like this made the sacrifice of my teaching career worthwhile.

After breakfast, I returned to the hostel and went through my rucksack, re-arranging everything in its order of importance. Somehow it seemed, no matter how careful I had tried to be before leaving England, I had still managed to bring along a number of items that were of little or no use to me. I extricated my expensive half-plate hiking boots, which had been packed away for a more suitable terrain and climate, at the bottom of my rucksack, to find them covered in a thick growth of mould. I began to panic, wondering what to do next, until a Brazilian roommate, noticing my predicament, came over and advised me to wash them in neat alcohol. I wisely followed his advice and immediately left, returning within the hour to bathe my boots and solve the problem, as the mould literally fell off, probably dying from cirrhosis of the liver!

This place was an alcoholic's paradise; after all, half a litre of 96% proof alcohol cost a mere fifty cruzeiros, which was approximately 27p.

Furthermore, it was also an architectural historian's paradise, with over 20,000 buildings which were over 250 years old located in the region.

Alcohol played an important part in the Brazilian economy, as the government had overcome its problems relating to an oil shortage by growing vast quantities of sugar beet, refining it into pure alcohol and then running their cars on it (it's called Alcool). The trouble was, alcoholics were now going around the petrol stations at night-time sucking the last few drops out of each petrol pump and getting pissed in the process. So that when the staff arrived in the morning to open up the station they sometimes found an unconscious body of an alcoholic lying on the forecourt.

In the evening, Roman and I were both invited to the twentieth birthday party of one of our Brazilian roommates. As the celebrations got under way, the Cachaça appeared and there was much singing and drinking, as bottle after bottle was passed around until everyone was well and truly drunk. The only problem was a total lack of female company to share the festivities with. Although, judging by the state of everyone at the end of it, it would have been purely wishful thinking anyway.

**

Alcohol-powered cars tended to stall in the wet.

Day 32

February 26, 1981

I woke up late. There was no doubt about it that I was beginning to sleep much better and at long last seemed to be adjusting to the hot and humid climate of the tropics. I spent a quiet day pottering around the hostel, biding my time and generally taking things easy. Tonight heralded the start of the Mardi Gras, so I was conserving all of my energies for what I hoped would be an eventful evening.

The city was full of people rushing around doing last-minute shopping or making other final preparations, and the air was filled with a mounting excitement as the streets became choked with a solid mass of people. South American cities were surrounded by large shanty towns and for the duration of the carnival practically everyone moved into the city. At night-time the pavements became covered in an uneven blanket of bodies as hundreds of thousands of people slept out in the open.

Roman and I left the 'Republica' (the Brazilian name for a student hostel) in the early evening and slowly made our way towards the city centre, stopping off en route for a bite to eat and the occasional liquid refreshment. On the way, we passed a small park which had been temporarily overrun by a mass of tiny stalls, each one hand-built that day using odd bits of wood, string and pieces of plastic sheeting. Here, several hundred shanty town dwellers lived for the duration of the carnival, selling local delicacies prepared before our very eyes over small fires. They stayed open throughout the carnival, both night and day, and there was always someone around ready and willing to serve you, while the rest of the family were either out enjoying themselves or sleeping on the grass at the back of the stall.

We reached the main square and joined the masses already waiting. Evidently, a famous band was going to officially open the carnival and it was to the large stage at the far end of the square that the throng of people pushed.

The evening began with a supporting band coming on to warm up the audience and this was quickly achieved, but not by the band – as their music was rather bland and uninspiring – but with the amiable help of three delectable bunny girls. The South American bunny was somewhat different to its English counterpart. *Obviously Darwin's Theory of Evolution was creeping in here*, I thought. They were tall, bronzed and beautiful, wearing very little, and the little there was, was not doing a very good job of covering up the parts that other bunny suits always reached.

They wore seamed stockings and high heels, a very small G-string which left nothing to the imagination when they turned around, a tiny half-cup bra which was at times more than overflowing, and a large pair of fluffy white ears. They stood at the front of the stage going through a number of interesting body exercises to the beat of the music and both Roman and I could have quite happily watched them for the rest of the evening. In fact, judging from the barrage of encouragement aimed at the stage, so could the rest of the audience as well. But, try as they may, these cuddly creatures were unable to hog the limelight all to themselves as they were accompanied on stage by a mischievous midget.

He really seemed to be enjoying himself as he tried to imitate their amazing belly and thigh movements, stopping every so often to watch the real thing to check that he was doing it right. At times though he got rather carried away, which was only to be expected considering he was eye level to their writhing navels. He'd stand beside them facing the audience with a huge grin on his face before turning around to stare at a jumping G-string, rhythmically pulsating in the air a matter of centimetres away from his nose. Several seconds later he'd turn back, eyes nearly popping out of his head, mouth open wide and tongue hanging out. To the delight of the crowd, he then pretended to demonstrate in vivid detail with the aid of his finger, nose and mouth exactly what to do if you were ever fortunate enough to be confronted by one of these energetic creatures!

Unfortunately though, they all left with the supporting band and after a few sound checks, the place erupted as the main band came on. Their arrival heralded the official start of the carnival and people responded by beginning to jump up and down in a frenzied display of excitement until the place resembled more of a riot than a concert. At this juncture, Roman and I quickly decided it was high time to make a hasty retreat and try to extricate ourselves from the swirling bedlam that was now boiling up all around us. However, we quickly realised that this was practically impossible as there were so many people pushing and jumping forward, that we were merely swept along with the crowd. I began to get worried as the earlier excitement turned into a genuine fear, because as much as I pushed and shoved, I hardly seemed to be making any headway. My main worry was being accidentally tripped up, as anyone who would be unfortunate enough to fall to the ground would most likely be trampled to death in no time.

After an anxious fifteen to twenty minutes, we eventually escaped with a few bruises and headed for the nearest bar for several liquid top-ups. By then, it was quite late so we slowly made our way home. No guesses as to what I dreamed of that night, but it was the nearest thing I'd ever come to bestiality!

***

West of Salvador flows the Rio (river) São Francisco which is the legendary home of the Bicho da agua (Beast of the water). This mythical creature which is part animal, part man, spends its time walking along the bottom of the riverbed snoring. The crews of the riverboats regularly throw offerings of tobacco into the river to placate the beast and ensure its protection against misfortune.

*

Picoaza is a small town near Ecuador's Pacific coast and during its 1967 mayoral elections, a foot deodorant company ran a series of politically themed adverts on leaflets which were handed out promoting their product, 'Pulvapies'.

In the last few days before election day, their message simply read: "Vote for any candidate, but if you want well-being and hygiene, vote for Pulvapies." The ballot papers being used in Picoaza were very basic on which the voter wrote on to the voting slip the name of the candidate they wanted to vote for. Needless to say Pulvapies won by a landslide!

*

Salvador had recently closed its medical school's museum and its most famous exhibits. The severed heads of the bandit Lampeao, his mistress and eight of his followers, were finally buried in a local cemetery.

Between 1920 and 1938, when he was eventually killed, Virgilio Ferreira da Silva known as Lampeao (the lightning), acted as a latter-day Brazilian Robin Hood. Often stealing from the rich merchants of the region, who grew wealthy from the proceeds of charging exorbitant prices to the local impoverished workers, he would regularly redistribute his plunder to the poor to help alleviate their suffering.

*

Brazil has a total population of 148 million, sixty million of whom live in squalor without proper sanitation, clean water or housing. Fifty-four percent of the country's wealth is owned by ten percent of the population.

Day 33

February 27, 1981

For the duration of the carnival, the military police patrolled the streets in groups of between eight and ten men with an officer at the front and his men obediently following on behind, like a mother hen leading her chicks. Each man wore a gun strapped to his side and carried a nasty-looking metre-long riot baton lovingly cradled in his arms. It seemed that although the Mardi Gras was regarded as a time of celebration, it was also the most dangerous period of the year.

One of the main dangers were the poor people, who during the carnival would flock to the cities in their hundreds of thousands from the surrounding shanty towns, wildly taking to the streets eating, drinking and dancing the days and nights away. For five days and six nights (most carnivals lasted four days and five nights but Salvador's carnival was the exception to the rule), they would forget their poverty and depressing existence and just celebrate, continually savouring each moment as if it were their last, as they tried to squeeze the maximum amount of enjoyment out of the 132 hours of festivities and celebrations. The trouble was that many of them would quickly spend what little money they had saved, and so in order to obtain more, they would often take to the side streets and lay in wait for some unsuspecting victim to walk by. At which point they would leap out and attack, knife at the ready to overcome any determined resistance with a frenzied cut and slash policy. Then, with their victim either lying dead or wounded at their feet or cowering into submission, they would take what few possessions they had and return to the festivities until their trusty knives were once more called upon to deliver them temporarily out of the hands of poverty. With so many people in the city, the police could seldom do little more than merely take details of the robbery or remove the body off the street.

Another problem was street fighting, for the typical South American was hot blooded and short tempered at the best of times and with the additional combination of carnival hysteria, alcohol and a lack of sleep, fighting invariably broke out. In fact, during the 1980 Mardi Gras in Rio de Janeiro, well over 150 people died from a mixture of murders, suicide, accidents or drunkenness, and throughout South America over 10,000 people met an untimely end to their celebrations.

For the last couple of days I had been in a permanent state of lustful desire over a devastatingly dynamic Argentinian. She was petite and very feminine, with long jet-black hair and the most enormous assets that I had ever seen. She was the sort of girl that you would love to squeeze past in a narrow corridor except it would have been practically impossible. If she could have only sung, she would have undoubtedly become South America's answer to Dolly Parton. I had desperately wanted to get to know her, but felt any attempts with my lack of vocabulary would have only resulted in me making a complete and utter fool of myself. *After all*, I thought, *how can you sweet talk a girl with phrases like, 'I do not understand'* (especially when I wanted to), *'sorry', 'pardon', and 'no money'*?

However as luck would have it, on this particular morning I was talking to Roman when she happened to walk past and overheard us. She immediately stopped and turned around, at which point my pupils dilated and my breathing became erratic, and she announced that she was learning English at university. I jumped at the opportunity and quickly offered to help her practice her conversational English which she readily accepted with great enthusiasm, much to my utter surprise, but obvious delight.

She stood before me, this celestial vision of beauty with pouting lips and big ...... brown eyes, asking me to correct her English, saying, 'Teacher, teacher, teach me, teach me,' and what I kept on thinking was, *Woman, what I want to teach you, you may not want to learn!* Of course it turned out that she was leaving for Fortaleza the next day and so regrettably it seemed unlikely that I stood any real chance of getting to know her intimately. Still, the two girls from Belo Horizonte were due in that night so all was not yet lost.

Roman and I prepared for their impending arrival by leaving a large notice, in which Roman had used all of his linguistic powers of diplomacy and persuasion, in the student hostel which we had recently moved from and had arranged to meet the girls at.

The notice read: 'IF YOU WANT TO MAKE LOVE, CONTACT US AT *****.' We then walked into town to buy a large bottle of vodka and a bottle of rum with an ample supply of mixers. We were both eager, ready and impatiently awaiting their arrival.

While waiting for our two companions to appear, Roman and I invited several other girls from the hostel into our bunk-room for a drink and a friendly get-together. Then, having come to the conclusion that the Belo girls weren't going to show up that night after all, we – by now both of us well on the way to getting plastered – went into town with a couple of the girls from the hostel. Being no fool, or at least that's what I thought at the time, I ensured we had ample supplies for the journey by filling up my two-litre water bottle with rum and Coke. But alas, within a comparatively short space of time we had lost the girls and Roman and I were left wandering through the streets on our own. We stupidly proceeded to drown our sorrows by finishing off the contents of the water bottle, whereupon it was decided that I should stagger back to the hostel for a refill of vodka and mixers.

What happened next I am still not too sure, but I remember being chatted up by a young lady near the city centre, while staggering around looking for Roman, and that she had invited me home for a good time.

Good time! I couldn't have stood to attention even if she had played the national anthem. However, as I was well and truly smashed, and by now had lost all sense of reasoning, I obediently followed her, trying unsuccessfully to walk in a straight line. I staggered forward wearing a stupid grin on my face thinking to myself, *Roman will never believe this!*

Being helpful, my newly found companion (I never did get her name) insisted on easing the burden I was carrying by ignoring my drunken protests and slipping my kit bag off my shoulder and then proceeding to walk away with it. I tried to stop her but for some reason had great difficulty in controlling my body.

By this point I was obviously overdue for a check-up, as I had lost the ability to co-ordinate my limbs. There I stood, swaying from side to side while my brain signalled to my right hand to reach out and grab hold of my portable drinks cabinet which was quickly disappearing in front of my eyes, when I suddenly started walking backwards. She vanished into the crowd and left me feeling helpless, confused and for some reason still walking backwards up a gently sloping hill, as once I had started I couldn't stop. Pity though, I would have loved to have seen her face when she opened up the kit bag. By the weight of it, she probably thought she had procured something valuable such as an expensive camera and accessories.

I didn't (and still don't) remember anything else that night, although I woke up the next morning lying on my mattress fully clothed. I had lost my silver cross and chain, was covered in dried blood and had cuts and bruises all over my body with a particularly deep and nasty-looking twenty-centimetre gash along my right arm.

Whatever happened I never did find out, but my automatic

instinct to get home could well have saved my life. If I had stayed out on the streets I might well have wandered into a knife-wielding drunk looking for some easy money. That night, I learnt one lesson that I would never forget and have adhered to ever since: never get rat-arsed in unfamiliar surroundings without a sober friend close at hand to look after you.

***

In 1984, the official death toll in Rio de Janeiro, as reported in the Times for the four-day carnival, was ninety-six. According to the local authorities, 'it had been a quiet year!'

*

Roman had met an American woman on Lake Titicaca on the borders of Peru and Bolivia who couldn't speak a word of Spanish, but was convinced that if she spoke English very sloooooowly the local peasants had to understand her!

*

Most Brazilian women marry while still in their teens and the average household contains 4-5 children. It is not uncommon for families to have as many as twenty children.

*

Some years later, I met a Brit in Singapore who, while travelling through a small mid-western town in America, stopped to ask a local for directions. The local, finding out that he was English, proceeded to exclaim, 'My, don't you speak good American!'

*

In Brazil armed robberies are known as 'Bangie-Bangies'.

*

While South America's rain forests are some of the wettest places on earth, the Atacama desert in Chile is considered the driest place on earth.

Day 34

February 28, 1981

I awoke with a blinding headache and began to survey my numerous wounds through a pair of bloodshot eyes. I had trouble focusing and it felt as if my eyeballs were rolling around inside my head on sheets of fine sandpaper. Dragging myself off my bed, I slowly undressed and headed for the showers where I carefully began bathing my newly acquired collection of cuts and bruises.

Once dressed, I went downstairs to look for Brazil's answer to the British Milk Marketing Board, only to be informed that she had already left. Furthermore, it seemed unlikely that the girls from Belo Horizonte would be putting in an appearance as they still hadn't turned up, and on top of my wounds and my frustration at losing my cross and chain, it didn't seem a very promising start to a new day. Several Brazilian friends advised me that the only safe place to keep anything was down my underpants, and the way I was currently feeling, I considered going one stage further and wrapping my money around a currently redundant part of my anatomy. *At least it would then have some useful purpose in life.* Who knows? *I might have even come into some money in the process!* I pondered. Still things could

TALES FROM A SOUTH AMERICAN STORM DRAIN

be worse, Gerard, a French friend who had been one of our roommates in Rio and was now staying in the same hostel as we were in Salvador, had lost US$400 the day before.

At the time, he had been on his way to the bank to change some money when he happened to meet two French guys that he had previously shared a room with in São Paulo. They were going for a swim and invited Gerard to join them, which he unfortunately did, nipping back to the hostel to collect his trunks. A couple of minutes later he had returned with trunks and towel in hand, still wearing his money belt underneath his clothes as he intended to go directly to the bank from the beach, as it happened to be on the way. He went in for a swim with one of his friends while the other lay on the beach sun bathing and supposedly looking after, among other things, Gerard's money belt.

Gerard came out, dried himself, got dressed and said goodbye, arranging to meet them later that evening for a drink. At the bank though, he found out to his cost that one of his supposed friends had gone through his money belt while he was swimming and had stolen all of his American currency. Gerard immediately left for the hostel where his compatriots were staying, only to find that they had returned shortly before him, packed their belongings and left in the direction of the bus station. It just went to show, you could never be too careful when travelling abroad.[8]

I, on the other hand, had a great evening, following a samba school through the streets of Salvador. The school had assembled in the square outside the Republica we were staying in, close to the main road which led directly into the city centre

---

[8] *A British couple sold their business and rented out their home for six months in order to achieve a lifetime's ambition of travelling through South America. They flew into Rio, and having completed the necessary entry requirements, caught the airport bus into the city centre. Unfortunately for them, however, they had all of their valuables (passports, travellers' cheques, foreign currency, hotel reservations, aeroplane tickets and cameras) stored away in a shoulder bag. They momentarily put it down on the floor to admire the passing scenery only to find it had permanently disappeared seconds later never to be seen again.*

and were busily making last-minute preparations while their musicians filled the air with the deafening thud of an army of African drums. At the time, I was talking to Roman in the bunk-room, but before long found the beat irresistible so I quickly threw on my Greek kaftan and went outside to investigate further. At the front of the proceedings was a large float, partly covered by an assortment of green vegetation. Close by sat several scantily clad women, their clothes torn, wearing chains around their wrists and ankles.

Three men stood towering over them dressed in seaman's clothes, cutlasses dangling from their belts and brandishing whips in their hands. The samba club had chosen as their theme a scene from African history in which slave traders were capturing Africans and sending them to a life of slavery working in the sugar plantations of South America. The float depicted the capture while following on behind were thirty-five to forty dancers, once more clothed in rags and wearing manacles on their wrists, who represented the plantation workers at work. Behind them came a mass of over fifty brightly dressed drummers, each one beating out a pulsating rhythm on a large African drum, strapped across their shoulders. I stood surveying the scene before me, entranced by the profusion of noise, colour and commotion.

The float started slowly moving towards the city centre and I obediently followed, clapping my hands and gyrating my hips to the music which seemed to be controlling me, rather like a South American 'pied piper of Hamelin'. Everyone around including the performers themselves thought it was great to see a fair-haired, blue-eyed gringo dancing along to the beat. In fact, for a time I was actually invited into the rope cordon which surrounded the performers, to join in with them as they danced through the streets.

Each club was cordoned off from the crowds by a long rope which was held in place by four marshals, one in each corner, to form an elongated rectangle. Their sole task was to keep the rope about a metre off the ground as the parade slowly moved forward, hoping to dissuade the populous (like me!) from gatecrashing the proceedings and thereby ruining their performance which would be assessed by carnival judges along the way. After all, this was a serious business and the reputation of the samba club was at stake.

The word 'samba' is believed to have been derived from a West African Bantu word meaning 'to pray' and from an Angolan word meaning pelvis movements or thrusts. The dance is said to be capable of sending people into a trance. I could completely understand this as I found myself totally captivated, watching the nubile young women's pulsating bodies on the floats as they slowly moved along the road. I was told that it was traditionally a dance to encourage procreation. I needed no encouragement.

Unfortunately, I was noticed by one of the samba club officials after a few minutes and was unceremoniously removed from the cordoned area. Still, I can now say, hand on heart, that I temporarily became a guest performer of a samba club and danced through the streets of Salvador as part of their Mardi Gras celebrations.

I arrived home late, meeting up with an Ecuadorian student staying at a nearby hostel on the way back. She spoke good English and we were getting along fine, when suddenly she grabbed my hand and led me across the road. *Well, I thought, looks like my lucky number's come up after all.* I began to feel myself getting excited until she turned to me and explained that there had been a man hiding in the shadows of a tree just up ahead with a large rock in his hand. *Obviously hoping for a donation to his carnival fund.*

***

Along the coast from Salvador is the beautiful palm-fringed beach of Itapuã, where you can watch local fishermen at work on their traditional fishing rafts called Jangadas. Each raft is made up of six logs, each one approximately eight metres in length and are fitted together with wooden pegs and tapered at one end to form a bow.

The fishermen often spend several days out at a time, anchoring themselves in a particularly good fishing spot with a long piece of twine and a large stone. They precariously bob up and down on the water like a piece of cork until the raft is either full of drying fish or they run out of provisions, at which point they return home.

*

Brazil is the largest Catholic country in the world, with over 90% of the population identifying themselves as Catholic.

*

Salvador was, for over 200 years, the capital of Brazil until 1763, when Rio de Janeiro took its place. Then on the 21st April 1960 Brazilia was inaugurated as the federal capital after being purpose built for a mind boggling $2 trillion U.S. !

*

In the town of Plato, on the shore of Magdalena River in Columbia, a local man used to regularly spy on the townswomen bathing naked in the river. In order to avoid being caught, he had a magician make him up two potions: one to turn him into an caiman, and the other to turn him back into a human again. The man would arrange for a friend to come along to administer this second potion.

For a time, everything worked well. Until one day his friend wasn't available to administer the second potion and, in desperation, the young man asked someone else to take his friend's place. Unfortunately for the voyeur, the replacement was not as brave as his predecessor. Upon seeing Montenegro returning as a caiman, the replacement jumped in fright and spilled the restorative potion. A few drops landed on Saul Montenegro's head but the rest fell on the ground.

The drops of potion that fell on the caiman's head and upper body turned that part of the animal human. However, the lower half, untouched by the spilled potion, remained caiman, leaving the man a kind of caiman centaur – half man, half reptile. Shunned by the people of Plato and unable to find more of the potion, he supposedly roams the Magdalena River to this day as the El Hombre Caimán (The Caiman Man).

Day 35

March 1, 1981

Some of the locals used to try to rip you off for every cruzeiro they could get. Outside the Republica where we were staying stood a street vendor selling a variety of cold drinks. Two days ago he had charged fifteen cruzeiros for a bottle of lemonade, yesterday it had cost twenty-five, and today he actually had the cheek of trying to charge thirty-five cruzeiros. Needless to say I was not amused, and before walking off suggested what he could do with the lemonade bottle.

It was my ninth day in Salvador and I was starting to get itchy feet. The carnival was fantastic, but after three days and nights, my enthusiasm for it was beginning to wane a little. So in the afternoon, Roman and I discussed where our next port of call should be and when exactly we would grace it with our presence, for as we were still heading in the same direction, we had decided to temporarily team up. Over a small crinkled map of Brazil it was agreed that we would stay to the end of the carnival and then travel north, along the coast to Recife.

Realising that the demand for coaches leaving immediately after the Mardi Gras would probably be considerable, we took the precaution of buying our tickets in advance.

By nine o'clock in the evening, Roman had already finished off the vodka, so we headed out towards the city for a few beers. The trouble was, due to the alcohol he had already consumed, Roman was by now in a somewhat boisterous mood and began loudly proclaiming to the world that I was 'the "Great Mike"', and I would 'kiss all the girls'. Every woman he walked past, he announced with an enthusiastic zeal, 'Velly boutiful.' The trouble was, after a couple more beers, he was so drunk that he even began saying it to the military police as they marched by. Fortunately for him, they either couldn't understand him or chose to ignore it.

We carried on bar hopping until Roman suddenly stopped in his tracks and turned round to face me, displaying an enormous grin which spread across his face; he slapped me on my back and promised that he would find me a woman for the night. He then attempted to sell me for fifty US dollars. *Well*, I thought, *fifty isn't too bad, considering this is South America*. However, after another drink, I was rather hurt to hear – especially as it had been my round – when Roman returned to the street, announcing to all and sundry that I had been reduced to a special carnival price of five measly dollars. I tried in vain to increase my value to a more realistic price of something in the region of eight dollars, but Roman would not have it and began advertising this once in a lifetime offer with renewed determination and vigour.

It was at this point that Roman, who was fortunately not drunk enough to miss a young woman close by blowing a kiss in my direction, took the initiative and promptly grabbed me by the arm whereupon he led me over, introduced me in fluent Portuguese to a somewhat surprised young lady, and like any good agent promptly left the scene. I felt a little bit embarrassed at first, but with a few beers already necked back for courage, and by now feeling permanently randy, I decided to take the bull by the horns and stick around to see if anything developed. Unfortunately the young lady in question, called Cecilia, couldn't speak a word of English, but luckily one of her friends that she happened to be with could.

It was quickly suggested that we all went for a drink, and as the night wore on I learnt that you did not necessarily have to speak the language to get on with the natives. In fact, that night non-verbal communication took on a whole new meaning!

We left the bar and made our way along the street, meeting up with two of Cecilia's sisters, Anna and Tereza, on the way. I stayed with Cecilia for most of the night, saying goodbye to her friends early on in the proceedings, and as the hours slowly ticked by we became more intimately acquainted, which was quite an achievement considering we were still on the street watching the carnival procession. Our only chance of privacy being the odd shadow in a doorway which we happened to come across as we mingled with the crowds walking through the streets. We parted company at some early hour of the morning and I returned to the hostel a little after three thirty in the morning tired but contented, having arranged to meet Cecilia again later on that day.

***

The Curupira is a mythological creature of Brazilian folklore. Its name comes from the Tupi language kuru'pir, meaning 'covered in blisters'. According to the legend, the creature is a dwarf, covered in bright red and orange hair, whose feet are turned backwards. It lives in the forests of Brazil and uses its backward feet to create footprints that lead to its starting point, thus confusing hunters and travellers alike. It rides around the forests on a collared peccary, (which are medium-sized, hoofed pigs that are found throughout Central and South America) producing a high-pitched whistle which drives its victims to madness. It preys on poachers and hunters that take more than they need from the forest, and also attacks people who hunt animals that were taking care of their offspring.

Day 36

March 2, 1981

I reached the bar we had visited on the previous night at five minutes to eleven in the morning, and a little after eleven Cecilia arrived, wearing a skin-tight pair of jeans and a revealing top, along with her two sisters, Anna and Tereza. She was thirty-two years old, petite, slim and had the sort of body that any model would have been proud of. She had golden brown skin and long black hair which had been especially plaited for the carnival. Her body was that of someone ten years younger: supple and firm, and she was extremely affectionate and well versed in the arts of pleasing her respective partner. She had even taken the trouble of learning some English earlier that morning, although with phrases like 'kissy kissy, I love you' and 'my baby', we were still unable to hold much of a conversation.

During the morning I was taken by Cecilia and her sisters to a small square close to the city centre, to witness one or two of the more unusual sights of carnival time. For it was here that the city's gay population met, congregating around a platform made of scaffolding and wooden planks, specifically built for the carnival on which transvestites queued up to swagger around in front of the enthusiastic crowd. It seemed that in Brazil, during carnival time many men dressed up as women.

I broke out in a cold sweat when I realised where I had been taken to and clung on to Cecilia's hand as if it were a lifeline, while at the same time ensuring that we stayed close to her two sisters. It was unbelievable to watch and I stood there agape as they strutted around the platform like overripe peahens. The theme for the day seemed to be nursery rhymes as one of them started to parade across the stage wearing a long dress strategically raised to reveal several frilly petticoats and a pair of white stockings with suspenders. He wore a long blonde wig and bonnet, along with a basket full of flowers dangling from one hand, while a shepherd's crook was daintily manipulated in the other. The scene was completed by a toy sheep on wheels which was being obediently pulled along behind. This was surely Bo Peep as she had never been seen before!

We left shortly afterwards as the girls realised from the horrified expression on my face that I had seen more than enough, and adjourned to a nearby bar for a much needed drink.

In the afternoon, Cecilia and I got to know each other a little bit better in the privacy of Tereza's flat in the centre of the city, while her sisters were both out and about enjoying the carnival. The girls had all done very well for themselves and having worked their way through University, now held professional jobs. Cecilia was a technical designer, Anna a lawyer and Tereza a paediatric surgeon, while Maria their younger sister, who was away celebrating the carnival with friends in Rio, was still studying at University.

I returned to the Republica tired and weary. The last few days were beginning to catch up with me, but after collapsing onto my mattress (bedding wasn't supplied in these establishments), I had great difficulty in getting to sleep. The cause of this predicament was a new roommate who had moved in during the day and had unfortunately taken up residence in the bunk above mine. He was a grossly overweight German who snored like a foghorn and perspired to the point that his body and clothing became coated with a liberal supply of 'old sweat' aftershave, the stench of which hung around the room.

My other worry was a rather disturbing undulation which appeared in the centre of the underside of the top bunk whenever he climbed onto it and I was left wondering whether or not he might be 'dropping in' during the night for an informal introduction.

***

In 1624, Salvador was overrun by a Dutch force of 1,700 soldiers who arrived on twenty four boats. However, they only managed to keep hold of the city for one year before it was retaken by the Portuguese.

*

In 2005 Franasca dos Santos gave birth via caesarean section at the Albert Sabin Maternity Hospital in Salvador. Franasca was thirty eight years old at the time of her son's birth. The doctors at the hospital believed his unusual size was due to his mother's diabetes. The baby was the heaviest baby ever born in Brazil.

*

The heaviest baby ever, was born on 19 January 1879 to Anna Bates, who was 241.3 cm (7 ft 11 in) tall, and gave birth to a baby boy weighing 9.96 kgs (22 lbs) and measuring 71.12 cm (28 in) at her home in Seville, Ohio, USA. It was reported that when Anna's waters broke, she lost an estimated six gallons of fluid. She was married to Martin van Buren Bates who was 236.22 cm (7 ft 9 in) tall, and they both worked as sideshow attractions in a travelling circus.

*

The early sugar plantation owners of Salvador poured their fortunes into the building of churches, believing that it would help ensure them of a place in heaven.

Day 37

March 3, 1981

It was the last day of the carnival so I had decided to go a little bit mad, after all, if everyone else was dressing up why couldn't I? Having firmly implanted this message into my brain to help counter any pangs of embarrassment that might otherwise arise, I left the Republica and made my way into town. Wearing a pair of 'shreddies' (underpants to the uninformed), sandals and my genuine Japanese silk dressing gown (made in Birmingham, 100% Rayon). The only problem being that my dressing gown was so short that at times it barely covered my sperm banks!

Upon reaching Tereza's flat I was enthusiastically welcomed at the door by Cecilia. From the delighted expression on her face, I could tell that she approved of my choice of clothing and, having the place to ourselves, she quickly moved in for a closer inspection. Within a matter of seconds my dressing gown had been discarded, along with an assortment of other clothing, and we were rolling around on the floor trying to retrieve my biro which had disappeared underneath the settee, or at least that is the version of the story that I am sticking to!

Our frantic movements eventually sated having finally

managed to retrieve the biro, although at times it had been a struggle, we sat down to a well-earned lunch. We left the apartment afterwards and slowly made our way through the crowds to meet up with several of Cecilia's friends who were situated in a particularly good vantage point on top of a semi-demolished two-storey building at the corner of a major T-junction.

From here I received a grandstand view of the procession as it came down one street and turned sharp right some twenty metres away, before sometime later weaving its way back through the streets to pass directly in front of us. The procession carried on for several hours as float after float, along with its entourage, slowly wound its way along the route.

By now the samba competitions had finished and everyone was just out to enjoy themselves by making as much noise and causing as much commotion as possible. Each float was lavishly decorated and equipped with a performing band and several scantily clad women flaunting their bodies about to the music, some of whom were topless, although regrettably, Cecilia wouldn't let me take their photographs. We spent most of the afternoon and early evening there, after all we had everything: good view, ample food and a plentiful supply of cold beer, carefully stored away in a couple of large ice boxes strategically situated in the shade.

Cecilia wore a type of South American kaftan with extra-large sleeves, which came in very useful when it got dark as they were large enough for me to slip my arms in as well. She never wore a bra and, after a quick reconnoitre with my braille readers (*how would you read braille?*), I discovered that she was only wearing a pair of very small cotton panties underneath. What's more, I deduced that it must have been very hot down there as they were extremely damp in certain places!

At the end of the procession we made our way back to the flat for some further rest and relaxation, before once more returning to the streets to be lost in a seething mass of people. Everyone around was working themselves up into an elated frenzy as the music, which was by now being relayed over numerous loud speakers, became progressively faster as the night wore on. Everywhere people were dancing, singing, eating and drinking in a frantic display of activity as they attempted to savour every last moment out of the dying embers of the carnival.

Tomorrow was just another day, but tonight, tonight was special: one last chance for people to forget the pitiful existence that awaited their return. They had crawled out of the pits of poverty for five days and six nights and tomorrow would once more return from whence they came.

The carnival finished a little after midnight, whereupon Cecilia and I, footsore and tired from dancing, slowly walked back to the flat for a nightcap. Tomorrow evening, I would be leaving Salvador for good and now that the carnival was over, Cecilia had become quiet and sad. The light in her eyes which had shone so brightly over the last few days was now extinguished.

After an affectionate farewell, which lasted well into the early hours, I reluctantly left and made my way home, passing numerous street cleaners on the way (most of which were female) as they began the awesome task of clearing away the litter from the streets. The gutters were full to overflowing with empty beer cans, in places over a foot deep. Small groups of drunken youths waded through them, sending these discarded remnants of the carnival in all directions, oblivious to whether or not they hit any of the numerous people sleeping close by on the pavement, for tonight practically everybody slept out on the streets, too weary or drunk to care otherwise.

I noticed several people being carried away by what I assumed to be friends, their faces and/or bodies covered in blood, while others were being placed into ambulances and rushed off to hospital. It had been a memorable experience and one that I would cherish for many a year, but it was regrettable that it had to be tainted with so much violence. Although this was South America, not Europe, and here death was viewed differently, in fact some would have said it was the inevitable release from a life of pain, torment and hunger.

So many people facing the wrong way in life, travelling along a tunnel heading towards a black void of nothingness, they couldn't stop the conveyor belt of poverty, they couldn't get off and they couldn't turn back.

***

In the state of Amapa, in the far North of Brazil, archaeologists have located an ancient stone structure in a remote part of the Amazon rain forest. It is believed to have been used as an astrological observatory and/or place of worship for hundreds of years and pre-dates Cabral's discovery of Brazil in 1500 by at least 500 years.

It consists of 127 large blocks of granite, each one up to 4 metres tall, which had been embedded into the ground on top of a hill. The stones are well preserved, each weighing several tons and are arranged in an upright position, evenly spaced forming a circle roughly 30 meters in diameter.

It is not yet known when the structure was built, but fragments of indigenous pottery found at the site are over 1,000 years old.

The stones appear to have been laid out to help pinpoint the winter solstice, and it is thought the ancient people used the stars and phases of the moon to determine crop cycles.

Day 38

March 4, 1981

Having packed our rucksacks and exchanged addresses with several roommates, Roman and I left the Republica. Outside, Cecilia and her sister, Tereza, were waiting, and having safely deposited ourselves and our belongings into the car, Tereza drove off in a cloud of dust. She wasn't a particularly fast driver, it was just that the roads were all covered in a thick coating of dried mud. Tonight, 'the lads' (as we liked to refer to ourselves) were leaving for Recife, but I had arranged for us to spend our last day in pleasant company and so depart Salvador with fond memories.

Roman and Tereza immediately got on well together and were soon nattering away to each other in the front of the car, while Cecilia and I sat in the back trying to amuse ourselves. We drove along the coastline and spent an enjoyable morning on the beach swimming and sunbathing before being treated to lunch by the girls at a nearby restaurant. It soon became fairly obvious that Roman and Tereza were greatly attracted to one another and I was put in the dog house for not arranging an earlier meeting. In my defence, I had previously tried to acquaint the two, but didn't seem to have Roman's flair for working as an introduction agency.

Over dinner Roman, who by now had reached the stage of frustrated infatuation, suggested that we could always consider ripping up the tickets and staying on for a few days. That was as long as the girls could make it worth our while. I carefully considered the proposal while demolishing a plate of vegetables and rice, and after some thought agreed, feeling sure that Cecilia would easily achieve this challenge. However, it was agreed not to immediately tell them of our change in plans and instead savour the moment for later. From the restaurant we drove back to Tereza's flat for a cold beer where Roman, being the persistent showman, took out his ticket, asked for a match and proceeded to set light to it. Luckily for him though, Tereza quickly interpreted his gesture and immediately blew out the flame, explaining in Portuguese that as the carnival had just finished, the coach company might be prepared to change the tickets.

So with no time to lose, we all raced out of the flat down to the car and drove off at speed to the coach station. Fortunately for us, Cecilia's company often dealt with the coach company that we had bought our tickets from. Consequently, she dashed off to the nearest telephone box where she made several phone calls to try and pull a few strings, and although it was highly irregular and against company policy, they agreed to change the tickets for a small fee. As to who exactly received the transfer charge, whether it was the organisation itself or the employee at the counter, I never did find out. The final result was that we had managed to delay our departure date until the Sunday evening, meaning four more days of conjugal bliss.

It was while these frantic negotiations were taking place that my attention was diverted, when someone behind me started screaming. I turned around to find out what all the commotion was about, only to be confronted with one of the most horrifying and disturbing sights that I had ever witnessed.

Standing close by, approximately five metres away, was a small, middle-aged woman cradling a child in her arms. The child was suffering from an extreme case of 'hydrocephalus', that is

TALES FROM A SOUTH AMERICAN STORM DRAIN

water on the brain, and the sight of its deformity turned my stomach and made me shudder all over. The child, which I believed to be a girl probably in her early teens, was nearly as tall as her mother but must have been paralysed since birth as I could detect no sign of muscle development in her body. Her head was grotesquely large, over twice the size of a normal adult and was sparsely covered with long scraggily hair. The poor thing couldn't even blink and just lay helplessly in her mother's arms, mouth slightly ajar, eyes staring forward practically bulging out of their sockets.

Her mother, who not only looked but also acted as if she was completely insane, spent her time walking up and down a line of people queuing up to buy tickets from a nearby counter, continually laughing and screaming at the top of her voice. I stood there stunned, eyes transfixed on the sight that paraded before me, while my brain tried to come to terms with yet another example of the harsh realities of the third world.

We left shortly afterwards and returned to Tereza's flat, before driving on to Cecilia's ground-floor, two-bedroomed apartment which she shared with her sister Anna on the outskirts of the city. On arrival, total chaos broke out as heated discussions gave way to much coming and going between Cecilia, Tereza and Anna, which left both Roman and I totally confused.

By the evening, Cecilia and I had been left all alone in the flat and I had no idea of what was happening. Questions kept racing through my mind, but owing to my lack of knowledge of the Brazilian language, they had to remain unanswered. Did we have the flat to ourselves? Where was Anna? Where had Roman and Tereza gone and where were they going to stay?

Cecilia approached me and entangled me in her arms, slowly pulling me towards her lips which obediently awaited mine, and having delivered a long, lingering kiss, she enquired, by indicating with her hands, whether I wanted to take a shower. I nodded, and having stepped under the cool refreshing jets of water, closed my eyes and began to relax. My mind still confused by what was going on started to clear and everything began to fall into place, especially when I opened them to find Cecilia stepping through the shower curtains.

We spent a long time carefully soaping each other's bodies under the water, rubbing soapy naked flesh against soapy naked flesh. *Things certainly seem to be frothing up around here*, I thought, and I didn't just mean the soap. She took a sharp intake of breath as my arms wrapped around her, my hands exploring the sensual parts of her body, adding to the excitement of the moment. Her skin was soft to the touch and she oozed femininity. I stood back to watch as she washed her hair, my eyes carefully studying the beautiful curves and intricate parts of her body. There was no doubt at all in my mind that she was the perfect example of Bahian womanhood and I wanted her badly.

We left the confines of the shower and stepped out onto the bathroom floor dripping wet. Then armed with a couple of towels, slowly dried each other in preparation for our first night together. The slowness of our actions increasing the excitement between us until it became electric. We had all the time in the world, we were alone, together and besotted by each other's presence. Cecilia led me into the bedroom where we silently lay touching and caressing, holding and kissing, exploring each other's most intimate places, until, as the night wore on, we came together and our bodies joined as one.

***

Founded by the Portuguese in 1549 as the first capital of Brazil, Salvador is one of the oldest colonial cities in the Americas.

*

Salvador's carnival is the largest in the world and attracts up to two million visitors a year.

Day 39

March 5, 1981

With blurred vision from having just woken up, I began fumbling around the bed with my hands in a vain attempt at trying to locate Cecilia, but alas she was nowhere to be found. So instead I spent several minutes collecting my thoughts and recalling the events of the last few days until the bedroom door slowly opened and Cecilia quietly tiptoed in. She stood by the side of the bed looking down at me, hands on hips and breathing deeply, before leaning over to gently place a kiss on my lips and run her fingers through my hair, whispering softly, 'My baby, my baby.' Then communicating with her hands, she carefully coaxed me out of the bed and into some clothes before leading me out into the dining room.

There sat Roman looking relaxed and noticeably enjoying himself as Tereza busily fussed over him. Cecilia indicated with her hand as to where she wanted me to sit and then proceeded to imitate her sister by placing large quantities of food before me. For some reason, I had worked up a healthy appetite during the night and now that the opportunity arose, I heartily began to feed my hunger. Everything had been freshly prepared that morning by the two girls, who it seemed just couldn't do enough to please us, as it appeared that my and Roman's every wish became their immediate command!

Once we had finished breakfast, Cecilia collected up some official-looking documents and mysteriously disappeared, leaving me suddenly feeling rather left out.

Tereza had earlier explained to Roman that the two girls did not want either of us talking about them, which effectively meant that, at first, we were hardly even allowed to look at, let alone talk to each other. Consequently, I spent a couple of hours lounging around the flat reading my South American handbook, while Roman and Tereza passed the time away in the bedroom, doing what, I never enquired, but they both emerged sometime later breathless and panting. Obviously Tereza had an exercise bike or rowing machine in her bedroom!

By eleven o'clock Cecilia had returned and the reason for her disappearance was revealed: she had gone into work and made up some plausible excuse for taking the rest of the week off. Late morning drifted lazily by as Roman and I allowed ourselves to be waited upon hand and foot.

After lunch, and as if Roman hadn't already done enough exercise for the day, he agreed to go jogging with me. At first the girls were a little averse to this idea, but having issued strict instructions not to talk about them while we were out, they reluctantly waved us off. Outside the block of flats, we emerged into a blaze of sunlight. Squinting, we reached for our sunglasses, then having firmly placed them into position, we set off at a sedate and pleasantly slow pace. We continued jogging around the vicinity discussing, among other things, precisely what we had been told not to.

From our illegal conversation, I discovered that Anna, Roman and Tereza had all driven back in Tereza's car to her town flat the night before, where Anna had agreed to stay over the next few days. Then Tereza and Roman had driven down to the beach and gone for a long walk, during which time they had discussed their careers to date and their hopes and aspirations for the future, before eventually returning to Cecilia's flat in the early hours of the morning to spend their first night together.

Roman and I arrived back at the flat hot, thirsty and drenched in perspiration. The area had been extremely quiet and we had hardly seen anyone. *Mad dogs and Englishmen go out in the noonday sun*, I thought to myself. We were greeted at the door by a much-needed, ice-cold drink, followed shortly afterwards by a cool, refreshing shower with our respective lady-friends. Once more dressed, we succumbed to temptation and spent the rest of the afternoon lying back on a pile of cushions with a good woman and an endless supply of chilled drinks.

That night, Cecilia and I removed the mattress from the bed and placed it on the floor. The reason for this move was that Cecilia owned a large four-poster bed which suffered from one slight problem: it rocked back and forth, hitting the wall whenever vigorous exercise was performed upon it. Consequently, the neighbours had probably been kept awake for most of the previous night due to an incessant banging noise echoing around the walls of the building.

***

If you are a surfing connoisseur and are looking for the ultimate ride, then why not try surfing the Pororoca in the Amazon basin, as it allows surfers from all over the world to come and experience the truly rare challenge of surfing for miles, up the world's largest river. It's a fairly rare but natural phenomenon called a tidal bore, and during the months of February and March in the Amazon, it reaches epic proportions. The Pororoca is caused when the incoming ocean tide creates such an influx of water into the river, that it results in a freak wave that forms at the tide's leading edge.

Each year in São Domingos do Capim, Brazil, the National Pororoca Surfing Championship takes place as one of the world's most extreme surfing events. The waves' lack of regularity is made up for by the adrenaline-stoking ride of a lifetime. The competitors excitedly hanging around on the riverbank waiting for the early warning signs of the impending ride, namely the roaring noise that the tidal bore causes thirty minutes before the wave itself forms. This is where the name

Pororoca comes from, which in the local dialect means 'great destructive noise'.

The energy of the wave is so intense that it easily rips trees, structures and other debris from the shoreline as well as the riverbed, creating an ironically debris-filled (and highly dangerous) surfing environment. But each year many surfers decide that the risk is worth it to achieve a dream feat: to catch a wave that never stops. The wave can last for hours and travels up to 800 Kms upriver. In efforts that form the stuff of legends, surfers have ridden Pororoca for more than half an hour and travelled well over twelve kilometres on a single ride.

*

In 1922, a billy-goat named Ioiô (Yo-yo), was elected as a city councillor for the city of Fortaleza. It can still be seen on display at the Museum of Ceará in Fortaleza.

*

Brazilian police recently detained a parrot that was acting as a lookout for drug dealers. As the police approach the hideout it was heard to repeatedly squawk "Mummy police". A search of the house quickly uncovered a stash of crack cocaine and marijuana. The parrot has since been retired to a local zoo.

Day 40

March 6, 1981

Similar to the previous morning, I awoke to find Cecilia towering over me, softly calling my name. Evidently breakfast was ready and my presence was requested at the table. I had to admit that the service at this particular establishment was faultless, and what's more, the management even accepted payment in kind.

Over breakfast, the day's plan of action was discussed between Roman, Cecilia and Tereza which, once settled, was then translated and relayed to me by Roman. *I love to see democracy at work*, I thought. It seemed that we were going to spend the day on Itaparica, a tropical island forty minutes off the coast of Salvador. So without further delay, we all bundled into the car and drove off at speed hoping to catch the next available boat over.

At the harbour, Tereza drove down a wooden ramp which led to a rusty old weather-beaten ferry, more suited to the confines of a floating museum than the open seas. Having parked the car in its allotted space, we made our way up a flight of rusty old stairs to an equally rusty old bridge, from where we awaited the boat's departure.

After several minutes, the creaking ramp was raised and the engines grudgingly spluttered into life, sending shockwaves throughout the boat which started shaking like a vibrator going into overdrive. The car ferry lazily parted company with terra firma, and leaving the harbour behind, headed out into the Atlantic. As the minutes passed by, I watched as the Brazilian coastline grew smaller and smaller and the island grew steadily larger.

Upon docking, we returned to the car, and having successfully negotiated ourselves off the boat, started threading our way across the island past lush green vegetation and through tiny hamlets where time stood still and the modern world had long since passed them by.

On reaching our destination, we parked the car under the shade of a tree and then, laden with picnic hamper and several bottles of wine, made our way through the palm trees and undergrowth to the beach. It was a gorgeous day, the sun was burning in the sky, the golden sand was hot to the touch and a light breeze rolled in along the shoreline. At the water's edge we all sat down, discarding our clothing and unrolling our towels in the process. The sea was crystal clear and pleasantly warm, although I was practically the only one who actually ventured into its inviting and refreshing waters.

I spent the remainder of the morning sunbathing next to Cecilia, one of us periodically massaging suntan lotion into the other. I found it a very arousing experience to have a scantily clad woman sitting on top of me with her golden brown legs splayed out on either side of my body, rubbing suntan lotion all over me. The slow rhythmic movement of her hands glided up and down my heaving chest while her eyes remained transfixed and staring into mine. In the meantime, while Cecilia and I were absorbed in playing massage parlours, Roman and Tereza quietly and unobtrusively strolled off along the beach and into the undergrowth for some open air activities of their own and were not seen again until sometime later.

I occasionally ventured into the water to temporarily escape from the effects of the uncomfortably hot sun. On one such occasion, I re-emerged to rudely awaken Cecilia from her slumber by hoisting her over my shoulder in a fireman's lift and carrying her against her will, into the water. She hung over my shoulder screaming, her legs thrashing about and hands playfully hitting at my back. Unfortunately what I had not realised at the time, was that all of the commotion had persuaded Cecilia's breasts to escape from the confines of her swimming costume and she was desperately trying to put them back in, but with little success as each time she successfully put them back in I unwittingly bounced them back out again.

There were several young children playing in the water close by who began falling over backwards with laughter as they witnessed the comical proceedings unfold before them. Exhausted from laughing and drained of energy, we both wearily dragged ourselves back up the beach and flopped onto our towels for a much-needed rest.

At a mutually agreed time, and with Roman and Tereza having returned from their excursion into the undergrowth, we all left the shoreline and retired up the beach to partake in a picnic to end all picnics. Under the shade of a palm tree we found the perfect location: an upturned wooden canoe, hewn from a once large tree trunk, which now lay abandoned and half buried in the sand. Here the hamper was opened accordingly and an array of mouthwatering delights were placed before everyone. It was a feast to satisfy the hungry and was washed down, or maybe one should say submerged, by a more than ample supply of wine. Then gorged and stuffed to bursting point, we lay back on the sand with our respective lovers and dozed for an hour or so while our food digested.

Sometime later, we strolled back to the car and drove on to a second beach where Cecilia and Anna owned a small plot of land among tall majestic palm trees. Their idea was that one day they would both live on the island in idyllic isolation with their respective partners, and it seemed, or so Roman informed me, that Cecilia was offering this all to me. All I had to do was pay for it in kind!

We continued along the narrow path that we had been following for a few more yards until it opened out to reveal a deserted beach. It was here that a wild fantasy of mine came true. It was suggested that as there was no one else around, 'What about nude bathing?'

Well not surprisingly, Roman and I were both game and what's more, so was Cecilia, but unfortunately for Roman, Tereza wasn't, in fact she was somewhat horrified at the prospect. Consequently, I stripped off, Cecilia went topless and hand in hand we ran along the beach jumping the waves and lapping up the sun. After a couple of minutes Cecilia stopped, peered behind her to make sure no one was around, then peeled off the remnants of her swimming costume. She clasped it safely in her hands as we continued along the beach until, breathless and panting, we dropped to the wet sand and she fell into my arms. We sat there, our arms and legs wrapped around each other, laughing, kissing and cuddling as the waves crashed in all around us. We were pushed and pulled by the warm waters of the Atlantic and soaked from head to foot, but we didn't care: we were together and for one brief moment were joined as one, each knowing what the other was thinking, each sensing what the other was feeling. Words were not enough when a smile could say all there was to be said, and a glance even more besides. In my arms, I held a beautiful Bahian native woman, fit to grace the centre pages of any glamour magazine. *This is it*, I thought afterwards. *How many men spend their whole lives dreaming about such a moment, when if they could only understand that it is all out there and all they have to do is reach out and grab it?*

Eventually the harsh realities of life once more descended upon us both and we silently strolled back to the car, covered up our respective assets, then drove off.

On the way back to the boat, we stopped at the roadside and bought a couple of coconuts from a native boy. He carefully placed the precious money into his back pocket and then proceeded to pick up a seven-metre bamboo pole, and with an almighty smash, sent a couple of coconuts crashing to the ground from a nearby palm tree. Then with great agility and practiced hand, he chopped the tops off with his razor-sharp machete and passed them through the window. Having drunk the cool refreshing juice, we discarded the empty shells out of the window and drove off. It seemed that in Brazil they seldom ate the actual flesh of the coconut and Cecilia and Tereza found it highly amusing when I tried to explain, with Roman's help, that in England they only ate the flesh and poured the juice away. Although to be fair, by the time the coconuts reached Europe, the juice would have long since gone off.

We returned to the boat and spent a romantic trip back on deck standing by the vibrating railings, watching the sunset sink below the waters from a passionate, albeit shaky embrace.

It was only some days later that Roman happened to mention to me that during my passionate encounter with Cecilia on the beach, he had strolled along with his camera and taken several photos to preserve the occasion for prosperity. Roman assured me though that if I ever became famous, he would not charge me more than 500,000 US dollars for the negatives, as after all, we were friends!

Could this be the start of a promising political career? I thought. *Move over, Bill Clinton, Cecil Parkinson and David Mellor. At least I now had the necessary entry qualification!*

***

Many traditional Guaraní Indians of Brazil still believe in Kurupi, a mythological creature that made his home in the wild forests of the region, where he was considered to be the protector of wild animals and lord of the forests. He was said to be short, hairy and extremely ugly. However, his most distinctive feature, for which he became legendary, was his enormous penis that he would invariably wrap around his waist several times, rather like a cummerbund. Due to this feature, he was at one time revered as the spirit of fertility. Consequently, he is often blamed for unexpected or unwanted pregnancies.

His penis is said to be prehensile, and owing to its length, he is supposed to be able to extend it through windows and doors to impregnate a sleeping woman, without even having to enter the house. In truth, however, Kurupi was merely a scapegoat used by adulterous women to avoid the wrath of their husbands, or by single women having to explain their pregnancies to their parents and friends.

*

In ancient Rome it was customary to sculpture Priapus, the Roman god of fertility, weighing his oversized penis on a pair of scales. These statues were often placed in Roman gardens to ensure growth and act as a protector of crops.

*

'Pisadeira', which means 'she who steps' is a part of Brazilian folklore. She is an old hag that wears sneakers and stomps over people's stomachs at night, making them breathless when they go to bed on a full stomach.

Day 41

March 7, 1981

My early morning call and breakfast was as ever impeccably performed and meticulously prepared. It was day three of our extended stay in Salvador and the time was passing by all too quickly.

Most of the morning was spent lying on a beach soaking up the sun, before driving on to the infamous Laguna Abaete. It didn't look particularly ominous or threatening, in fact it appeared quite harmless. Elongated in shape, it measures between 250 and 300 metres across and a couple of kilometres long, and was surrounded by brilliant white undulating sand dunes. However, appearances can often be very deceptive as Roman and I were soon to find out. This was Brazil's answer to the Bermuda Triangle, where people who swam out to the centre of the lake would often simply disappear. One moment they would be contently swimming along and the next they would have silently vanished, leaving only ripples of water behind.

Some Bahians believed the lake to be haunted by the goddess Janaina, who it seemed was quite partial to swallowing up handsome young male swimmers. Numerous studies had been undertaken but they had failed to come up with a plausible explanation as to why the death rate should be so high.

Consequently, the beach was littered with notices warning people not to swim out too far and was regularly patrolled by armed police who acted as a further deterrent. Roman suggested that the disappearances might have been due to people being accidentally shot by the police as they forcibly tried to coax them back to the shallows, but he was assured by Tereza that this was not the case.

I tentatively ventured into the dark green waters of the lake for a dip with Cecilia as it was uncomfortably hot, but needless to say, we both paid special attention to the warnings and stayed close to the shore. I wasn't too proud to admit that I am a complete and utter coward and particularly didn't like the look of the police who could be seen walking around.

The lake was still a popular place with the locals, however, even with its formidable reputation for being dangerous. Along the beach several women stood up to their waists in water, washing clothes, while others were either stripped naked taking an outdoor bath or relieving themselves of their bodies' natural waste products! *Yes*, I thought, *I can now say that I've actually swam in an oversized launderette, cum bathtub, cum toilet. I wonder if I'll come out smelling of roses? I hope it's not the ones grown in Kenya!*

In the afternoon after much protest from the girls, Roman and I successfully treated them to lunch at a nearby open-air restaurant where we all wined and dined for a mere two US dollars per head. The rest of the day passed by quietly enough with the girls taking even more trouble than usual to please us. In fact, it reached the point where they would have willingly torn off our clothes and jumped into bed at the mere raising of a finger or the winking of an eyelid, for tomorrow we were leaving and this time everyone knew there would be no further delays in our departure.

At seven o'clock, Roman and Tereza left the flat and drove back to her apartment in the city. Shortly afterwards, Anna arrived having caught the local bus over. As she was not feeling too well and had a high temperature (or so she told us), she soon retired to her bedroom for the night, thus ensuring that Cecilia and I had the rest of the flat to ourselves. Cecilia then, with the aid of a translation dictionary, gave me strict instructions to lie back and relax on a Persian cushion to ensure that I would be well rested for the forthcoming night's nocturnal pursuits, while she disappeared into the kitchen to cook me a special meal.

The stage was set for a night to remember, and I obediently sat there biding my time, eagerly awaiting the feast to begin. There was a bottle of South American bubbly slowly chilling in the refrigerator (a birthday present from Anna to be kept for a special occasion such as tonight), mouthwatering aromas were escaping from the kitchen and the drinks cabinet beside me was fully equipped with a wide selection of beer, spirits and liqueurs to choose from. I lay there fastidiously sampling a selection of its contents in between updating my diary on the events of the last few days.

Sometime later Cecilia emerged from the kitchen and began explaining, once more with the help of the translation dictionary, the planned menu for our last night together: 'Meal, shower, champagne and love.'

I quickly suggested that a couple more courses of love would not go amiss in the program and Cecilia eagerly agreed, which was probably just as well as we did not finish off the champagne till nearly six the following morning!

***

In several parts of the world there are a number of watery regions where mysterious unexplained happenings regularly occur. These include the Bermuda Triangle, Laguna Abeate, the Devil's Sea in the Pacific Ocean and the Sargasso Sea in the North Atlantic Ocean where four currents converge forming an ocean gyre. Unlike all other regions in the world called seas, the Sargasso Sea has no land boundaries and is instead surrounded by ocean currents which accumulate huge quantities of marine plants and garbage, causing it to be full of a dense, brown, invasive seaweed known as Sargassum. Because of the build-up of this seaweed, the sea remains eerily warm and calm, despite it being surrounded by the freezing and choppy waters of the Atlantic Ocean which has contributed to the area's mystery. Over the centuries, a number of crewless ships have been found, gently drifting through its peaceful waters. For instance in 1840, the French merchant ship Rosalie sailed through the Sargasso Sea and was later discovered with its sails set but without any crew members on board. At the time, rumours abounded that the Sargasso Sea's carnivorous seaweed had devoured the sailors whole, leaving only the ship and its cargo behind.

The Devil's Sea, also known as the Pacific Bermuda Triangle or Dragon's Triangle, is a region of the Pacific Ocean around Miyake Island, approximately sixty miles south of Tokyo. Between 1952 and 1954 the area became recognised as a danger zone after Japan lost five military vessels, along with over 700 sailors.

Day 42

March 8, 1981

Cecilia was as ever up long before me, working away on one of her delicious sucro (fruit juice) mixtures. Her eyes had once more lost their sparkle and we sat there silently over breakfast, each one of us hardly daring to look at the other. She didn't even respond when I eventually caught her eye and gave her a mischievous wink.

Cecilia often wore a sleeveless cotton dress, of which she had several, around the house. Made from a simple design, they were held in place by a thin band of elastic sewn into the top of the garment. Consequently, whenever the opportunity had arisen that we were left alone for a few brief moments, she would often take great pleasure in teasing me by pulling out the front of her dress and allowing me a quick peep inside. She would then let go without warning, the elastic would once more pull the garment back into place and the breathtaking sight, which somewhat resembled a Santa's grotto with lots of goodies inside, would vanish before me. The disappointment that always registered upon my face would make Cecilia break out into fits of uncontrollable laughter each time.

By ten o'clock, we had been joined by Roman, Tereza and Maria, the girls' younger sister who had just returned from Rio that morning, where she had spent the Mardi Gras with friends. We had a late lunch which was lovingly prepared by Cecilia and Tereza, and included a local Bahian speciality called Vatapa, which comprised of king prawns, coconut milk and spices, mixed together in a blender with a liberal supply of Dende, a special oil extracted from a certain type of palm tree. This was then poured into a large pudding basin and carefully placed in the fridge where it was allowed to set. By the time it reached the table it resembled a bowl of pease pudding, except that it was pink in colour, and the taste was simply out of this world. We all helped ourselves by spreading it on an assortment of crackers which had accompanied it to the table.

The rest of the afternoon was quietly spent, locked away in separate bedrooms for one last fond farewell, before re-emerging to take a selection of photographs of the Bressy family in its entirety.

At around 6pm, we loaded up the car. Roman and I waved goodbye to Anna and Maria, and the four of us drove off for one last look around Salvador. We visited the main cathedral and several of the city's spectacular churches, along with one or two more secluded beauty spots, revealing spectacular views of the city and the ocean beyond. Eventually, we reluctantly made our way to the bus station, where a rather emotional farewell ensued, with both girls crying and us two macho men choking back the occasional tear. It was a moment that none of us had been looking forward to and now that it had arrived, we all wanted it to pass quickly.

On the coach, Roman managed to lay his sleeping bag out on the rear luggage compartment, which meant that I had the use of two seats to stretch out on. Consequently, we both slept well, admittedly having the most uninterrupted night's sleep we he had had since leaving the Republica.

Day 43

March 9, 1981

We reached Recife (known as the Venice of Brazil), capital of the Brazilian state of Pernambuco, by ten o'clock. Having queued up to buy tickets for the overnight coach to Fortaleza, we caught a local bus to Olinda, the region's former capital which was situated some six kilometres north of the city. Here we spent a pleasant morning walking around, during which time Roman sold some US dollars on the black market and I bought my first souvenir of the journey. It was a three-foot wooden carving, of what though, I was not quite sure. Nevertheless it was very eye-catching, looked typically Brazilian, and was well worth the one thousand cruzeiros that it cost me. It resembled an elongated head, perched upon the end of the big toe of a seven-toed foot, which was eating a pineapple, carefully balanced on another toe!

I also managed to get a pair of sandals mended for the ridiculous price of twenty cruzeiros, approximately eleven pence. However, I have since been assured by a friend that I could have had the same job done in India far cheaper.

During the afternoon we returned to Recife and took in a few of the sights, including a visit to the Casa da Cultura, the city's old municipal prison which had since been converted into a cultural centre. Inside, most of the cells were now used as arts and crafts or souvenir shops, and even the death cell had now become a thriving hub of commercial activity. It felt strange walking through the entrance, past the massive imposing gates of the old prison. In days gone by, men would have shuddered at the very thought of entering this place, and if the walls could have talked, I felt sure they would have told a different story to that of its new lease of life.

How unfair life can be, I thought, when England's prison community were treated better than the vast majority of the Brazilian population, many of whom would have given anything to have the privilege of residing in such luxury. After all, the very idea of having one good meal a day let alone three, clean clothes and a roof over their heads was often beyond their level of comprehension.

Every day the Brazilian newspapers carried column after column of tiny advertisements in which people offered to sell parts of their anatomy to the rich and affluent. If the price was right, you could buy anything from a living, breathing donor. The sacrifice of a donor's sight by selling the cornea of their eyes would result in blindness, but might pay for a proper education for their children. Alternatively, the loss of a kidney could help drag the donor's family out of the gutter and give them a basic level of existence. In fact, for the right price you could even buy a heart from a living human being.

***

Recife is located on two main islands and several small islands connected by forty-nine bridges, most of which were built during the Dutch colonial times. It is divided by a series of waterways and is made up of three districts connected by a number of bridges: Recife (the reef), which lies on a peninsula; Santo Antonio, on an island between the peninsula and the mainland; and Boa Vista, on the mainland.

Recife had the highest consumption of Scotch whisky per head of population in the whole world.

*

Gasoline is thirty percent more expensive if you don't have a sticker in your car window paying homage to Jesus or God.

*

Traffic clowns are actually employed by the Recife city council to dispense driving advice to bad drivers.

*

Some of the local nicknames for districts in Recife include: Cold Water, Conception Hill, Enchanted Lake, Good Trip, Good View, Little Fish, Little Mustard, Milk Island (which isn't an island at all), Piety, Rabbits, Sweet River, Two Sheep, Yellow Penis and Zombie.

*

In 2020 a Brazilian supermarket in Recife apologised for "making a mistake" after it concealed the body of a recently demised salesman for 3 ½ hours using garden umbrellas and crates of beer in order to ensure the shop could remain open!

Day 44

March 10, 1981

I had been looking forward to reaching Fortaleza (capital of the state of Ceará) ever since a Brazilian friend of mine in Rio had jokingly warned me, that if I ever went there with my white skin, fair hair, blue eyes and beard, I would probably never be allowed to leave! It seemed that the unofficial ratio of women to men was something in the region of ten to one. *Well*, I thought, *being an economist, I'm naturally interested in demography* (the study of the changing size and structure of a country's population), and I was hopefully looking forward to confirming this statistical anomaly.

At the bus station, having first booked tickets for the overnight coach to Belem, I kept an eye on our rucksacks while Roman made full use of the station's excellent washing facilities and took a much appreciated shower. Then upon his return, we swapped roles, and I was soon washing off the dust and grime of travel under the cool, refreshing waters. It was while this was taking place that Roman began talking to an attractive young Brazilian student called Lena who was studying English at Fortaleza University, and upon my return, I was immediately introduced to her. The formalities over, she generously offered to show us around the sights of the city, and looking at her, I was starting to think of a few that weren't in the official guide book!

At our request, she began by taking us to the lace market, for which the city was famous, where a profitable hour was spent haggling over the price of embroidered lace tablecloths: a surprise present for each of our respective parents. At times the haggling became somewhat heated, with raised voices and wild gesticulations of the arms, and on more than one occasion we pretended to lose interest and walk away, resulting in an amount being finally agreed at approximately a third of the original asking price. *It pays to be obstinate.*

Flushed with our success, we moved on to another stall to negotiate the purchase of two strong hammocks in preparation for our forthcoming trip up the River Amazon.

Lena then helped me obtain an injection against infectious hepatitis at a local pharmacy, although I was somewhat hesitant due to the lax attitude towards hygiene. It seemed they had never heard of disposable needles and instead simply placed their one needle in boiling water for three minutes to supposedly kill off all the germs. (It is recommended you should place medical equipment in boiling water for a minimum of twenty minutes in order to sterilise.)

Finally, she took us to the international post office where our newly acquired tablecloths, along with my wooden carving from Olinda, were wrapped up in cardboard and brown paper, acquired from a nearby shop, and sent home.

All this done, Lena invited us back to meet her family, to which we obligingly agreed, stopping off on the way for a meal at a roadside café where we appreciatively wined and dined our guide on a bottle of beer and a cheap meal. Yes, dear reader, no expense was spared, we were out to impress. The lavish banquet worked, and she proceeded to lead us through the back streets wearing a smile from ear to ear, noticeably overjoyed to be seen walking along with two blue-eyed gringos. As soon as she reached the immediate vicinity of her home, she began announcing to all and sundry, regardless of whether or not she actually knew them, that, 'Hey, these are my friends!'

We arrived at her home, a small stone-built shack surrounded by a low wall, and followed Lena inside to meet her family of three younger brothers and eight sisters; five of whom were attractive, fully developed and very friendly. One of them took an immediate liking to me and in no uncertain terms made this fact blatantly obvious by flinging her arms up into the air in a gesture of sheer delight and walking towards me shouting, 'Oh! You want take photo of my titties?' My mouth dropped open and my tongue practically fell out and rolled across the floor towards her as I turned to Roman in total disbelief, convinced that I was either dreaming or had just walked into a Monty Python sketch.

After several seconds of stunned silence, I finally regained my composure and began tentatively suggesting to Roman that as we had been travelling for a couple of days, maybe it was time we rested up and took things easy again. But alas he was not convinced, especially as time was running out for him and money for me. Unfortunately, Roman had a plane to catch back to LA from Manaus, for the start of his final semester in nine days' time, and as we were still nearly a thousand kilometres away from Belem, the main port at the mouth of the River Amazon, and there was the prospect of a five- or six-day boat trip up the river, he was working to a very tight schedule as it was.

Now you may well be wondering why on earth I didn't stay on my own. Trust me, I've asked myself that very question on many an occasion, especially when I consider what happened three days later in Monte Alegre! But the simple answer was that I had grown quite fond of travelling with Roman and making the most of his linguistic skills to help keep me out of trouble; we were a team. It was true that the ticket to Belem had been rather expensive and that my finances were beginning to dwindle to the point that I could not have afforded to waste the ticket, but I could have at least asked Lena or one of her other sisters to return to the bus station with me to see if I could have changed my ticket, as had been done in Salvador. However, as everything was happening so quickly, I never really had enough time to properly think things through. No sooner had we arrived than it was time to leave and so regrettably, I left this potential nest of eager-to-please, nubile young ladies.

I was almost certain though that had I remained in Fortaleza, I would have been given a proper welcome later that night by Lena and her smiling sisters, possibly all six of them![9] *Would I have survived?* I later asked myself. I would unfortunately never know, but what a lovely way to go!

I reluctantly left the house, saying goodbye to my newest fan, before catching the bus back to the coach station. Although not before the "Oh you want take photo of my titties?" sister grabbed me in her arms and gave me a parting snog grinding her body into mine.

***

The state of Ceará, of which Fortaleza is the capital, was the first Brazilian state to abolish slavery in 1884. For this reason it has the nickname of 'Land of Light'.

*

The Amazon Rainforest is home to more than one third of all species in the world.

*

The Bullet Ant is the world's largest ant that can grow up to four centimetres in length. It has known for having one of the most painful stings of any insect on the planet as it contains a neurotoxin. The Satere-Mawe tribe who live in the North East part of the Amazon, perform a coming of age ceremony in which the young boy has to endure repeated stings from these ants without making a sound. The ants are initially drugged by submerging them into a solution of sedative and then hundreds of them are woven into a glove made out of leaves (which resembles a large oven mitt), stinger facing inward.

[9] *Recollections of Dustin Hoffman's lead role in the film 'Little Big Man' always spring to mind when I think of Lena and her family, although Hoffman only had to contend with four sisters in the tipi.*

When the ants regain consciousness, the boy slips the gloves onto his hands and must keep the gloves on for a full ten minutes. When finished, the boy's hands

are temporarily paralysed due to the ant venom, and they may end up shaking uncontrollably for several days. The only 'protection' provided is a coating of charcoal rubbed into each hand, which tends to confuse the ants and thereby reduces their stinging. The warrior's initiation is only complete once they have worn the gloves on twenty separate occasions over the course of several years!

*

Brazilian scientists have found a new river in the Amazon basin – around 3.9 km underneath the Amazon river. The Rio Hamza appears to be as long as the Amazon river at 6,000km. But whereas the Amazon ranges from 1km to 100km in width, the Hamza ranges from 200km to 400km wide.

*

20% of the world's oxygen is created from the Amazon jungle.

*

A recent study in the Amazon rain forest had confirmed that the White bellbird has the loudest bird song ever recorded, 125 decibels, which is equivalent to standing next to fighter jet as it takes off. It uses this impressive call along with a half-hearted attempt at a dance to try to swoon its mate by performing then screaming

*

In 2014, following the shooting of an off-duty policeman on the streets of Belem, messages were posted on social media advising people to stay indoors as 'several areas of the city would be cleaned up'. Then several men on motorbikes went on a six-hour killing spree, shooting dead nine people. Six of the killings were carried out like executions, police said.

Day 45

March 11, 2018

The journey to Belem (which is Portuguese for Bethlehem) was largely uneventful apart from the antics of some of the passengers. The coach appeared to be overrun by a large Brazilian family of thirteen who throughout the night and following day, participated in a non-stop game of musical chairs. Every five to ten minutes, one of them would get up and change places with another, while at the same time the youngest member of the family, the baby, would be passed around from one pair of willing hands to another, rather like a relay baton. I wondered what the forfeit was if you were left holding the baby when the coach stopped and came to the conclusion that it was probably having to change its nappy.

Furthermore, the mother of this prestigious band of Amazonian Indians seemed to be suffering from a virulent throat infection which restricted her ability to swallow. As at regular intervals she would walk over to the window above the seat in front of Roman and I, where two of her children were sitting, lean over them, and spit out of it. The trouble was that her spit kept on hitting the outside of our window, making it difficult for us to see out as parts of it became coated in a thick veil of frothy saliva. Our patience eventually stretched to its limits, Roman asked, in his best Portuguese, if she would mind spitting out of her own window instead. She glared at us menacingly while muttering something under her breath, but did end up complying with our request. Two of her own children happened to be occupying the seat behind where she was sitting, and by the time the coach finally reached Belem, their window resembled Nelson's column in Trafalgar Square after the pigeons had been in residence.

We arrived shortly after seven in the evening, and before leaving the coach station, were approached by an enterprising young Brazilian offering his services for a small fee. He 'wanted to help us' find whatever we were looking for, whether it be a place to change travellers' cheques, a boat up the river, a cheap hotel for the night or a good woman. Roman and I considered the alternatives open to us and with some reservations accepted his help. His eyes lit up like two raging forest fires and a broad grin spread across his face as he proceeded to lead us to a nearby hotel, where after several minutes of negotiations, we had agreed upon an exchange rate and changed some travellers' cheques. From here, he took us to the home of the owner of a large cargo ship which was heading upriver to Santarem, exactly halfway between Belem and Manaus, from where he assured us that we would easily be able to catch a boat on to Manaus.[10]

The ship's owner resided in a luxurious house full of expensive decor and furniture more attune to the landed gentry of the English countryside than Belem, gateway to the Amazon. This should have set alarm bells ringing in my ears, but if they were, I chose to ignore them. Supposedly, or so we were informed as the sales patter began to seep out of the ship owner's mouth like a leaking cesspit, it was a very large ship with room for well over 200 passengers, fully equipped with shower and toilet facilities, and all meals were included in the

---

[10] *Manaus, the capital of the Amazon, was some 1,600 kilometres away from the coastline, yet surprisingly only thirty-two metres above sea level.*

price which was a mere 3,000 cruzeiros each (approx. sixteen US dollars). Furthermore, for an extra 1,000 cruzeiros apiece, we could have our own two-berthed cabin.

Fortunately for us, we had already decided to rough it like two fearless adventurers and equipped ourselves accordingly in Fortaleza with hammocks. It turned out that the boat was leaving at one o'clock the next morning, and although Roman and I had planned on spending a day in Belem, we decided to grab what we were offered, not knowing when the next boat would be leaving and whether or not we would be able to get on it.

We enquired about how to get to the boat and were told that the owner's son was first mate and that he would take us there. *Well, at least that sounds promising,* I thought.

That was of course until we left with him, and instead of walking to his car, he hailed a taxi and at the other end dived out without saying a word, leaving Roman and I to pay the fare. Obviously the son had been learning from his father.

We followed him down a gloomy-looking road by the water's edge which was largely comprised of cracked tarmac, assorted rubbish and pot holes of various sizes full of oily-looking water, and were appalled by the sight that lay before us. Our luxury merchant ship had obviously not returned to port in time after the ball and like Cinderella's coach, had changed back into its former self: an old weather-beaten rust bucket. A floating – *but for how long?* – wreck of a monument to an era long passed.

The boat was about twenty-five metres in length and had been built in 1896, or so the plaque at the front of the bow informed us. We climbed aboard to discover that the top deck was covered in a sea of swinging hammocks, so retreated swiftly to the deck below in a vain attempt to find a suitable location where we could set up residence for our forthcoming voyage.

We ended up lashing our hammocks between a couple of wooden beams so that they hung precariously over a large number of oil drums stored away for future use. It wasn't the most sought-after part of the boat, but it suited our needs and we were soon trying out our recently acquired sleeping facilities for size and comfort. The ship did not possess a radio, so we instead listened to the dulcet tones of the engine room, which lay close by. Periodically when the wind changed direction, we were also graced with the fresh aroma of diesel fumes escaping from its hatchway.

Everybody on board shared communal washing facilities. There were four wash-hand basins on the top deck and two toilet-cum-shower rooms (although initially one of these toilets was occupied by several chickens) situated below to be shared between 140 passengers and twelve crew members. Finally to top everything else off, the lower deck seemed to be reserved for insomniacs, as it was lit up all night and every night. We later found out that this was a necessary precaution to help avoid night-time collisions with other river users.[11]

However, Roman and I received some comfort later on, when we by chance saw the inside of one of the luxury, two-berthed cabins that we had been offered for an extra thousand cruzeiros each. It was small, dark and dingy with no windows, just a door, about the size of a British Rail toilet and consisted of a couple of bunkbeds.

There was no furniture inside as there was not enough room for any. In fact, it was so small you would have even had trouble fitting in a small chair. Needless to say, the recipients of these overpriced boxes were not at all pleased, especially as the rooms became unbearably hot in the daytime whereas the other passengers could at least lie in their hammocks in the shade, gently swaying from side to side while being cooled by a steady breeze caused by the boat as it steadily ploughed its way upstream.

Having dumped our gear safely on board, we headed back

---

[11] *During the previous week, on the night of March 6th, a riverboat with engine trouble collided with a large cargo ship and sank in the upper reaches of the Amazon. It was carrying 209 people a sizable proportion of which were children returning from Iquitos to a jungle village at the beginning of their school holidays; 134 were missing feared dead.*

down the road and entered a sleazy-looking hut which professed to be a restaurant. Here we ate a rather uninspired meal consisting of curried chicken skin and stodgy rice, before returning to the rust bucket and the confines of our hammocks.

'Rust bucket' cast off a little after one in the morning. I slept uneasily throughout the night, periodically waking up, either from the excitement that I felt inside at the start of fulfilling one of the most important challenges on my bucket list, or from the cold. It became extremely cold at night-time, which I found somewhat surprising considering the boat was sailing virtually on the equator.

***

Belem's main market on the docks are teeming with numerous street vendors selling exotic tropical fruits, freshly caught fish and shrimp, along with many illegal products. These include manatee fat, which is used to aid runny noses, and pink river dolphin vaginas, which are used to make a love potion. Also available are snake and frog oils, toucan beaks and an array of potions and soaps made from the endangered Amazon turtle. All of them, plus live animals such as baby tamarins, are often offered for sale even though the market is regularly patrolled by policemen.

*

The jigger flea (Tunga penetrans) is a tiny, pinhead-sized parasitic creature that lives in the sandy terrain of warm, dry climates. When the opportunity arises, the pregnant female will burrow into its victims skin to begin feeding on its host's blood, leaving her posterior exposed through which she breathes, shits and drops eggs. It will grow up to a centimetre in length and has to be surgically removed. In Kenya alone, an estimated 1.4 million people suffer from jigger infestation.

Day 46

March 12, 1981

Having slept through breakfast, I ignored the pangs of hunger permeating from my stomach and after carefully negotiating my way out of my hammock, slowly made my way forward. I was already dressed, as like everyone else (with one exception: Roman Kurowski!) I had slept fully clothed to help combat the cold night air. At the bow of the boat, much to my surprise, all I could see was water with just a faint outline of terra firma on the distant horizon. I was about to learn some important geographical facts regarding the River Amazon which I had failed to appreciate, like so many other things at school.

Evidently it was not the meandering little river that I had presupposed it to be. In fact it is the largest river in the world, being 6,275 kilometres long with well over a thousand tributaries, seventeen of which are over one and a half kilometres in width when they flow into the river Amazon (the Amazon basin has over 80,000 kilometres of navigable rivers). By the time it reaches the Atlantic, the Amazon River is over eighty kilometres wide and there is so much fresh water flowing out into the ocean, that it is said to be drinkable for up to 300 kilometres from the coast. It has been estimated that a fifth of the world's fresh water flows down the river. That is twelve billion litres of fresh water every minute (around 209,000 cubic metres per second)! That is more than the next seven largest rivers combined.

There was a famous story of a group of shipwrecked mariners in the middle of the 18th century, who had been drifting in a rowing boat for several days. Without drinking water to quench their thirsts, they languidly lay in the boat attempting to gain what little shelter there was from the sun. Finally one of them could take no more and in desperation stuck his head over the side and started drinking the sea water. His colleagues lay, watching him commit suicide, as they all knew that it would lead to certain death as the salt would make his tongue swell up and he would die from suffocation. However, much to his (and their) surprise, the water was drinkable as they were passing the mouth of the River Amazon without realising (they were too far out to see the coastline). They were picked up the next day by a passing ship and all survived to tell the tale.

Roman was amazing. He was the only person on board who actually changed into pyjamas before retiring to his hammock. I doubted if the natives had ever heard of pyjamas, let alone seen them before. But Roman was a man of principle and most insistent in not letting his standards slip or as he put it, to maintain an order of culture and civilisation upon this floating rust heap. Sometimes he would have to wait for up to twenty minutes until one of the toilets became vacant so that he could change in privacy, but he didn't seem to mind and never complained. He would then casually stroll back to his hammock wearing a pair of brightly coloured and garishly patterned nightwear that most of the locals probably mistook for the western equivalent to war paint.

On board, the whole boat functioned around the river. Every morning the decks were washed down in brown Amazon water: the crockery, cutlery, pots and pans were cleaned in it. The coffee was made with it and even the only source of drinking water on board, a drinking fountain located on the top deck, produced it. Furthermore, you showered under it, cleaned your teeth with it and if you ever wanted to flush the toilet, you simply slung a bucket on a rope over the side, hauled it in and used the contents.

The toilet itself was unbelievable. I had come across some dire cases before on my travels, but this one had to be placed in a league of its own. It had no seat and the outflow pipe that opened straight into the waters below was coated in an ugly-looking and pungent-smelling algae, that looked like it was slowly crawling up the toilet bowl to get you. Whenever I relieved myself into the toilet, no sooner had the urine hit the algae, than it let off the most overpowering stench that my nostrils had ever had the misfortune of coming into contact with. The smell was so bad that it left me coughing and staggering on my feet as I hurriedly fumbled for the door handle in order to get out.

One of the problems of travelling on a boat such as this, was that it became a statistical probability that most of the people on board would contract some form of intestinal infection. Being the tropics, it was likely that most of the locals would have already contracted intestinal worms and/or a large variety of other infections prior to boarding. Consequently after the first day, both Roman and I tried to drink as little water-based refreshment offered to us on board as possible, relying instead on bottled water, beer or Coke which we managed to procure whenever the boat stopped to offload supplies at the small settlements built on, or close to, the water's edge.

Lunch and dinner consisted of chicken, boiled rice and spaghetti, all cooked in a large cooking pot. What really made the meal memorable was the realisation that we now had the use of the second toilet. Unfortunately, however, I have to report that the former occupants of this room were by now very much deceased.

It rained throughout most of the day, so the canvas side-flaps on the boat were rolled down. Roman and I passed the day lazily away, lying in our respective hammocks, gently swaying from side to side as the boat made slow progress up the river against the current. In the evening, I even managed to grab myself a cold shower.

At eleven o'clock that night, the boat slowly chugged up to a small village which was perched on the riverbank between water and jungle. Roman and I seized the opportunity to go ashore to buy some provisions from the village shop, but only once we had been assured by some of the crew that a small shop actually existed. We ran all the way there and back and hurriedly completed our purchases, returning as quickly as possible, a little nervous and unsure as to whether we would find our river transport still waiting for us upon our return. Luckily, Roman had informed the captain of our intended expedition, which was probably just as well considering that no sooner had we clambered aboard, than the crew were casting off. By the time we had reached our hammocks, the boat was once more underway. We hungrily devoured our spoils: four bottles of Coke and two packets of plain biscuits, then contentedly lay back in our hammocks and fell asleep.

We later discovered, by chance, that the only reason the boat had stopped that evening was because the crew had miscalculated their beer supplies for the trip and a request to replenish their sadly depleted stock had been granted by the captain.

***

The machete is often used by the Amazonian Indians as an extra leg: sticking it in a nearby log for balance or as a walking stick to help climb a muddy bank. It is also razor sharp for cutting.

Some years later while back packing through South East Asia, I was staying in a White Karen village in Northern Thailand. I had been riding an elephant bare back for a couple of hours through the jungle when we stopped to give them a rest. Upon alighting from Epoh, a 34 year old Burmese elephant, I borrowed a machete and went into the bush to cut some bamboo for our elephants. Having found a clump I proceeded to cut it but the machete was so sharp it went through the bamboo like a knife through butter to the point I very nearly sliced into my leg! **Important life lesson** *whenever using a machete always cut away from your body.*

*

There are over a hundred different species of poison dart frog, although only three are extremely dangerous to humans. The most deadly species is the golden poison arrow frog whose toxin is so virulent, that merely touching the creature can deliver a lethal dose.

*

The glass frog's flesh is completely transparent, which allows you to see its internal organs, including its heart pumping away. The flesh merges with the surrounding vegetation, making the frog extremely hard to see.

*

The bush or savannah dog can be found in the Amazon basin and other parts of South America. They have short stumpy legs, a solid muscular body, rounded face with round ears and a bushy tail. But what really makes them unique is that they are the only dog species on the planet that has webbed feet. Hence they are as at home in the water as they are on land.

*

Over the past 13 year Physiotherapist Igor Andrade has been giving monthly swimming sessions to children suffering from a wide range of physical and mental disabilities. Based in the city of Novo Airão in the Amazon basin he takes them swimming with freshwater pink dolphins in the Rio Negro, a tributary of the river Amazon.

Leonardo Araujo was born without arms and has legs of different lengths and began swimming with wild pink dolphins when he was seven. At the time he was unable to walk, had trouble standing up, and kept falling over, but by learning how to swim like a dolphin it strengthened his muscles and significantly improved his mobility and independence.

He is now 21, has recently passed his driving test (he steers his automatic car with his feet) and has a positive attitude to life. The scheme is supported by the Brazilian government's environment agencies.

Day 47

March 13, 1981

I awoke to find the sun shining through a fine veil of mist which was rising above the jungle. While below, the mighty waters of the Amazon silently flowed by with an air of peace and tranquillity, as if still sleeping from the night before. I lay back, contentedly wrapped in my sleeping bag and hammock, gently swaying from side to side, letting my mind wander as the boat continued to make its slow progress up the river.

This morning I actually managed to get up in time for breakfast. However, I regretted it soon after, wishing that I hadn't bothered to make the effort and simply stayed in my hammock instead. Outside the cookhouse, which I felt was an extremely generous title, situated on the lower deck, they were handing out tiny cups of thick, sweet, black coffee with two biscuits apiece. I readily accepted and devoured it on the spot. Once finished, I patiently waited for the main course to be served, assuming this to be an appetiser to help keep the swelling masses at bay. But alas, this was not only the first course but also the last and so I was, therefore, left feeling hungrier than when I had first arrived.

We were by now chugging along the side of the river approximately eight to ten metres away from its bank, which was covered by a thick, choking mass of what seemed impenetrable jungle. We were slowly threading our way through the region of the thousand islands, known as the Breves Narrows, which consisted of a veritable maze of large and small islands, located between the Xingu River and the Amazon River mouth.

A wave of excitement swept through my body as I realised that I was witnessing one of the last frontiers of the world which remained at least partly unexplored and untarnished by progress and civilisation. Somewhere out there in that vast seven and a half million square kilometres of rainforest, lived tribes that had never seen a white man; rivers that had yet to be navigated; plants, trees and animals waiting to be discovered, classified and named. *Could I discover them?* I asked myself as I quietly mused over the prospect of becoming *Plummer the intrepid explorer. Hacking his way through the jungle with blazing machete and fearless determination, like a real-life Indiana Jones. Warding off hunger, thirst, wild animals and unfriendly natives.* I silently pondered over the idea, leaning against the boat's rusty side rail, watching the passing scenery before reaching the inevitable conclusion: No. Let's face it, I was a complete and utter coward, I bled far too easily and would probably give the locals indigestion.

A recent British Royal Geographical Society expedition was sent to the Mato Grosso region of Brazil with the specific aim of collecting a wide range of specimens of local fish. They found upon their return to the UK that approximately fifty percent of the specimens collected were totally new to science.

Dinner consisted of a few scraps of corned beef, some black beans and the inevitable plateful of rice and spaghetti, which looked like a tangled sticky lump of stodge, guaranteed to make the meal look unappetising. However, on this particular occasion it wasn't so much the food that worried me, but the company I kept while eating it. Sitting opposite me was a loud-mouthed, egotistical American woman, dressed in a sickly-looking, luminous green swimming costume. Now I have nothing against Americans, but this was hardly the sort of emissary they would have wanted to represent their country in the eyes of the third world.

During the afternoon the boat pulled into Gurupa, a small hamlet of wooden huts situated at the edge of the narrows and it was here that Roman and I once more managed to buy some provisions of Coke and crackers to help supplement the boat's somewhat meagre supply of food. Afterwards we retired to our hammocks, where we lay devouring our acquisitions like two hungry children who had just spent their pocket money at the tuck shop.

Later on in the day, an amusing interlude arose which helped break up the river boat's monotonous routine. As usual we were lying in our hammocks talking, when our conversation was broken by the sound of someone tapping on the deck above. Roman, without hesitation, instinctively picked up an empty Coke bottle which was lying close by on an upturned oil drum and started tapping back on the ceiling. After a moment a reply came back, to which Roman once more responded. This continued for a minute or two until the responses from above suddenly ceased. At this point he put the Coke bottle down and we carried on talking.

A few seconds later, a podgy-looking Argentinian girl came rushing down the stairs, and breathless with anticipation, stopped by our hammocks to enquire if either of us had been tapping on the ceiling. Roman took one look at her and convincingly lied saying, 'No!' Disappointed, she began rushing around the lower deck like a brooding hen looking for a prospective mate. Being unsuccessful in locating him, she sullenly returned upstairs and resumed moving around the upper deck, tapping on the floor in the vain hope of resuming lost contact.

As evening approached, I watched the sun slowly sink below the treeline from the upper deck, fascinated by the ever-changing colours of the sky, the night gradually placing its blanket of blackness across the jungle. It felt strange, as if I was witnessing a scene devoid of time itself, for the Amazon seemed ageless. I could have been making the same journey thousands of years ago and little would have changed.

Unfortunately, this special moment was somewhat ruined by

the sound of Miss America, whose voice broke through the evening calls of the jungle like nails on a chalkboard. She sat surrounded by a group of gormless travellers who lapped up her sickening humour, relishing her superimposed mannerisms and marvelling at her uneventful travel stories. It seemed that during her journeys through South America, the most exciting event that had happened to her was when she met a Brazilian transvestite at a bus station in Rio de Janeiro. She frequently recalled this encounter in great graphic detail and at every conceivable opportunity to anyone who was unfortunate enough to be listening.

***

The Amazon represents over half of the planet's remaining rainforests and comprises the largest and most biodiverse tract of tropical rainforest in the world. It has an estimated 390 billion trees, over 18,000 plant species and 15,000 species of animal, which include 319 species of hummingbird (North America has only nineteen), 250 species of mosquito, and over 2,000 species of fish. It covers forty percent of the South American continent and is located in the countries of Bolivia, Brazil, Colombia, Ecuador, Guyana, Peru, Suriname and Venezuela. It is larger than the whole of Western Europe.

*

One square kilometre of virgin rainforest in the Amazon has more variety of trees than the whole of the United States of America.

*

When fleeing from predators, the Jesus lizard can run along the surface of a pond or stream. It propels itself along the water using surface tension to briefly support its weight. The lizard's toes have flaps of skin that create a broad surface and trap air pockets to enhance the surface tension. For a short distance, it can reach speeds of up to five miles per hour.

Day 48

March 14, 1981

During the previous day's stopover in Gurupa, the boat had picked up another fifteen to twenty passengers, several of which had lashed their hammocks on the lower deck close to our own. It was to the screams of one of them, a little girl, barely two years old, lying close by in the arms of her father, that I awoke.

Now I had heard children crying before on numerous occasions, but this time was different. It was not attention seeking nor a cry from hunger or a soiled nappy, this was a heart-wrenching scream from acute pain and immense discomfort and was something that I had not experienced before and would prefer never to hear again. She had apparently been suffering from dysentery for a little over two weeks and her worried parents were taking her upriver to the hospital in Santarem.

The boat continued chugging along up the side of the river with monotonous regularity, which left one feeling helpless and isolated. We were surrounded by so much open space, yet I felt trapped and imprisoned upon this floating heap of corroding metal and rotting wood.

Occasionally we would pass by a native dressed in a simple but effective loincloth, sitting cross-legged in their dugout canoe going about their business. Upon the boat's arrival on the scene, they would stop paddling and watch our progress with great interest, while bobbing up and down on the water. Through the eyes of the natives, this wreck of a bygone era probably resembled a floating Aladdin's cave, a kind of watery equivalent to Cinderella's coach racing off to faraway places, full of valuable raw materials and commodities which they could never hope to possess. Yet through my westernised eyes, used to the fruits of an industrialised nation with all of its wealth and prosperity which I all too often took for granted, I saw it in a different light and consequently, often despised myself for it. If nothing else, this trip had made me appreciate the British economy far more than I could ever have imagined.

We had the usual boiled spaghetti, rice and black beans for lunch and supper again, and the afternoon passed off quietly. That was until I decided to volunteer to play doctor.

Around four in the afternoon, the captain, who by now had realised that Roman could speak Portuguese, approached us to enquire if we had any aspirin for one of the passengers. Of course being a qualified first aider, I put my foot in it and pretended to know what I was talking about. *After all*, I thought, *anything to add a bit of excitement to the boat's daily routine*. It seemed that this particular passenger had just returned from the Mato Grosso area[12] of Brazil and the crew, who believed he had probably either contracted yellow fever or some form of swamp fever, were understandably keeping their distance.

However, I nonchalantly and rather recklessly approached him, comforted with the knowledge that my yellow fever, cholera and infectious hepatitis jabs were still active. Having then stood around like an idiot for several minutes, I eventually diagnosed that the patient was burning up with fever as he had a

---

[12] *Mato Grosso is part of the Brazilian interior well known for its swamps which cover over 130,000 square kilometres of the region (England is the exact same size).*

pulse rate of 128 beats a minute, dilated pupils and was sweating profusely. I gave him a couple of paracetamol tablets and told him to take things easy, which probably did not help much as he could not understand a word I was saying and by the time I had finished fart-arsing around, he was probably more afraid of the crazy 'Englander' than the fever. I returned to my hammock. Chest puffed out and head held high; full of self-admiration and convinced that the medical profession had missed out on a potentially gifted doctor.

During the afternoon, Roman and I witnessed a spectacular fly-past of thousands of pelicans. Flying in small groups, columns of them flew overhead in perfect 'V' formations as wave after wave of them appeared over the treetops, only to disappear once more on the other side of the river.

Throughout our journey up the Amazon River, Roman had frequently used two catchphrases. Firstly, he would refer to our vessel as the 'Love Boat', a title whose christening had been further substantiated by the now legendary 'Lesser Spotted, South American Coke-tapper'. Secondly, he would invariably poke his head over the side of his hammock and deliver the profound statement, *'There's a lot of water out there!'*

The captain and crew seemed to know very little of what was happening. We were both confidently informed that the boat would reach the little port of Monte Alegre sometime in the evening, but the estimated time of arrival varied from six in the evening until ten at night. In fact, we decided to stop asking silly questions like, 'Where are we going?' and, 'When will we get there?' after trying to ascertain the estimated time of arrival in Santarem, as this varied from six o'clock Sunday morning to four o'clock Tuesday afternoon.

We eventually reached Monte Alegre shortly after ten at night, so as it turned out they were all wrong, and that included the captain who had assured Roman that we would definitely be arriving by six at the very latest that evening. Just before reaching land, as the sun was beginning to slowly sink below the treeline, I went up to the bow of the boat and sat, legs dangling over the side. In the distance I could make out the glittering lights of a curious tree-cleared hill which was surrounded by jungle. A strange eerie silence seemed to descend over me and I could not put my finger on why, but I felt uneasy and a little tense as the village came ever closer. It was as if I was slowly being drawn to an important event in my life and there was no way out. Little did I realise just how much of an effect this little backwater village would have upon me and my plans for the future as I sat calmly, although a little apprehensively, surveying the surroundings, oblivious of the hand of fate gradually closing in around me.

Shortly after docking, Roman and I left to pick up some provisions, return our empty Coke bottles and if possible, grab a couple of beers. Unfortunately, by the time we had arrived the area was in total darkness due to a power failure. Monte Alegre proudly possessed three street lights that occasionally worked when the generator was behaving itself, but on this occasion fate had decided that they would not. Using the light emanating from the boat, we slowly walked into the inky blackness of the night. We had been assured by the crew that a couple of bars would be open and lit by candles. So we tentatively stumbled forward, straining our eyes searching for the dim lights of flickering candles. I've often thought to myself in the years that have followed why I had not dug out the torch which I had carefully stored in the bottom recesses of my rucksack for just such an emergency, but have come to the conclusion that you cannot cheat fate.

We cautiously walked across the road that ran along the riverbank and headed towards candle light that we could vaguely make out ahead of us. There we bought some biscuits and drank a couple of beers apiece before re-emerging into the night with our bag of empty bottles, as they would not accept them in the bar (each bottle carried a five cents deposit). In the distance we could make out the lights of the Love Boat. So using that as our compass bearing, we started heading directly towards it, talking away, paying little attention to our surroundings. It was so dark you could not see your hand in front of your face, let alone what was happening on the ground. Suddenly, we both disappeared into a one and a half metre deep storm drain that ran down the centre of the road. It felt as if the jaws of mother earth had opened up before us and swallowed us whole. Roman was virtually unscathed, just a few scratches and the odd bruise – he had previously undertaken several parachute jumps in America and this training served him well as he automatically rolled with the fall – whereas I was not so lucky and sustained a dislocated right wrist.

Dazed and shaken, I could sense something was wrong with my arm and held it up before me, straining my eyes in the darkness, silhouetting it against the distant lights of the Love Boat, desperately trying to assess the damage.

To my dismay, my right wrist was badly disfigured. Without letting myself think too much about what I was about to do, I immediately seized hold of it with my left hand, gritted my teeth and yanked it back into place. Once the pain had subsided, I once more held it up and was very glad to see that it looked just fine. I breathed a sigh of relief, optimistically believing that the worst was over. However, I then decided, that I would check to see if my wrist was still in good working order by moving it from side to side. At which point it alarmingly, slipped once again out of place.

Confused and disorientated, I stood still not knowing what to do next. I considered the predicament I found myself in: I was standing up to my chest in an empty storm drain, three and a half days up the River Amazon, in a small jungle outpost which did not even appear on any map of the region and was more than 8,300 kilometres away from home. In addition, I could not speak the language of the country I was travelling in and fast running out of money. My conclusion was simple. I was not scared, I was f****** petrified!

After a few moments of uncontrollable panic, during which I stood shaking like a leaf, tears streaming down my face, I closed my eyes and prayed: *If there is a God, I could do with your help right now.* I then opened my eyes, took a couple of deep breaths and slowly came to my senses. I reappraised my situation and quickly decided that skulking in a storm drain was not going to solve any problems. So carefully cradling my right wrist in my left hand to try and protect it from any further damage, I attempted to climb out using my elbows as levers. However, finding this virtually impossible due to the depth of the drain, I turned to Roman for assistance and was somewhat annoyed to find him grovelling around on his hands and knees, trying to locate the empty bottles which he had understandably dropped during the fall. This mercenary exhibition, coupled with the intense pain from my wrist as it started to swell up, resulted in me telling Roman, in no uncertain terms, where I would shove the bottles if he did not immediately desist his futile search and help me out of this pit and back to the boat. He sensibly realised that I was not joking and quickly took my advice.

Once back on board, my luck began to change as the good guy upstairs had heeded my request as a couple of German med students, followed us back onto the boat and, upon seeing my predicament, came to the rescue. They carefully examined my wrist and collectively agreed upon an appropriate course of action.

The first job was to correct its position, and at their request I wrapped my left arm around one of the wooden posts on the lower deck and gritted my teeth once more. One of the med students then took hold of my right wrist and pulled it back into place. After three painful attempts, this was finally accomplished to their satisfaction and then they proceeded to bandage it tightly to prevent any further swelling. Upon completion of this task, I asked Roman if he would go back to the bar, this time accompanied by a torch, and buy a few beers.

He returned shortly afterwards laden with cold beers and the news that the electricity had miraculously come back on. Evidently, we had unwittingly walked across a flat bridge on the way in, but had attempted to take an ill-advised shortcut on the way back. The four of us (myself, Roman and the two med students) had a cold night-cap toasting each other's health, along with my wrist, and talking about home, before parting company and going to our respective hammocks.

TALES FROM A SOUTH AMERICAN STORM DRAIN

***

In the 17th century, members of the Leco tribe were being chased through the Bolivian jungle by Spanish conquistadors, when they came across a piranha-infested river which they had to cross. Several young warriors immediately ran back down the path they had just cut to where they had previously noticed a large anaconda hanging from an overhead branch. Then having dragged it from the tree, they killed it, sliced it open and stuffed it full with the leaves of a local vine which they used as an anaesthetic. They then roughly stitched it up and threw it into the piranha-infested river. The piranhas ravenously ate the snake and its complimentary side salad and became briefly stunned by the anaesthetic, allowing the tribe to cross safely.

Several of these young warriors then stayed behind close to the riverbank so that when the conquistadors reached the river, they saw the warriors disappearing and a number of them immediately gave chase and entered the river. The unlucky conquistadors were promptly attacked and killed by the piranhas that had by then fully recovered from the Lecos' homemade anaesthetic.

*

In June 2019 a United States Coast Guard Cutter out on patrol in international waters off the coast of South America successfully intercepted a self-propelled semi-submersible, commonly known as a "narco sub". They seized 6.9 tonnes of cocaine with an estimated street value of $US 232 million.

During a three months tour at sea, the Cutter had conducted 14 'narco sub' interceptions, confiscating over 23.9 tonnes of cocaine and 420 kilograms of marijuana.

*

In 2019, a 43-year-old man was arrested in the Northern state of Rhondonia, after dressing up as his mother and trying to take her driving test.

When Heitor Schiave's 60-year-old mother, Maria, failed her test three times, her son decided to step in and try to help her out. So, wearing a floral blouse, lashings of make-up, an array of jewellery and a wig, he turned up at the test centre feeling confident.

However, suspicions were quickly raised by the instructor as the woman in the driving seat next to her looked nothing like the woman on 'her' ID.

The police were called and he was arrested at the driving school for fraud and misuse of someone's identity.

*

The fishing bat is the world's largest species of bat and has claws similar to an osprey's. At night it can detect surface ripples made by swimming fish then using its echolocation swoop down and grab the fish using its talons. No other species of bat is able to fish.

*

In Peru, it's traditional to give friends and family yellow underpants on New Year's Eve.

*

In the run up to the 1932 Olympics, Brazil could not afford to fly its team to Los Angeles, so instead it put them all on a ship and made them sell coffee on the way.

*

The state of Amazonas is one and a half million square kilometres (the size of the UK, France, Belgium, Holland, Luxembourg, Spain, Portugal and Denmark combined), yet only has a

*

The largest ever gold nugget found in the Amazonian gold belt, weighed thirty-four and a half kilograms and was worth £500,000 sterling.total population of two million.

Day 49

March 15, 1981

The haunting cries of a child locked in the jaws of pain entered my world of make-believe and quickly dragged me back to reality. I lay swinging from side to side, wrapped in the supporting cocoon of my hammock, realising the discomfort that I felt from my wrist was probably nothing to what that poor little girl was going through.

I opened my eyes to find, much to my surprise, that the boat had not moved in the night and was still tied up at Monte Alegre, and it appeared would remain so until eight that evening. I was beginning to wonder if we would ever reach Santarem, let alone Manaus.

The morning was spent wandering around, renewing our acquaintance with our previous night's drinking hole in the process. Roman noticed that the empty coke bottles[13] had been retrieved from the storm drain and were now carefully stored

---

[13] *Coca-Cola in Peru is sold under the brand name of 'Inca Cola'. The company's marketing department believed it would significantly increase sales. McDonald's have also used the same ploy in Israel, trading under the name of 'McDavid's'.*

away on the bottom shelf, behind the bar. The thought momentarily flashed through my mind that this whole saga of the power failure and the positioning of the open storm drain was probably a cunning ruse, hatched by some devious mind in order to obtain our supply of empty coka cola bottles.

Monte Alegre itself was built on a large hill that rose out of the jungle, and it was at the base of this hill that the tiny harbour lay. It had a total population of approximately 850 and was surprisingly modern for a small back-water outpost 720 kilometres up the River Amazon. It had two dirt tracks, one running alongside the riverbank while the other ran up to the top of the hill, the view from which was well worth the steep climb up to its summit. The only other note of interest was that the harbour area was inundated with pharmacists. In fact there were five of them in a row of eleven shops.

By now news of my unfortunate accident had spread around the boat and on several occasions passengers approached Roman to ask, in Portuguese, if I had been to the village's medical health centre. After all, it was free!

So under the heat of the afternoon sun, we slowly retraced our steps up the hill, where we were successful in locating the clinic. It was a small building set back from the road and surrounded by lush vegetation and green foliage with its very own defunct fountain, which Brazil seemed to specialise in. Although this time its circular concrete surround was filled with water and largely covered by an assortment of flowering waterlilies. It all looked very tranquil and picturesque but was definitely not the place to go paddling in. We sat on the rim of the surround talking as the cottage hospital was closed for lunch. My wrist was by now throbbing and unpleasantly hot. The thought of dipping it into the cool, refreshing waters was becoming more and more tempting. It was at this moment that Roman asked if I knew that we were being watched. I looked around, but couldn't see anyone, until he told me to look again carefully among the water lilies. I scoured the aquatic plants to see a number of eyes looking back at me, watching my every move with unblinking attention. It appeared the water was inhabited, not with goldfish, but a number of caiman alligators of varying sizes, some over a metre long.

Lunch break over, we entered the building which was more like an elongated wooden hut with a matted roof of leaves. Inside stood a few iron-framed beds, most of which were occupied by smiling faces and inquisitive eyes which followed our progress through the room with great interest. There was a small waiting room and an adjoining treatment room. I felt comparatively fine when I arrived with just a continuous, dull throbbing ache in my wrist, but when the doctor removed the bandage, it revealed several large dark patches on my arm where the bandage had restricted the swelling. I became acutely alarmed. However, displaying true British grit, I attempted to conceal my fear as best I could, remained silent and kept very still throughout the examination, even though I was sweating profusely and could feel the blood draining away from my face in sheer terror.

The doctor shook his head from side to side and carefully placed the wrist under an infrared lamp for a few minutes before writing a prescription for some tablets and cream to ease the pain. He then issued the strongest possible warning, via Roman, that no matter what advice I may receive, I should not allow my wrist to be bandaged up again.

We walked back down the hill and attempted to obtain the prescribed medication, but inexplicably, all five of the pharmacists were closed. Returning to the riverboat we discovered that the old boat was devoid of life. Apparently it was leaking badly and shipping so much water that the passengers had been transferred onto a smaller, single-decked boat, no more than fifteen metres in length, which was leaving for Santarem that night. Evidently boats regularly sank on this route and a couple of weeks earlier, a boat had gone down taking well over 230 passengers with it.

I definitely did not want to become another tasty human meal for all the carnivorous inhabitants of the murky waters which include creatures such as:

- Cachorro, the Amazonian dogfish, whose teeth were so large and sharp that the Amazonian Indians use them to shave with
- Caiman, Amazonian alligators
- Piranha
- Poraque, a form of electric eel
- Payara or vampire fish that has two huge fangs growing from their lower jaws (up to 15cm long) that fit into conical nasal slots in their upper jaws. It's a ferocious hunter that is constantly on the prowl for its next meal. They eat fish and are particular partial to Piranha in fact it has been witnessed that they can even make an entire shoal of piranhas turn tail and swim away when it comes across them. It has no known preditors.

They live in rivers and streams with strong currents, and often populate the bottoms of dams, waterfalls and rapids where there's always motion and activity. Their fangs basically function as spears that can be used to stab, grab and hold its prey.

These flesh eaters presented a genuine danger to the lives of the local population and had to be taken seriously, especially when one was contemplating a quick dip in the water to cool down.

In addition to the original passengers from the boat, there were a number of locals joining us for the trip upriver to Santarém.

However, before anyone could take up residence, one of the crew had to forcibly evict a squatter: a large tarantula that was taking a quiet siesta on the ceiling. Once this task had been completed, the place quickly became a choking mass of swinging hammocks slung from anything that would support the occupant's weight. The proverb of the day seemed to be *'keep moving or you will have a hammock lashed to you!'* In some places the hammocks were three deep, inducing a sense of rocking claustrophobia. The mere thought of being boxed in with a swinging hammock above, below and on either side of me sent a cold shiver down my spine.

If you needed to cross from one side of the boat to the other, your only option was to crawl on your hands and knees, commando style, beneath a sea of swaying hammocks, that is assuming that you could thread your way through the carpet of people lying on the deck itself.

The journey was an extremely rough one for me and probably the most painful night of my life: when I arrived back from the health centre, the medical students had strongly advised me to allow them to re-bandage my wrist. However, I stupidly assumed that the doctor at the clinic knew best. Later on though, I doubted whether this doctor even had the medical knowledge to apply a plaster, let alone deliver a proper medical diagnosis and course of treatment.

As the night wore on, my wrist and arm, no longer restricted by the tight bandage, began to swell until it was more than double its normal size. It felt as if my whole arm was on fire while at the same time someone was continually twisting a red-hot poker into my wrist. I could do little more than quietly groan and cry due to the agonising pain that I was now experiencing.

My companions had thoughtfully hung my hammock down the side of the boat, close to the wheel-house, which seemed to be the only place that was not already full of heaving masses of suspended humanity. However, no sooner had this been accomplished than the reason for the comparative emptiness of the position became clear as one of the boat's crew stormed up, shouting in Portuguese, telling us to move using a vast array of expletives. Roman substantially increased his Portuguese vocabulary that night with a large number of colourful words and phrases.

We tried reasoning with the crew member, but to no avail as he kept insisting loudly that he would go and fetch the captain. By now I was sinking into an abyss of tortuous pain, so responded angrily by telling him to fetch the (insert expletive of choice here) captain.

The squat, scowling crewman eventually stomped off in the direction from which he had first appeared, never to be seen again. I retired in exhaustion to my hammock. However, I was unable to sleep or even restlessly doze due to the intense pain. Consequently I awkwardly rolled out of my hammock and spent the night slumped against the side of the boat, slowly rocking backwards and forwards whilst holding my wrist against my chest, gently moaning in extreme torment as the tears continued to roll down my face. All the time I prayed for the morning to come and with it our destination of Santarém.

Yet even in the midst of this living hell, I still noted that Roman had contrived to somehow change into his pyjamas. Where he had performed this feat, I never did manage to find out.

***

Girls from remote settlements in the North East of Brazil, some as young as nine years old, were being recruited to work as waitresses in bars in the Eastern Amazonian gold belt mining community, in the jungle.

When they're first recruited, they're given money in the form of a loan to buy new clothes and to pay for the cost of the flight out. However, upon their arrival, they are immediately informed of their actual duties: that of working as unpaid prostitutes for the mine workers. During their first night at the camp, each girl is forced to parade in front of a large crowd of drunken, vociferous gold miners, whereupon their virginity is auctioned off to the highest bidder. They are forced to sleep, huddled together in a number of small rooms with little or no bedding and are constantly under armed guard.

If caught trying to escape, they are killed in front of the others to act as a deterrent. If the girls become pregnant, they are beaten up until they have a miscarriage. Their only form of release, albeit temporary, is through the use of drugs which they quickly become addicted to. Needless to say, the level of suicide among the girls is very high and consequently, there is a constant need for new recruits.

Day 50

March 16, 1981

The boat finally reached Santarem around four in the morning and the crew tied it up to an adjoining boat, which in turn was lashed to another, which was finally tied up to the harbour's mooring.

At 07:00 the gangplank was run out to enable us to climb onto the adjoining boat, releasing everyone from their forced captivity.

Once ashore, with the help of Roman and the two German medical students, Eugene and Gunther, we proceeded to stop people and ask for directions to the nearest hospital. Unfortunately, it seemed that in Santarem each doctor had a local monopoly on various parts of the anatomy, for the hospital would not even look at my wrist, and instead simply referred me to the city's one and only bone specialist. It seemed totally incomprehensible that in such a large city of over 112,000 people, there was only one person who was qualified to perform a simple operation like fixing a wrist.

Still, needs must, and having received directions on how to get there, we set about trying to locate the bone specialists clinic.

I was by now half expecting to come across a large mud hut in the middle of the jungle: *I could just imagine walking through an open doorway to be confronted by the gaze of a young native woman, semi-clad in a grass skirt, nurse's hat and little else, seated behind a bamboo table. She would indicate that we should sit down and make ourselves comfortable on the floor as there were no chairs.*

Shortly afterwards, the doctor would arrive jumping through the doorway grunting obscenities, throwing handfuls of powder into the air like a sumo wrestler and dancing around as if he was stepping on hot coals. He would be wearing a large bone through his nose, hence the title 'the bone doctor' and have a cluster of tiny shrunken heads dangling from his belt. He obviously didn't accept credit!

Gyrating his body from side to side, like someone throwing an epileptic fit, he would slowly advance towards me, and having briefly examined my wrist, would lead me outside and try coaxing me into a large cooking pot, standing in the middle of an open fireplace. He would then proceed to fill the pot with water, light the fire and hand me a potato peeler, along with an assortment of vegetables, suggesting I should be as quick as possible and not to forget to throw the potato peeler out when I had finished.

I returned to the harsh and painful realities of life upon reaching our destination and proceeded to breathe a sigh of relief at seeing a large, whitish building standing before me and not a mud hut in sight. What is more, I could not even see a cooking pot in the front garden. *Obviously,* I thought, *they keep it hidden away around the back.* We were informed that the doctor was due in at 09:00 and as it was ten minutes to, we decided to sit out on the verandas and await his impending arrival.

He eventually strolled in an hour and a half later and for a thousand cruzeiros consultation fee, agreed to see me. I obligingly paid the money and entered his surgery with Roman to act as translator. He examined my wrist for a few seconds while Roman explained how the accident had occurred, then told me to get an X-ray and proceeded to write the name and address of where we had to go to on a piece of paper. I left feeling resentful, convinced that it must have been the easiest money that he had ever made.

After all, within a couple of minutes of the bone specialist entering the surgery, we were back out on the road again, heading this time for the city's one and only X-ray centre. Before long, we were all sitting in the waiting room, nervously awaiting the next calamity to arise, when a nurse walked out from an adjoining room and casually announced, 'No X-ray!'

The shock immediately registered on my face as Roman began to enquire as to why we could not have an X-ray. The nurse seemed somewhat taken aback by the question as if the answer should have been fairly obvious, but then decided that these strange gringos must know nothing, so she began to explain that the centre could not take any X-rays because it had no electricity. Undeterred, Roman relentlessly continued with his questioning and asked her when she expected the electricity to be turned on. She momentarily stood still, silently contemplating the scene before her, then shrugging her shoulders, explained that she didn't know, before disappearing through another doorway.

I left thoroughly depressed and, quite frankly, in a state of stunned shock, wondering what on earth to do next. In the meantime my entourage followed on behind, each one silently mulling the problem over in their mind, trying to come up with a solution. We reached the bottom of the road and were about to turn the corner, when someone ran out of the X-ray centre and started shouting and waving their arms, beckoning us to come back. It seemed that fortune had shined upon me, my prayers had yet again been answered and the power had miraculously been restored. Not knowing how long it would last, we all ran back as fast as we could. I dived into the X-ray room, discarding my rucksack on the way in. The two X-rays set me back a further two thousand cruzeiros, but holding them up to the light, it did not exactly require a trained eye to see that I had badly dislocated my wrist.

Unfortunately, the bone specialist that I had seen earlier at the clinic was not due back until four that afternoon. He usually came in at five, but as Roman and I were hoping to catch a connecting boat to Manaus which was due to leave at six that evening, he had agreed to come in early. In the meantime, we all returned to the docks where Eugene and Gunther booked their passage on the aforementioned boat, before retiring to a bar to while away a few hours.

Roman and I returned to the clinic on time for our appointment. However, the doctor was nowhere to be seen and being a man of habit, remained true to form and eventually appeared a little after five forty-five. We followed him into his surgery and, after a brief examination of the X-rays, he declared that four of my carpal bones were out of place and that in order to correct my wrist, he would have to give a general anaesthetic. This announcement worried me considerably, as having already experienced the proficiency of a member of the Brazilian medical profession in Monte Alegre, I began contemplating the likelihood of the anaesthetist arriving with a wooden mallet! But the pain was excruciating, so I reluctantly resigned myself to accepting whatever course of treatment was necessary to rid me of this living nightmare.

It was then that the doctor informed me of the cost: 20,000 cruzeiros. A new worry caused my face to momentarily lose its suntan as I calculated in my mind that the total expenditure would come to over 25,000 cruzeiros, approximately 400 US dollars. I reluctantly agreed to use the doctor's services; after all, I didn't exactly have much choice, and with Roman's help, we began piling up a thick wad of notes on the table. The doctor seemed suitably impressed with the proceedings and immediately phoned up the anaesthetist.

I looked up from the operating table, a long wooden bench covered by a white sheet with a lumpy pillow at one end, through a pair of terrified eyes as the two doctors stood over me, preparing for the operation. I lay there praying over and over again that everything would be alright and that the anaesthetist actually knew what he was doing.

Sometime later, my prayers once again answered , I awoke to find them putting the finishing touches to my newly acquired plaster cast. I thanked everyone in the building and left with Roman shortly afterwards, poorer than when I had arrived, relieved that I had taken out an insurance policy before leaving England, and for the first time in two days, virtually free from pain.

It felt a little strange walking along the road afterwards though and I was convinced that the doctors had got a little carried away with their plastering. *Obviously they wanted to ensure that I had got my money's worth*, I thought. I had only dislocated my wrist, yet was now in plaster up to my armpit and the cast had been set so that my arm was now permanently bent at a ninety-degree angle. I looked like a standard bearer who had forgotten to pick up his flag before leaving the building. I walked on slowly down the road with Roman, carefully balancing my rucksack over one shoulder to try and ensure that no unnecessary pressure was placed upon my right arm.

We procured a room in the first cheap hotel we came across for 300 cruzeiros. Dumping our gear, we then went out to change some travellers' cheques. I repaid Roman the money he had lent me earlier and we both bought a plane ticket to Manaus for the following day. I was in no condition to undertake another two- to three-day journey by boat and Roman could not risk the boat arriving late for his return flight to Los Angeles to finish his MBA.

After something to eat and a couple of beers, we retired early and I eventually fell asleep on my side with my plastered arm protruding into the air like the leaning tower of Pisa.

***

Santarem was established in 1865 by a large number of Americans fleeing South Carolina and Tennessee following the confederate defeat in the American civil war. In fact, the Confederate flag is still displayed in a number of bars around the city. Brazil abolished slavery twenty-three years later in 1888.

*

There are currently over 550,000 gold miners and slightly less diamond and tin miners working throughout the Amazon region. The gold miners are causing irreparable damage to the environment through sustained mercury pollution and there seems nothing the government can do to curtail this practice. The miners use mercury to form an amalgam with the gold which they then burn off later. This causes a considerable quantity of metallic mercury and mercury vapour, approximately six tons per annum, to escape into the Amazon ecosystem.

Many of the fish now being caught and sold in the local markets have high levels of mercury, and doctors in Santarem and Manaus frequently have to treat people, especially children, for mercury poisoning.

Mercury poisoning is fast becoming a major cause of illness throughout the Amazon basin.

*

It has been estimated that for every ton of gold produced two tons of mercury are released into the atmosphere.

*

Brazil is the fifth largest producer of gold, although an estimated eighty percent disappears on the black market in order to avoid paying government taxes.

*

In 2016, Brazilian construction workers in the Northern state of Para set off a controlled explosion while extending a road in the jungle. Upon returning to the immediate area, once the dust had cleared, they found the recently deceased corpse of a gigantic 10 metre long anaconda weighing over 400kgs.

*

You are strongly advised by some superstitious locals to never walk the streets of Santarem late at night as you may come face to face with the city's equivalent to the Loch Ness monster. It is a fire-breathing pig that will roast you on sight!

Day 51

March 17, 1981

I awoke from an uneasy sleep as the alarm clock broke into a controlled bout of high-pitched beeping. It was half past five in the morning and I cautiously viewed the new day through a pair of squinting eyes. I lay there, slowly collecting my thoughts, before begrudgingly responding to the age of technology by getting dressed and joining Roman outside in the hotel's lobby/lounge/restaurant for breakfast. Once finished, we picked up our rucksacks and abruptly left to catch a bus to the airport and our early-morning flight to Manaus.

We had been reliably informed that the standard taxi fare to the airport was 700 cruzeiros. Not surprisingly, we had agreed to get up especially early and catch the bus instead. Although somewhat slower, it only cost a mere twelve cruzeiros each. Within a few minutes we were watching the local scenery slowly trundle past the window, happy in the knowledge that we had saved ourselves just over 300 cruzeiros each.

Minutes later though, the bus pulled into a half-built and deserted shopping centre, where we were informed by the driver that the bus had developed a fault and that we would have to get off and await his return with a replacement.

Before leaving, he assured Roman that this would not take long and that he would be back within fifteen minutes at the very latest. The driver left, leaving us alone by the steps of the shopping centre. Things soon turned decidedly fishy as a taxi immediately appeared from around the corner and pulled up directly in front of us, obediently awaiting our pleasure. We looked at each other and came to the obvious conclusion, the driver not only looked but even smelt like a fishmonger, this was too much of a coincidence.

After forty-five minutes Roman was becoming increasingly aggravated as there was still no sign of the replacement bus and the taxi driver confirmed our suspicions by getting out of his car, approaching us and saying that if we wanted to catch our plane, we had better use his taxi. We briefly considered his extortionate terms and agreed to use his services, having successfully renegotiated the fare from 600 down to 400 cruzeiros. As we drove off, I began wondering how much the taxi driver had paid the bus driver for this deception and how many other travellers they had blackmailed in this way.

We reached the airport, checked in and passed straight through the various boarding procedures as we were the last passengers to arrive, and were soon strapped in our seats, ready for take-off. The journey took a little over an hour, during which we passed over an endless sea of rainforest, filling the window from horizon to horizon. A seemingly impenetrable mass of tree tops, occasionally broken by the brief glimpse of a winding river as it snaked its way through a thick blanket of jungle.

The plane touched down in Manaus at approximately nine in the morning, and after what seemed a frustratingly long wait under the scorching heat of the sun, we caught a bus into the city. Once there, we began searching the streets for some suitably priced refuge and were soon settling into our latest sanctuary.

The bone specialist in Santarem had been unable to take an

X-ray of my wrist, due to not having the facilities, to check that everything was healing correctly and the carpal bones were back in the right place. He had, therefore, written a letter to a consultant friend of his in Manaus, asking him to X-ray my wrist for him as a precaution. My first priority, then, was to try and contact the consultant to put my mind at rest. We eventually reached the hospital where he worked, only to find that said consultant was visiting another hospital! And the nursing staff had no idea of when he would return. Somehow I felt that I had heard all of these excuses before and promptly left.

We reached the British Consulate, a poky little room tucked away in its obscurity, on the twentieth floor of a skyscraper. It resembled a back-street turf accountants more than the representative office of a once great nation, with its dank and dingy walls, sparse furniture, peeling paintwork and wire-netting frontage which you had to talk through. It was here that I checked to see if there was a letter from Lima in Peru, offering me a job. Needless to say there was not, it was just not my lucky day. That evening, I wrote in my diary: *'This means I will shortly be leaving South America,'* but at the time I had no idea of just how true this statement would soon turn out to be.

I spent the rest of the afternoon walking to and from the city's main bus station, where I collated as much information as possible about the next leg of my travels, a coach trip into Venezuela. It seemed that the journey would take me along the trans-American highway, which in this region would often be full of surprises. *Never a dull moment practically guaranteed*, I thought. Evidently, completion on this particular part of the highway had been long held up by hostile Indians who demonstrated their distaste for the road by chopping up a number of its road workers with their machetes during the construction and still remained a potential threat. Consequently, traffic which was intermittent normally travelled in convoy, it was a case of safety in numbers and on this occasion I just loved a crowd.

The evening was spent gorging ourselves in a tiny restaurant before moving on to an adjoining bar to pour litres of ice-cold beer down our throats till the early hours of the morning. During these festivities, Roman kindly offered to lend me 500 US dollars to help me out till I was reimbursed by the insurance company for my medical expenses and I, needless to say, gratefully accepted his kind offer. Roman would be flying back to LA for the start of his semester in a couple of days' time and was evidently in no great need of the money on his return.

***

The Indians had become hostile because the construction workers had bought with them a variety of diseases, including: VD, tuberculosis and malaria, which had decimated the local native population. This has been true throughout the Amazon basin whenever Indian tribes had come into contact with people from the outside world.

*

The governor of Amazonas, Gilberto Mestrinho, currently in his fourth term of office, recently stated in an interview, 'There are hardly any healthy trees in Amazonia and they should all be cut down and used before the woodworm gets to them.' He continued, 'I wasn't elected by the trees, I was elected by the people!'

*

It has been estimated by a number of academics that the native population of the Americas, before Columbus's arrival in 1492, could have been as high as 112 million. However, due to the prevalence of the slave trade, the introduction of diseases, military action, and the general disruption of the social systems of the native tribes, this native population had declined to less than six million by 1650.

*

During the 1920s, Henry Ford bought over six million acres of Amazon jungle from the Brazilian authorities and proceeded to create the world's largest rubber plantation, named Fordlândia.

In it he built a modern hospital, power plant, hotel, library and even a golf course, along with thousands of little white clapboard houses for the employees to live in. Eventually, as the community grew, other businesses such as bakeries, butcher shops, restaurants, and shoemakers, were also established.

Ford employees from mainland USA were then relocated to this little piece of the States along the Amazon River where they, along with native Brazilian workers who moved into the settlement in order to work at the factory, were forced to live the mandatory 'healthy lifestyle'. This included attending poetry readings, square dances, and English-language-only singalongs, and abstaining from alcohol, which was strictly prohibited.

Unfortunately, Fordlândia proved to be wildly unsuccessful. The rubber saplings that Ford had planted (without the help of a botanist) barely grew, and those that did were soon hit by a leaf blight, which ruined the remaining trees. By the end of the 1920s, malaria had also became a serious problem.

In December 1930, agitated workers rioted, breaking windows and overturning vehicles in the road. After the riots, which lasted less than three days, work continued, but there was almost no product to show for the millions of dollars that Ford had poured into the jungle.

In 1933, after coming to terms with the failure, Ford purchased a new plot of land downriver and called it Belterra. At first the land showed promise, but progress was slow. After 10 years of work, Ford realized that his goal of 38,000 tons of latex was a far cry from his factory's output of just 750 tons.

Ford retired from the rubber industry in 1945 after losing over $20 million in the Amazon (over $430 million in today's terms). The Brazilian government purchased all of Ford's land for a measly $250,000. Today, some of the structures of Fordlândia and Belterra still remain and are visited by Amazon tourists.

*

The leaves of the royal waterlily are so large (60-180cm in diameter) and strong that they can support the weight of a small child.

Day 52

March 18, 1981

I spent the morning on the trail of the elusive consultant, following him around the city from one clinic or hospital to another. Yet every time he stayed one step ahead of me. When I eventually caught up with him though, I was immediately impressed by his professional manner. *No wonder he was in such demand*, I thought to myself. To top it all off, he could even speak English! This guy at least acted as if he knew what he was talking about, unlike his counterparts with whom I had previously come into contact. The consultant listened in earnest to all the events of the last few days and read the letter that his friend and colleague from Santarem had written. He then quickly arranged an appointment for a series of X-rays to be taken of my wrist at the particular hospital he was visiting that afternoon, followed by a further appointment with him afterwards. *At long last things seem to be sorting themselves out and I will able to draw a line under this episode.*

That afternoon, I arrived at the hospital in good time for my appointment and was soon being guided through a maze of corridors which led down into the dark recesses of the hospital. Here, a smiling radiographer, without a polaroid camera in sight, seemed eager to make a memorable impression upon me, as he proceeded to take a collection of X-rays of my wrist from every conceivable angle.

When the consultant arrived for the prearranged meeting, he carefully studied my latest batch of holiday snaps with a well-trained eye and then announced that his findings were not good. To begin with, it appeared that the bone specialist in Santarem was not so special after all, and fairly incompetent at jigsaw puzzles. My arm, and especially the wrist, had swollen so much that the carpal bones had moved and he had put two of them back in the wrong place (which has resulted in me only ever regaining partial movement in my right wrist), and that he had also failed to notice that I had badly fractured my scaphoid, the small bone at the base of the thumb. The super-consultant went on to inform me, that after four days it would be a very difficult and very expensive operation to correct, with less than a fifty percent success rate.

Consequently, he strongly advised me to return home immediately to England, where the facilities and equipment available were far superior to those anywhere in South America, and have my wrist operated on as soon as possible, in any case within the next few days. He let that sink in for a few moments, before adding that if I stayed on in South America, I would most likely end up having my wrist, and possibly even my arm amputated, as gangrene would set in within the next week.

Manaus was situated on the equator and had an extremely high level of humidity. Consequently, doctors seldom bothered trying to reset broken limbs and amputation was the normal procedure throughout Brazil, for all but the richest of families, who could afford to fly their injured family members away to a more suitable climate in which to recover. So it was a case of 'Bye-bye world trip,' for the time being at least, and, 'Hello England.'

I returned to the hotel with the doctor's words still ringing in my ears. I had thrown away a promising career to achieve a dream trip around the world and I would be back home before two months were up. *Well I'm not finished yet*, I promised myself.

They can't keep a Plummer down!

That night, Roman lent me even more money to help buy the ticket home and informed that me he believed he had caught parasitic worms, as he had been suffering from the runs for the last two days; the first time in his whole trip. His suspicions were reinforced when he found out that afternoon that the Republica's ice-cold drinking water, that we had liberally been helping ourselves to from the fridge, was not sterilised as we had wrongly assumed, and was instead merely chilled tap water.

It seems that in Manaus virtually everybody had worms, because the water system was so unhygienic due to the lack of any proper sanitation. I then casually dropped into the conversation that I too had started marathon training that morning and I didn't mean jogging! *Oh well,* I thought. *I wonder if customs will impound my intestinal worms for six months quarantine when I reach the UK, in case they're carrying rabies!*

***

Manaus's main market is situated close to the water front. At the back end of the market stands a dirty-looking cafeteria, situated under the roof of an old and badly dilapidated warehouse, whose sides had long since disappeared. The raw fish and slabs of meat which the café use when cooking, are laid out on the ground nearby for all to see and were invariably covered in a thick blanket of flies.

The open-air larder is kept cool by a continuous stream of dirty water which flows out from the market stalls, before mingling with grey water, a mixture of urine and toilet water, overflowing from a nearby toilet. This runoff then flows around, and sometimes over, the fly-infested meat and fish, before reaching the river to join all the other raw sewage of Manaus. However, this culinary curiosity had a further USP to its reputation as Urubu vultures, roost in the rusty ironwork of the cafeteria roof and you are advised never to leave your food unattended as the vultures will often swoop down and help themselves if the opportunity arises.

*

The difference between high and low water levels of the river at Manaus harbour in an average year is eleven metres. The record set in

1990 is over fifteen metres.

*

Over 700 different species of fish have been caught within a thirty-five-kilometre radius of Manaus.

*

One of the more unusual inhabitants of the river is the manatee, a harmless vegetarian water mammal. When fully grown, its hairless body can measure over two metres in length and up to one and a half metres in circumference, at its thickest part. It is also known as the sea-cow because of the way the female suckles its young by lying on its back out at sea, whereupon the young pup climbs onto her stomach and suckles from her breasts. While this is happening, she wraps her flippers around the pup to help hold it firmly in place and produces woeful sighing noises.

It is believed by many that it is these sounds that helped create the mermaid legends. For one can easily imagine homesick sailors, trapped on sailing ships for months at a time, a long way from land and prone to wishful thinking, to have heard these strange melodic sounds and let their imaginations run riot.

Unfortunately, the manatee has been practically hunted to the point of extinction in many parts of the world. Local Indians used the manatee's fat to produce oil for cooking and lighting and its tough hide for shields, while the Europeans used the hides for making engine belts.

I am sorry to admit that I haven't helped its survival either, as some years later, while working as the international director for Bournemouth and Poole College, I inadvertently ate part of one at a private banquet on Hainan Island, off the China coast. Its meat was very spongy and is evidently a much sought-after delicacy in China, but very expensive.

Day 53

March 19, 1981

Breakfast complete and farewells exchanged, I promptly left to catch a bus to the airport from where I attempted to buy a ticket to Miami. Unfortunately though, I had considerable difficulty trying to make myself understood as it seemed that no one at the airport could actually speak English. But thankfully luck was close at hand, as a young backpacker, newly arrived from Switzerland, noticed my predicament and came over to help, acting as a translator. She began carefully explaining the situation and before long, I was offered a flight to Miami via of all places: Rio de Janeiro! But this was double the normal charge.

By now, I had been patiently trying to buy a ticket for nearly three-quarters of an hour and after being assured that this was the only flight available, I finally gave up in sheer frustration, told them what they could do with their flight to Miami via Rio and walked off, saying I would visit the Varig agent, the Brazilian national airline, in the city centre instead.

As we left the building and started walking towards the bus stop, surprise, surprise, a booking clerk came rushing out after us, announcing that they had found a spare seat on a flight to Miami, via Caracas, which left early the following morning, costing me the usual charge of 444 dollars, plus the airport tax. *Typical,* I thought, *the businesses here try and screw you out of every last Cruzeiro you possess.* They could easily see from my appearance how desperate I was to reach Miami, and were probably working on commission, so were consequently trying to take full advantage of my unfortunate predicament. After all, how could I conceal a seventy-centimetre plaster cast that ran from my fingers to my armpit?

I quickly decided to play safe and followed the clerk back into the airport building to book the flight and then promptly left for the city, my immediate worries finally resolved. I later realised that I had forgotten to go through the normal booking procedures of bribing the official behind the desk beforehand.

I caught the bus into Manaus with my new linguistics assistant, as I had promised at the airport to return the favour and help her locate a suitably priced hotel. Upon reaching the city centre, I led the way through the streets, to an area where I had previously noted several small hotels. We then entered the first one that we came to and approaching the desk clerk, we enquired the cost of a single room. Upon hearing the ridiculously inflated price of over a thousand cruzeiros, I was about to leave, when much to my amazement, my fellow backpacker readily agreed to the price, saying that it would do her nicely. In fact, she was only too happy to part with the money. *This girl is way out of my league,* I thought to myself, and bidding her a safe journey through Brazil, left shortly afterwards.

I decided to spend the afternoon visiting the city's famous Maneus opera house, the 'Teatro do Amazonas'. It was built in the 1890s during the rubber boom, when the city exploded into a thriving hub of entrepreneurial activity. At the height of the boom, Manaus became one of the wealthiest cities in the world and extravagant behaviour became the norm. For instance, the wealthy rubber plantation owners would send their shirts to London to be laundered and to have their collars starched. The round trip would have taken approximately fifty days. They must have owned in excess of at least 170 or more shirts and collars, when you took into account the number of ships that never reached their destination in the 19th century, for a myriad of reasons.

Architects and artists from all over Europe were bought to Manaus to help create this extravagant masterpiece. After which Italian marble, English porcelain and French furniture was then imported to adorn its elaborate structure. The ceiling and walls of the lobby were decorated with mirrors, while murals of harp-playing angels and Amazonian Indians looked on. In the centre of the room stood a large fountain that continuously flowed with champagne, which the guests would scoop up with their elegantly designed glass flutes. The city then paid exorbitant sums of money in order to book world famous performers such as the Ballet Russe, Sarah Bernhardt, Caruso and Anna Pavlova (the Russian ballerina that the famous Pavlova dessert is named after).

On the opening night in 1896, the rich and affluent members of Manaus society turned out in style. The ladies wore the latest Paris fashions, while the men donned top hats and woollen tailcoats. In the humidity of the equator, the air must have been heavy with the stench of sweating bodies inside that building.

Situated some fifteen kilometres downriver from the 'meeting of the waters', where the black waters of the River Negro flow into the yellow-brown waters of the River Amazon (the two rivers run alongside each other for approximately six kilometres, before the waters finally mix together). The two rivers run side by side because of their differences in water density, temperature and speed.

Manaus was the furthermost point to which large cargo ships could safely navigate. Consequently, it rapidly expanded and became the collection point for all the rubber brought down from the vast regions of the Amazon and beyond, including parts of Peru, Bolivia and Columbia. It was during this period that the impressive, and now legendary opera house was built with its huge domed roof, covered in green, yellow, red and blue tiles which could be seen from practically anywhere in the city.

En route to the opera house, I took temporary refuge from the glare of the afternoon sun by entering a local bar for a liquid top-up. Entering the bar, I was met with the pleasing sound of harmonious singing and immediately caught sight of two locals leaning up against the bar happily singing away. During a lull in the proceedings, and using my full Portuguese vocabulary, I complimented them on their harmonising and was quickly drawn into conversation as they both happened to be learning English at night school.

Before long, a constant supply of beer bottles, courtesy of my newly found drinking companions, began to be placed before me as I temporarily delayed my departure. They were both well educated, one being a doctor, while the other was a botanist and the sudden realisation that if I had not broken my wrist, I could have been talking to my passport to an expedition into the Amazon jungle. This obviously filled me with a feeling of frustration and remorse. The botanist began describing the jungle around Manaus along with some of its lesser known legendary inhabitants such as the 'Capelobo'. This was a mythical Amazonian creature with the body of a man and the head of an anteater. It was evidently reputed to silently creep up on its intended victim, squeeze them to death in a Capelobo bear hug, that would crush their ribcage and then pierce their skull with its horny snout, rather like a woodpecker attacking a tree, and suck out their brains with its elongated tongue.

He continued by explaining that most visitors to the jungle were surprised to find that the ground was not choking with undergrowth, as was portrayed in most films. It seemed that large areas of the Amazon basin were regularly flooded and that only ten percent of the sunlight actually reached the jungle floor, due to the thick tree canopy above. Consequently, most flowers had long ago forsaken the ground and evolved into anchoring themselves to tree branches instead. They were called epiphytes or air plants, and flourished by absorbing moisture from the humid atmosphere or trapping rainwater in their own tailor-made mini reservoirs.

Several beers later, I bid my newfound drinking partners

farewell (having successfully ignored the advances of one of their male friends, who had taken an immediate liking to me and attempted to proposition me, even offering US dollars in payment!) and left the bar, heading for the opera house, gently swaying from side to side. I never could drink in the afternoon.

I arrived just in time to join a party of four Germans on a guided tour of the building. Their guide was an attractive student who was studying languages at the Federal University of Amazonas and working as a tour guide during her holidays. She began by escorting us from room to room while giving a running commentary in German, until that is, she found out that I was British, at which point she quickly conducted everyone into a large, lavishly decorated room.

Once inside, she informed the other members of the tour group that she would let them browse around the room for a few minutes to appreciate its beauty, before continuing on with the tour. At this point she grabbed my good arm and quickly led me out of the room and along a series of corridors to where a small group of guides were seated. There I stood, surrounded by four young Amazonian women, all of whom were studying English at University, and they immediately began bombarding me with an array of questions relating to England itself and the correct pronunciation and use of various words and phrases. Unfortunately, it seemed that the only non-Brazilian English teachers in Manaus were all American and spoke with a pronounced American drawl. I spent the next ten minutes correcting their use of grammar and pronunciation as they proceeded to verbally abuse the English language, by speaking with a rich embellishment of American jargon and slang.

Then quite unexpectedly, one of the guides, a particularly well-developed, young amazon maiden, looked me straight in the eyes and declared that she wanted to eat me as I was so beautiful! Needless to say, my big blue eyes and beard were a major contributing factor to this statement and I could tell from her gaze she meant every word. She followed up this mind-boggling statement by then casually informing me that she was already two months pregnant. In other words, *'How about it?'*

and, 'Don't worry, I can't get pregnant twice!'

There I stood, surrounded by empty rooms at my disposal and I missed the opportunity. She sat there looking up at me, openly offering me an incredible ending to my trip up the east coast of South America, to sample the delights of a beautiful Amazonian woman, possibly in the royal box of the famous Manaus opera house. But me, no, I was so naïve I just swam right past the deliciously tempting bait that was being dangled before my very eyes. Looking back, I can't believe it. It was Fortaleza all over again.

Shortly afterwards, I returned with my guide to continue the tour, before leaving to meet up with Roman, and Gunther and Eugene, the German med students, who had arrived in Manaus early that morning. We all adjourned to the nearest bar upon meeting, and began some serious drinking to catch up on each other's news and while away the few hours before I left for my flight.

A little after ten, I left with Roman to walk to the bus stop. The night felt strange. Tomorrow I would be back in England, two years and ten months earlier than anticipated, and the realisation of what was about to happen was just beginning to have an impact on me.

Over those eight weeks I had made some really stupid mistakes and stumbled into several situations that I was lucky to have walked away from. I had also omitted to budget my meagre financial resources properly, which was one of the first rules of survival for any experienced traveller. So in some ways I was quite excited about returning home, knowing full well that once my wrist had fully recovered, I had received the money back from the insurance company and worked for a few months to help replenish my sadly depleted finances, I would be dusting down my rucksack once more and flying off to a new continent to continue my travels. Except this time, I would not be the innocent and naive young traveller that had flown out of Heathrow two months earlier.

While waiting at the bus stop, we were fortunate enough to

witness one of the Amazon's natural phenomena: an electrical storm. Every two to three seconds, the sky would be lit up for as far as the eye could see by sheet lightning. It seemed, or so we were informed by several locals also awaiting the arrival of the impending bus, that this was a regular occurrence in these parts and would sometimes last for up to three hours. The sight of this was made even more astonishing by the fact that during the spectacle, there was not the slightest breeze, drop of rain or sound of thunder. The night was still and strangely silent. It was as if two superhuman magicians, each one standing at either side of the Amazon basin, were battling away with each other, casting spell after spell which lit up the night sky as they met above the jungle.

The bus finally appeared and trundled along the road. Roman helped me on with my rucksack, before we once more said goodbye, each of us promising to keep in touch with the other.

I checked in at the airport not long after and quickly passed through customs. The airport itself was quite respectable by South American standards. It was clean, tidy and there was a noticeable absence of armed guards and scraggily-looking chickens, unlike its counterpart at Santa Cruz in Bolivia. I found a soft chair and sank into its welcoming embrace. The plane left on time and I spent the night drifting in and out of an uneasy sleep, as events of the past two months kept flashing into my dreams.

***

As previously mentioned, piranha fish are not always as deadly as people believe them to be, unless of course the river is absolutely teeming with them or when food is in short supply. Usually, all you have to do to ensure you won't be eaten alive, is to keep moving, but above all, do not stop swimming and float, unless of course you are tired of living.

There is a wonderful story of a river boat captain that I heard about while travelling. He was working out of Manaus and would regularly take his tourist boat upriver to catch piranha. After a successful day's fishing the boat would 'develop engine trouble' when it was time to go back and the captain would call the young cabin boy over to discuss what they should do next.

After a close inspection of the engine, under the watchful gaze of an increasingly worried group of passengers, they would purposefully walk to the stern of the boat and start peering at the propeller shaft, disappearing into the murky piranha-infested waters below. After further deliberations and a heated discussion, the heroic cabin boy would reluctantly take off his T-shirt and dive over the side.

Women would often openly be seen crying through fear and admiration, while the men would look on wide-eyed, with gaping mouths and worried expressions, wondering if they would pick the short straw and be next to go over the side to become the piranhas' second course while trying to free the propeller.

After half a minute or so of frantically thrashing about in the water, the heroic boy would surface and be quickly hauled in to rapturous applause and given outrageous tips, which he would later share with the captain. A week later, the dramatic events would yet again unfold as the cabin boy would once more be forced to dive overboard and save the day, while giving the tourists a story that they would recall over and over again, when they returned home.

*

If you are ever out fishing for piranha, I would strongly recommend bird's heart, as it makes an excellent and irresistible bait that the hungry carnivores cannot resist.

*

When an Amazonian Indian has a bad cut that needs stitching, they use the impressive sickle-shaped jaws of the army ant to close up the wound. They carefully hold the body of each ant between their fingers, then press it up against the wound. Once the ant sinks its jaws into the two sides of the wound, they decapitate the body and continue closing the wound with another ant. Who needs sutures when you have a plentiful supply of army ants?

*

The arapaima, is a gigantic carnivorous fish that lives in the

Amazon basin. They tend to stay close to the surface of the water, because they need to breathe oxygen through their gills, and make a distinctive coughing sound when they emerge for air. It is one of the largest freshwater fish on the planet and can reach 2.75 metres (nine feet) in length and weigh up to 200 kilograms. These fish are so vicious that even have teeth on their tongue.

*

The pacu is a larger relative of the piranha, known for its distinctive, human-like teeth. and it's omnivorous, with a good part of its diet being made up of fruit and nuts. Unfortunately though, this doesn't just include the nuts that grow on trees as there have been cases reported, mostly from Papua New Guinea, where they have occasionally bitten off the testicles of male swimmers.

*

According to legend the Mboya Jagwa or dog-snake, is a ten-metre-long water serpent with the head of a dog, whose call is that of the yelp of a puppy. It is a sex-mad creature that grabs hold of native women when they go down to the river bank to bathe or wash, molests and rapes them.

*

Police in Rio de Janeiro killed 731 people in the first five months of 2019 marking a 20 % increase on the same period in 2018, according to Rio's Public Security Institute figures. At a press conference on Governor Wilson Witzel shrugged off the increase as "normal", saying it was due to police "hitting hard" at criminals.

Day 54

March 20, 1981

I arrived in Miami at seven in the morning, went through customs and tried to book an ongoing flight to London. Unfortunately, however, the first plane with available seats was a Pan Am, flying out late afternoon. Being a true Brit though, I decided to hang on and fly with Laker Airlines instead, later on in the evening. Although the flight ended up being delayed by a couple of hours, so I actually ended up spending the whole day at Miami airport.

While booking my flight at the Laker desk, the air hostess serving me was most intrigued by my plaster cast and enquired how it had occurred. After hearing that it had happened while travelling up the River Amazon, she told me that she was off soon and asked if I would like to meet her for a drink, so I could regale her about my adventures. She even said she would pay for the drinks! As you know by now, I don't like to be rude when it comes to women, so I readily accepted the invitation. She smiled and then told me that she would make an announcement and call my name over the loudspeaker system, when she had finished.

In the meantime, and with time to kill, I wandered off around the airport, which turned out to be huge, and soon got lost making my way through an endless number of check-in desks, for what seemed like every airline on the planet.

I entered a bar, and carefully sorting through a pile of foreign currency, managed to scrape enough together for a beer and sat on a bar stool, every so often checking the clock on the wall behind the bar. My attention was soon drawn, however, to an attractive American blonde who was sitting close by, looking straight at me and frequently sighing, implying she was obviously bored, possibly waiting for her flight and if I read the signs correctly, looking for company to help while away the time. Still, as the old saying goes, 'a bird in the hand is worth two in the bush'. Much to her frustration, especially as there was hardly anyone else in the bar at the time, I ignored her, finished my beer and walked out, giving her a smile. She did not look amused, but I was tired and wanted to find somewhere to sit quietly and doze until my appointed hour.

As it turned out, I fell asleep and awoke a little after five in the afternoon to realise that I had missed my very special appointment. In the end I spent the rest of my Miami stopover on my own.

The plane eventually took off at the rescheduled time and I was pleased to find that I had been given a seat right at the back of the plane, with no passengers on either side of me, so I had plenty of room to stretch out. Evidently, my mistimed date had logged on the computer system that I should be given special attention by the cabin crew due to the severity of my injuries, and I am happy to report that they followed their instructions to the letter.

Due to the delayed departure, the Laker airline kindly offered to send a telex to my parents informing them of my estimated time of arrival, so all being well, they would be waiting to pick me up at the airport.

**

When Spanish conquistadors first arrived in the Yucatan peninsula in Mexico, they asked the local natives what the area was called, to which they replied 'Yucatan', which in Yucatec Maya means, 'what are you saying?'

*

Ayahuasca a plant-based potion, that contains a natural hallucinogen known as DMT, has been used in spiritual medicine by indigenous Amazon indians for over 1,000 years.

The hallucinogenic concoction, traditionally administered during shamanic ceremonies, has led to a tourism boom in the upper reaches of the Amazon as thousands of western backpackers are drawn to the area in search of spiritual awakening, psychological healing and out-of-body experiences.

Researchers from the University of Exeter and University College London used data from more than 96,000 people worldwide in the largest study on the effects of the drug to date.

Respondents who had taken Ayahuasca in the past year reported better general well-being than those who had not and it is currently being considered as a possible psychiatric therapy in treating alcoholism, depression and post-traumatic stress disorder.

Day 55

March 21, 1981

The plane touched down at Gatwick Airport at midday, and after a slight delay while waiting for my rucksack to appear on the conveyor belt, I successfully negotiated my way through customs. However, outside in the arrivals lounge, my parents were nowhere to be seen. Not only that, I also could not contact them on the telephone. It seems that while I had been away, they had sold their house and moved and the new owners did not have a forwarding address or telephone number or so they said. I then phoned my brother, only to shockingly find that he had mysteriously disappeared from his flat and had not been seen by his flatmates for a few days. A little perturbed, I phoned his girlfriend, Talie, only to be told that she had not seen him for a couple of days either, and was also starting to get worried.

Ever get that feeling that you're not wanted? I momentarily thought. Fortunately though, I managed to contact an old school friend and arranged for him to meet me at Victoria Station to help with my luggage.

Steve Brett could not believe that I was back so soon, as he and everyone else had thought they had finally got rid of me for at least three years. Formalities over, we got down to more serious business, and with Steve weighed down with my rucksack and kit bag, we aimed for the nearest pub, where over a couple of beers I attempted to recall the last fifty-five days.

Our glasses drained, we headed back to Steve's flat to meet a somewhat bewildered Christine, Steve's wife, and daughter Lucy. We dumped my luggage and then drove over to the University College Hospital, where I underwent a further series of X-rays, which for the first time revealed the full extent of my injuries. Apparently I had not fractured my scaphoid as the specialist had informed me in Manaus, I had actually broken it in three places. As a result, I was asked to check into the hospital first thing Monday morning for an operation to be carried out the following day.

Whilst in hospital the medical staff also performed a series of unpleasant tests upon me, as they thought I had also contracted paratyphoid and intestinal worms. As you can imagine, after the wild and exhausting events of the last two months, I was pleased to find out that the results came back negative on both accounts.

***

Three weeks later I read in the newspaper that another boat had sunk in the Amazon near Obidos, over a hundred kilometres upriver from Santarem. Over 150 people had died and the captain, who had survived, had to be escorted to the nearest town and locked up in the jail for his own protection. It appears a lynch mob of angry survivors were after his blood and some sort of revenge after losing everything: family, friends and what few possessions they had carried with them. These boats would regularly travel up and down the river with between two to three times as many passengers as they were legally licensed to carry.

*

The Brazilian wandering spider is the most venomous arachnid on the planet. The spiders got their name because they are known to wander the jungle floor at night-time, rather than residing in a lair or maintaining their web. During the day, they hide inside termite mounds, under fallen logs and rocks, and in banana plants.

Their venom contains a toxin called PhTx3 which causes extremely painful swelling, skin cell destruction, paralysis, fatal breathing complications, heart attacks and painful erections (priapism) in men, which last up to four hours. It is because of this that the venom is currently being studied for use in erectile dysfunction treatments.

In 2014, a Brazilian wandering spider carrying a sac of several thousand eggs was found hidden among a bunch of bananas at a Waitrose shop in South London. Once correctly identified, both spider and eggs were quickly killed.

*

In 2019 Jair Bolsonaro (dubbed Trump of the Tropics" by the Brazilian media), was elected the 39th president of Brazil on "the promise of jailing crooked politicians and zero tolerance towards the country's drugs trade. So there was some embarrassment when a member of his official military detail was arrested en route to this week's G20 summit in Japan after being found with 39kg of cocaine in his hand luggage.

The Brazilian Air Force officer was detained during a stopover in Seville, Spain.

*

Seven percent of Brazilians believe that the Earth is flat, according to a recent survey conducted by the Datafolha Institute in July 2019. The survey had 2,086 respondents over 16 years of age in 103 cities across the country and was the first to estimate how many in the country doubt the planet is spherical - about 11 million people.

*

There are two kinds of fresh water dolphin in the Amazon region, the Pink Dolphin (Boto) and the Black Dolphin. During the month of June, the feast of St.John takes place when bonfires are lit, people dance and there is an abundance supply of food and alcohol.

TALES FROM A SOUTH AMERICAN STORM DRAIN

Tradition states that during these festivities, the Boto will often leave the water and gate crash the party disguised as a handsome young man wearing a hat to cover his blow hole on top of his head.

At these parties he dances with the most beautiful young woman he can find and then lures her to come with him to the depths of the river and to her death. Consequently, during these festivities, it is common practice to ask every man to take off their hat to make sure that there are no dolphins among them.

*

In Brazil voting is compulsory for men and women between the ages of 18-70 and optional for illiterates, 16-18-year-olds and people over the age of 70.

*

The Oxford English dictionary defines a prison as "A building in which convicted offenders (prisoners) are incarcerated for the duration of a custodial sentence. However the level of punishment varies from prison to prison for instance;

When more than 11,000 Venezuelan troops raided and regained control of the notorious Tocorón prison in Aragua they were amazed at what they found inside.

It had effectively been taken over and run by one of the country's most powerful gangs, the Tren de Aragua, for years. The gang which has over 5,000 members and operates in at least 8 Latin American countries had been using the prison as its headquarters from where they organised human trafficking, drug trafficking, extortion rackets and kidnappings.

Among items seized from the prison were bitcoin mining machines, rocket launchers, machine guns, grenades and large quantities of ammunition.

Some of the relatives and partners of the inmates had even moved into the prison and were able to roam freely throughout the detention facility and enjoy its resort like facilities, these included;

A small zoo, children's playground, swimming pool, gaming room, casino and even a baseball field. The inmates could watch horse racing on television and place bets, arrange loans at a makeshift bank and even spend the night dancing at a nightclub dubbed "Tokio."

Locals used the prison as a food bank when basic necessities became hard to come by during Venezuela's economic crisis.

Local media reported that many of the leaders had managed to escape and leave the country before the army arrived having received a tip off beforehand.

The Venezuelan Army reported one casualty during the raid, a major who died after hitting his head on the door of his armoured vehicle.

Cecilia's Song

Tropical lover
Be mine tonight
Together we'll make music
Till the early morning light
Caress your naked body
As you lie here in my arms
Run my hands across your features
And concede to your demands

Chorus:
Bahian beauty
Brazil's centre of delight
My hot-blooded lover
We'll make love throughout the night

On paradise beach
Walking hand in hand
We sat upon the shoreline
As the waves crashed on the land
Wrapped around each other
Our arms and legs held tight
As the waters pushed and pulled us

MIKE PLUMMER

We were lost in our delight

Chorus

Now we are both silent
For tomorrow I must leave
As my journey has not ended
There are places still to see
So one last night of passion
Slowly promises to unfold
As I'll take your nubile body
Your sensual curves I'll firmly hold

Chorus

MIP, 1981

TALES FROM A SOUTH AMERICAN STORM DRAIN

Iguacu falls on the borders of Argentina, Brazil and Paraguay.

The devil's throat Iguacu falls.

My Rio de Janeiro room mates

Mike and Roman traveling up the River Amazon

TALES FROM A SOUTH AMERICAN STORM DRAIN

Itaparica Island with Cecilia and Teresa

Olinda.

MIKE PLUMMER

Cecilia

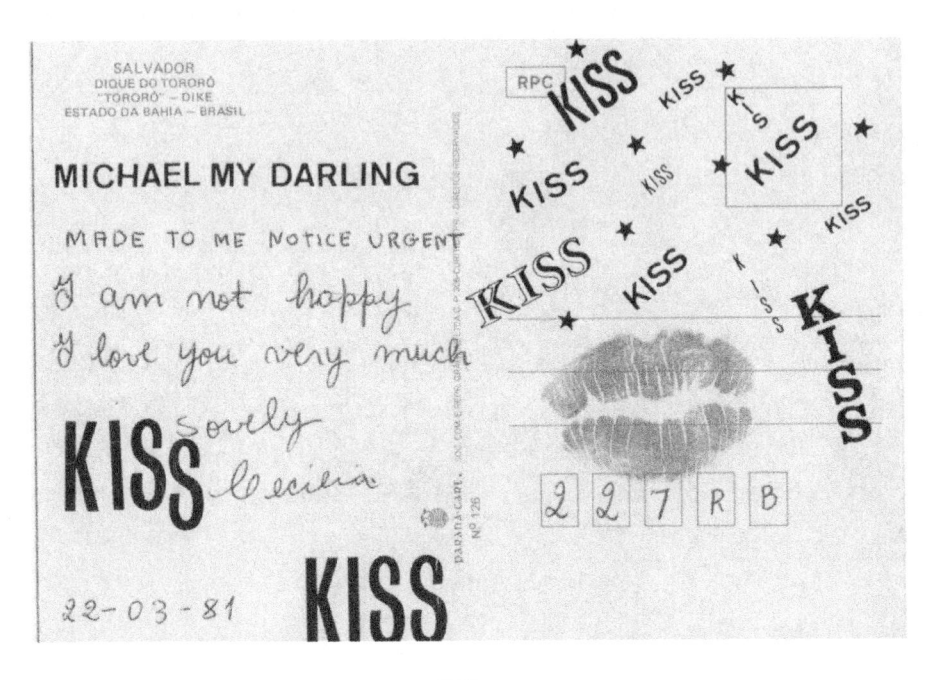

MICHAEL MY DARLING

MADE TO ME NOTICE URGENT

I am not happy
I love you very much

lovely
Cecilia

22-03-81

TALES FROM A SOUTH AMERICAN STORM DRAIN

Original cover for First edition of book.

A jaw dropping adventure

of a lifetime !

ABOUT THE AUTHOR

Mike Plummer

His career path to date has been somewhat unorthodox. Having left school virtually unqualified and starting work as a sales assistant, six years later he had obtained his post-graduate Diploma in Management Studies and was working as a full-time lecturer. He now has five post-grad Qualifications and recently retired as a University academic in Business and Management.

He is a man of action and not just words, and has backpacked across four continents, travelled up the River Amazon, lived with white Karen hill tribe people of Northern Thailand and worked as the road manager of a rock band in Canada, backpacked around Europe and Iceland..

He was a Liberal Democrat councillor for fourteen years, has stood for Parliament five times and is one of those people who can't sit on his hands and ignore the abuse of power and manipulation of people. For instance;

In 2005 he walked 120 miles rom Poole council offices to the House of Commons to deliver a petition demanding more money for education in Dorset which resulted in £1.25 million in additional funding. Shortly afterwards he was awarded the first ever Dorset Education Award by Dorset County Council.

In 2007 he saved a disabled REMPLOY factory from closure, and some years later in 2012 saved a local primary school from closure as well.

In 2022 he was granted two patents for 'Novel aspects' relating to Vertical Axis Wind Trubines.

He is happily for 37 years, married to Janet, lives in Dorset, has two grown-up daughters and is a confirmed Christian.

Tim Foster

Following a wonderful childhood growing up in Northern France, Tim Foster returned to the UK where he kept up his ability for languages, eventually attaining a bachelor's degree in French with Spanish and German.

A keen runner and cyclist, Tim has completed several long-distance cycling challenges for charity, including Land's End to John O'Groats twice and London to Paris. Tim is a lover of literature and modern history, writes poetry in his spare time and is currently working on his first novel.

'Tim lives in Dorset with his wife Rute and their two children. He works full-time as an Inclusion Lead in a mainstream junior school.'

MIKE PLUMMER

Printed in Great Britain
by Amazon